Your Next
Five Moves

Your Next Five Moves

■ ■ ■ ■ ■

Master the Art of
Business Strategy

Patrick Bet-David
with Greg Dinkin

GALLERY BOOKS

New York   London   Toronto   Sydney   New Delhi

G

Gallery Books
An Imprint of Simon & Schuster, Inc.
1230 Avenue of the Americas
New York, NY 10020

First Gallery Books trade paperback edition June 2021

GALLERY BOOKS and colophon are registered
trademarks of Simon & Schuster, Inc.

For information about special discounts for bulk purchases,
please contact Simon & Schuster Special Sales at 1-866-506-1949
or business@simonandschuster.com.

The Simon & Schuster Speakers Bureau can bring authors
to your live event. For more information or to book an event,
contact the Simon & Schuster Speakers Bureau at 1-866-248-3049
or visit our website at www.simonspeakers.com.

Interior design by Michelle Marchese

Printed and bound by CPI Group (UK) Ltd, Croydon, CR0 4YY

11

The Library of Congress has cataloged the hardcover edition as follows:

Names: Bet-David, Patrick, author.
Title: Your next five moves : master the art of business strategy /
Patrick Bet-David, with Greg Dinkin.
Description: New York : Gallery Books, [2020] | Includes bibliographical references. |
Identifiers: LCCN 2020010273 (print) | LCCN 2020010274 (ebook) |
ISBN 9781982154806 (hardcover) | ISBN 9781982154820 (ebook)
Subjects: LCSH: Strategic planning. | Entrepreneurship. | Success in business.
Classification: LCC HD30.28 .B4585 2020 (print) | LCC HD30.28 (ebook) |
DDC 658.4/012—dc23
LC record available at https://lccn.loc.gov/2020010273
LC ebook record available at https://lccn.loc.gov/2020010274

ISBN 978-1-9821-5480-6
ISBN 978-1-9821-5481-3 (pbk)
ISBN 978-1-9821-5482-0 (ebook)

To my father, Gabreal Bet-David,
the Aristotle of my life

Author's Note

I tell stories that go back more than thirty years and do my best to describe those events accurately. The people in the book identified by their first and last names are real people. Those mentioned only by first name are either composite characters or people whose names and identifying details have been changed. The essence of their stories is factual.

Contents

Introduction

Before Your First Move

When I first watched *Magnus*, the documentary about Magnus Carlsen, I couldn't stop thinking about the parallels to business. Carlsen is a Norwegian chess prodigy who became a grand master at thirteen. Talk about a visionary; he is constantly thinking as many as fifteen moves ahead. In doing so, he has the uncanny ability to predict (and control) what his opponents will do. I was also impressed by his meticulous preparation. Because Carlsen has played the game in his mind so many times *before* it actually happens, he is unflappable in the heat of battle. Plus, he has to deal with something founders and CEOs face all the time. He said, "If you want to get to the top, there's always the risk that it will isolate you from other people."

After watching *Magnus*, I continued to think about how much successful entrepreneurs and chess masters have in common. It didn't surprise me when I learned that Tesla and SpaceX founder Elon Musk started playing chess at a young age. "He's able to see things more clearly in a way that no one else I know of can understand," his brother, Kimbal, said. "There's a thing in chess where you can see twelve moves ahead if you're a grand master. And in any particular situation, Elon can see things twelve moves ahead."

That quote about Musk put everything into perspective. Most people don't think more than one or two moves ahead. Those people are amateurs and flame out quickly in business. Effective strategy is about making a move and being prepared to launch another series of moves based on how the market or your competition reacts. You must think beyond your first strike to execute an effective strategy. When you start to get really good, you anticipate how others will react and can deploy a series of moves that are nearly impossible to counteract.

Though business is a game of thinking several moves ahead, this is not a book about chess. This book is about taking the vision and mindset of a chess master and applying it to business. In fact, you don't even have to know anything about the game. There aren't any specific chess examples in the pages that follow, but there are plenty of examples of successful men and women who *think* like winning chess players.

People who don't think more than one move ahead are driven by *ego*, *emotion*, and *fear*. Your top salesman threatens to quit if you don't give him a raise. The emotional amateur responds by saying "Nobody threatens me" or "We don't need him anyway." The practical strategist, on the other hand, is plotting his next moves.

The same approach applies to parenting. Giving kids whatever they demand—whether it's candy, an iPad, or permission to skip piano practice—feels fantastic. They smile and tell you how much they love you. You also know that the alternative—an all-out tantrum during which venom and hatred will be hurled at you—will feel awful. This scenario shows you that, as with most business decisions, one is clearly the *easier* choice; the other—which entails thinking five moves ahead—is the *more effective* choice.

I wish somebody had taught me to think this way when I was transitioning from salesman to sales manager to founder to CEO. At every stage of my development, this kind of critical thinking would have saved me millions of dollars and dozens of panic attacks. When I reflect on how I went from a hot-tempered, insecure, cocky health club salesman to a strategic, self-aware, confident CEO, I see that the key was learning how to think at least five moves ahead.

Some of you overachievers may be wondering why *only* five moves ahead. There are two reasons. First, five moves is the sweet spot of thoughtful strategy and swift action. Though there may be times when you will want to think beyond five moves, such as at an annual off-site meeting or when you are analyzing a possible acquisition (or building a colony on Mars), thinking too many moves ahead can lead to paralysis by analysis. Five moves is enough to make sure you are anticipating future outcomes and seeing moves and countermoves. The second reason is that, on a macro level, there are five moves you need to master to succeed in business. I've divided the book into these five moves to make sure you know exactly what you need to do to achieve success.

There are many things I can't do. I'm six foot five and 240 pounds but can't play basketball or throw a football. I can't write code or rebuild an engine from scratch. But if there's one thing I can do, it's help entrepreneurs and C-suite executives put together a strategy to conquer a market. When I sit down in a boardroom with a founder or a CEO, we approach strategy as a game. The only difference between business and chess (or Monopoly or Final Fantasy, for that matter) is that we're playing for millions (or billions) of dollars instead of bragging rights. With this mindset, leaders learn how to create the strategies that position them for growth.

As an adviser to executives and a guide to students and aspiring entrepreneurs, one of the most common questions I get is: Should I quit my job to start a business? Other frequent questions are: Should I raise money by giving up equity or issuing debt? How do I set up my compensation structure to attract and retain C-suite executives or a 1099-based sales team? Should I expand globally now or wait until market conditions change?

The simple questions in business are binary. Their answer is either yes or no. The trap is believing that *all* answers are binary. The answer to any question is actually a series of moves deployed in the proper sequence. "Experts" often make things worse by giving yes or no answers as if everyone fits into the same box. That's why, as you'll see, our first move is figuring out who you are and what you want.

The other problem I see is a lack of planning. Enthusiasm can be powerful, as long as it's coupled with planning five moves ahead. Too many people want to make move number five without first going through the first four moves. There's a sequence to it. To reach the next level, you have to shift from one-track (and one-move) thinking to seeing many moves ahead.

If you are clear that you want to be an entrepreneur, quitting your job may be move four, or it could lead to a series of moves to create a lucrative position within your current company (becoming an intrapreneur, which we'll cover in chapter 3). If you have a family and don't have any savings, quitting your job is definitely not move one. In fact, you may not ever have to quit your job to become exactly who you want to be. The information in this book applies to people in all phases of life and at all levels of business. You may be a CFO who loves being a CFO or a freelancer who enjoys the variety and flexibility of being a "solopreneur." One of the things I love so much about business is that there's a path for everyone—as long as you have self-awareness and the willingness to think five moves ahead.

Regardless of which sequence fits your circumstances, what sets shrewd strategists apart is their ability to *anticipate*. The best military leaders have a knack for planning several moves ahead. The top fighters know how to set up their opponent. They may be willing to lose round one because a move that seems to be working against them early in the fight is actually being used to bait their opponent into a mistake in a later round. World-class poker players do the same thing, making a bluff and sacrificing chips early in the game to set into motion a series of moves that will ultimately bust their opponent. And though we don't necessarily think of Warren Buffett as a chess master, his sustained success comes from his patient, strategic approach. Buffett isn't trying to win a particular trade or even the quarter or year. He's making a series of moves to win the long game.

NBA legend Kobe Bryant told me, less than six months before his tragic death, that when he was thirteen, he already knew he wanted to be one of the greatest basketball players of all time. At that time he was the fifty-sixth-ranked player in the nation. He created a hit list of all the names ahead of him until, five years later, he passed them all and became a first-round pick right out of high school. Rumor has it that Michael Jordan used playing for the 1992 US Olympic "Dream Team" as a way to learn the weaknesses of his teammates and use those weaknesses against them when he returned to the NBA. Both of these players were master strategists who were always thinking at least five moves ahead. You will need to think this way, too, especially if you plan on competing in your market and eventually dominating your industry.

■ ■ ■ ■ ■

In the pages that follow, I'll give you everything you need to think like a master strategist. I'm also going to show you how to:

1. Differentiate yourself and communicate your unique value
2. Find investors and build a high valuation for a lucrative exit
3. Attract top talent and design incentives to cultivate and keep them
4. Maintain systems during rapid growth and staying power/sanity during chaos
5. Process issues, make decisions, and effectively solve problems
6. Identify who you want to be and the legacy you will create
7. Negotiate, sell, and strategize as if your life depended on it

Maybe you picked up this book thinking that you lack the education or resources to build a business. Or you might be the person with a high IQ who can't make a decision to save your life because you're always overthinking it. It doesn't matter where you start. If you have any doubt that someone can't grow to be an entrepreneur, consider my story.

Anyone who knew me growing up would have labeled me "least likely to succeed." You're going to see how I went from a guy who couldn't think ahead at all (and as a result had twenty-six credit cards with a total of $49,000 in debt) to a CEO. You'll see how I founded PHP Agency, a financial services marketing company with sixty-six agents in one office in Northridge, California, and, ten years later, had grown it to more than fifteen thousand agents with 120 offices in forty-nine states and Puerto Rico.

I'm proud of the fact that our agency is recognized for its unique diversity, millennial culture, and social media presence. We did it in the life insurance industry, which has a "boring" reputation. (The average life insurance agent is a fifty-seven-year-old white man; our average agent is a thirty-four-year-old Latino woman.) We haven't been successful because of our connections or thanks to any good fortune. In fact, my personal background proves that entrepreneurs can come from anywhere and don't have any qualities that you don't also possess.

The Least Likely CEO

I grew up in Tehran, the capital of Iran. During the Iran-Iraq war in 1987, my family lived with the possibility of an attack at any moment. Even though I was only eight, the sounds still stick with me. Every attack began with a siren, and the sound alone could pierce your soul. Then a voice would warn of enemy planes crossing the border. Finally, we would hear the whistling sound of bombs falling through the air.

After each whistle, we prayed that our shelter wouldn't get hit. I remember sitting next to my parents, frightened beyond belief. Finally, my mother had had enough. She told my dad that if we didn't leave the country, their son was going to get stuck and have to serve in the Iranian army. My dad realized that the surest way to fail would be to fail to act.

My sister, my parents, and I got into our white, two-door Renault and headed toward Karaj, a city two hours from Tehran. To get there we had to cross a bridge. Right after we crossed, there was a massive flash behind us. Dad told my sister and me not to look back, but we couldn't help ourselves. I wish we had listened. When we turned around, we saw the devastation of a bomb that had dropped onto the bridge less than a hundred yards behind us—right after we had crossed safely. I still have no words for it, other than to say that no one, much less two terrified kids, should ever have to witness something like that.

I can replay that moment in my head as if it were yesterday. Times like that can break you, or they can build in you an amazing tolerance for pain and adversity. Somehow we managed to skirt disaster and escape. We lived in a refugee camp for two years in Erlangen, Germany, before eventually moving to Glendale, California, on November 28, 1990. When we arrived in the United States, I had just turned twelve, spoke little English, and couldn't escape the horrible mental images of fleeing a war-ravaged country.

Thanks to my parents' decision to make the right move in the face of life and death, I'm alive today, a proud US citizen with a thriving business and a beautiful family of my own.

■ ■ ■ ■ ■

When you learn to think five moves ahead, it may seem as though you're becoming a mind reader. What's actually happening is you've seen the moves so many times that you can anticipate what your opponent is going to say or do next. I bet you are wondering: Can I do this? Can I truly go from a person who lacks experience to someone who thinks strategically and builds an empire?

You might be saying, "But, Pat, you have the gift of gab. You have the pedigree of an entrepreneur. You, Pat, are a lot smarter than I am."

Smarter than you? Really?

Consider the following:

1. I barely graduated high school. I had a 1.8 GPA, got 880 on my SATs (out of a possible 1,600), and never set foot inside a four-year college. I was constantly told by friends and relatives that I would never amount to anything in life.

2. You think I have the gift of gab? At age forty-one, I *still* get teased about my accent. As an immigrant teenager, I was more scared of pronouncing certain words than I was of war. Words such as "Wednesday," "island," and "government" challenged me the most. That was when reruns of *Gilligan's Island* made the TV show really popular. You can only imagine how I pronounced both words—and how brutally I was teased for it.

3. My parents divorced after they arrived in the United States. I lived mostly with my mom, who was on welfare. Even though I was a tall kid who loved sports, I didn't play any because my mom couldn't afford the $13.50 monthly membership fee for the YMCA.

4. I enlisted in the army at age eighteen because I believed I had no other choice. At age twenty-one, when those with the real brains were starting their careers, I was selling gym memberships at Bally Total Fitness.

On the one hand, it would seem as though I had no business beating the odds. On the other, it was those very challenges that fueled my success. Had it not been for all the adversity I experienced, I wouldn't have had such a strong desire to succeed.

Let's get this straight right now: I cannot teach you desire. If you prefer to avoid hard work, if you feel no desire to do something important with your life, there's not much I can do for you. This book is for people who are curious to find out what their best looks like and are looking for the right strategies to help them get there. They're not just looking for motivation; they're looking for proven strategies that work. They want to find effective formulas to speed up the process of getting to the next level. Does that sound like you?

■ ■ ■ ■ ■

Speaking of formulas, I've been as diligent in looking for them as I've been in sharing them. Back in 2013, I started making videos about what worked for me in business. It was just me, my right-hand man, Mario, and a small Canon EOS Rebel T3 camera (which is typically used only for still photography). We first called those videos "Two Minutes with Pat" and put them on YouTube. Within a year, we had sixty subscribers and changed the name to Value-tainment. Three years later, we had 100,000 subscribers and created a reputation for producing useful and practical content. In March 2020, we passed 2 million YouTube subscribers. Along the way, I advised people from all walks of life. At our first big conference in May 2019, called the Vault, 600 entrepreneurs from 43 countries in 140 industries traveled to Dallas to attend. They ranged from small start-ups to executives to a CEO running a business with top-line revenue of half a billion dollars.

Why did people spend their hard-earned money to fly halfway around the globe to attend that conference? Why all those subscribers? It's because all the philosophies and strategies I've learned are *transferable*. You can easily understand them and put them to use immediately. Many of my followers began calling themselves "Valuetainers" and seeing positive results. Though we're not a traditional business school like Harvard, Stanford, or Wharton, Valuetainment has become a breeding ground for both successful executives and entrepreneurs worldwide.

I firmly believe that entrepreneurship can solve most of the world's problems, and I have learned from experience not only how it can be done but how to teach it to others. From my personal conversations to our group meetings to tense negotiations, I'm putting every bit of wisdom I have into this book because I've seen it work and know you can achieve similar success.

The Path to Achieving Your Goals in Business

In your hands is a complete playbook for accomplishing whatever vision you create. You'll learn not only the skills required but also the *mindset* required. Along the way, you'll see what it takes to be a better leader and human being. By the time you have studied all five moves, you will have everything you need to achieve whatever type of success in business you are after. The five moves are:

1. Master Knowing Yourself
2. Master the Ability to Reason
3. Master Building the Right Team
4. Master Strategy to Scale
5. Master Power Plays

Move 1 is about **knowing yourself,** a topic rarely talked about in business circles. What you'll see is that thinking ahead is impossible without self-awareness. With self-awareness, you gain the power of choice and control over your actions. Above all, with the knowledge of who you want to be, you will know which direction to take as well as why it matters.

Move 2 is about **the ability to reason.** I'll show you how to process issues and provide a methodology to deal with any decision you'll face, no matter what the stakes. No decision is black and white, and this section will teach you how to see all the shades of gray and move forward decisively despite the uncertainty.

Move 3 is about understanding others so you can **build the right team** around you—the team that will help you grow. Though you may view some of my tactics as Machiavellian, at the heart of everything I do is leading people to find the best in themselves. I do so by asking questions that uncover their deepest desires. Just as I challenge people to understand themselves, I will challenge you to understand your relationships. Building trust in employees and partners creates profitable alliances, speeds up all parts of your business, and helps you sleep at night.

Move 4 is about how to implement **strategy to scale** to create exponential growth. We'll cover everything from how to raise capital to how to create rapid growth and how to hold people accountable for their actions. By the time you get to this section, you'll be thinking like a seasoned CEO and learning how to gain—and maintain—momentum as well as how to create systems that allow you to track and measure the key parts of your business.

Move 5 is about **power plays.** We'll discuss how you can beat the Goliath in your industry. You'll also see how to control your narrative and leverage social media to frame your story. You'll learn about psychology and gain insider secrets from one of the most notorious business organizations in the world: the Mob (yes, the Mob—and you'll soon see why!). We'll close out with some incredible stories that show how winning entrepreneurs think five moves ahead.

■ ■ ■ ■ ■

Even though I have no formal education, I have read more than 1,500 business-related books. I was, and remain, obsessed with learning. I've squeezed every bit of wisdom out of these readings and applied it to my business. As Valuetainment started to take off, I was able to interview many brilliant minds and strategists. It has served and continues to serve a dual purpose: I have been able to improve my own business and life, and, as a by-product, viewers from all over the globe have benefited from this wisdom.

To help you understand how the most successful entrepreneurs and strategists think and operate, I'm going to share their stories. These include people I've interviewed, such as Ray Dalio, Billy Beane, Robert Greene, Kobe Bryant, Patty McCord, and a host of mobsters including Salvatore "Sammy the Bull" Gravano. The book also includes people I've studied and admired from afar, such as Steve Jobs, Sheryl Sandberg, and Bill Gates. All of them are fascinating, and their stories will help bring my advice to life.

The entire purpose of this book is to enable *you*, regardless of the position you're currently in, to thrive. By the time you're finished reading, you'll know exactly how to make your next five moves.

My goal is for you to create a series of "Aha!" moments—and to teach your brain to process information and strategize in a new way. Imagine the frustration of trying to unlock a safe without the right combination. Then imagine discovering the combination and opening up a vault of business wisdom. By reading this book, you'll gain the level of confidence of knowing not only what to do but also how to do it. And as a result, you'll gain the wherewithal to solve problems at all levels while growing your personal brand and business.

MOVE 1

■ ■ ■ ■ ■

MASTER
KNOWING
YOURSELF

1

Who Do You Want to Be?

> I believe that having questions is better than having answers
> because it leads to more learning. After all, isn't the point of
> learning to help you get what you want? Don't you have to
> start with what you want and figure out what you have to learn
> in order to get it?
>
> —Ray Dalio, author of *Principles: Life and Work* and investor,
> on 2012 *Time* list of world's 100 most influential people

Michael Douglas, playing Gordon Gekko in the 1987 film *Wall Street*, says to Bud Fox, played by Charlie Sheen, "And I'm not talking a $400,000-a-year working Wall Street stiff flying first class and being comfortable. I'm talking about liquid. Rich enough to have your own jet."

Some people read that quote and say, "Making $400,000 a year and being comfortable sounds like a dream come true." Some say nothing at all and claim they have no interest in material things. Others pound their chest and scream to the heavens that they're going to have their own jet. What matters to me is what *you* think, since all your choices will be dictated by where you want to go.

Whether it's a high school student asking for direction or a CEO running a $500 million company, when someone asks me a question,

I respond by saying, "It all depends on how honestly you can answer this question: Who do you want to be?"

In this chapter, I'll guide you to answer that question with clarity. I'll also show you how to go back to the blackboard of your life and set a new vision for yourself that will fire you up and set you in motion. I'll show you why making a plan and committing to it will unleash all the energy and discipline you'll ever need.

Answer Questions to Reveal Your Deepest Desire

Nothing matters unless you understand what makes you tick and who you want to be. Far too often, consultants and influencers assume that everyone wants the same thing. When I'm speaking to a CEO or a founder, I start by asking questions. Before making any recommendations, I gather as much info as I can about who the person wants to be and what he or she wants out of life.

I understand that not everyone knows who he or she wants to be. It's normal not to have all the answers immediately. Remember that this question—and every move in this book—is a process. All the examples I give and stories I tell exist for *you*. They're meant to get you to reflect and better understand yourself. If you don't have a clear answer at this point in time, you're in the majority. All I ask is that you keep an open mind and keep reading with the goal, in due time, of answering this question.

The purpose of this Move is to identify what matters to you the most and help put a strategy together that fits your level of commitment and vision. I may influence you to question certain decisions or ways you'll go about fulfilling your vision, but it's up to you to decide to stretch yourself and think bigger.

Who do you want to be?

As you continue to ask yourself this question, your answer will determine your level of urgency. If you want to build a little mom-and-pop corner store, you don't have to treat business like war and you can be laid back in your approach. If you're looking to disrupt an industry, you'd better be armed with the right story, right team, right data, and right strategies. Really take the time to get clear about your story—exactly who you want to be—or you won't be able to soldier on when things get tough. And in business, things always get tough.

Make Pain Your Fuel

I could sit here and tell you about the life that you may live one day. Talking about the cars, the jets, and the celebrities you meet all sounds wonderful, but first things first. You are going to have to endure more anguish than you can imagine to get there. Those who can tolerate pain the most—the ones with the most endurance—give themselves the highest chance of winning in business.

By the time we've been on our own for a few years, many of us have become cynical. It's an ugly thing, but I've seen it happen too often. We all have big dreams growing up, and we make a lot of plans for ourselves. Then life gets in the way, the plans don't happen the way we thought they would, and we lose faith in our ability to focus on who we want to be. You may not notice it, but it also hurts your ability to make your next moves.

We may even start to think, "Hey, what's the point in saying I'm going to do something big if I'm not going to follow through? Better to just aim low and play it safe."

The only thing separating us from greatness is a vision and a plan for achieving greatness. When you're fighting for a cause, a dream, something greater than yourself, you will find the enthusiasm, passion, and joy that make life a great adventure. The key is identifying your cause and knowing who you want to be.

In the summer of 1999, I was twenty years old and had left the army. My plan: to become the Middle Eastern Arnold Schwarzenegger. That June, I felt certain I would become the next Mr. Olympia, marry a Kennedy, become an actor, and eventually govern the state of California.

As the first step in my plan, I got a job at a local gym, hoping to be noticed as soon as possible. At the time, the biggest fitness chain in the area was Bally Total Fitness. With the help of my sister, I got an offer from a Bally in Culver City. It had to have been the smallest and most antiquated Bally location in the state of California.

Despite the less-than-ideal circumstances, I was promoted and transferred to the largest Bally gym, which happened to be in Hollywood. My plan was working! Because I kept getting better at selling memberships, I was making $3,500 a month. Compared to what I had made in the army, it felt like millions.

One day, my supervisor, Robby, offered me an assistant manager position at the Bally in Chatsworth, thirty miles outside Hollywood. He wanted me to turn the club around; it had been hitting only 40 percent of its monthly goal.

I didn't want to go to Chatsworth. I wanted to be a weekend manager in Hollywood, a position that paid $55,000 a year. Robby promised me that if I turned things around in Chatsworth, the job would be mine. The only other contender for it was a longtime employee named Edwin. As long as I outperformed him, I could bank on becoming the weekend manager in Hollywood.

Fast-forward ninety days. We were able to turn things around at the Chatsworth club, taking it from 40 percent of the monthly revenue goal to 115 percent. I was near the top of the leaderboard companywide, well ahead of Edwin. When I got a call from Robby to meet, I assumed that corporate must be pleased. My plans were coming together. I was going to meet the fitness legend Joe Weider, be spotted by a major Hollywood agent, get my acting career off the ground, and meet a Kennedy. I can vividly remember the anticipation I felt that afternoon before my meeting with Robby.

The moment I walked into Robby's office, I knew something was off. This wasn't the same guy who had promised me the position if I outperformed Edwin.

That's just paranoia, I reassured myself. Give him the benefit of the doubt and hear what he has to say.

"Patrick, I'm so proud of the performance you and your team put up the last ninety days," Robby said. "I want you to stay there for another six months and take the Chatsworth club to the next level."

"What do you mean?" I asked. "I made it very clear that I wanted the weekend manager position in Hollywood." That position, he said, had already been filled.

At that point, my blood was boiling. I couldn't believe a grown man could look me in the eye after going back on his word. I had been so focused on beating the goal that I hadn't put any thought into what I would do if it didn't work out.

Who'd gotten the position? You guessed it: Edwin. Why? Edwin had been with Bally for six years; I'd been there for only nine months. Never mind my accomplishments, kicking Edwin's tail on the national leaderboard. Never mind that, according to objective data, I had earned it.

In fairness to Robby, he wasn't being unethical. Because he had to follow marching orders from corporate, he was being political. In many ways it was a blessing to learn at a young age that corporations have agendas and that advancement is rarely based on merit alone. Robby could tell I was furious, and he asked me to step outside to cool off. I walked to the parking lot and tried to think. I imagined how these events were going to dictate the rest of my life. I played the movie in my mind, and I just couldn't accept how it would end if I accepted Robby's decision. I didn't realize it then, but I was already processing my next moves. The only challenge was that I was reacting to someone else's move rather than executing my own. I walked back into his office and asked him if the decision was final. He said it was.

At that point, I looked him in the eye and told him I quit. Initially, he thought I was kidding, but I was confident about my decision. What's the point of working somewhere that doesn't give you a clear direction on what you need to do to advance in the company? Why put myself through the misery? It was at that moment I realized I could not live another day with my destiny in someone else's control.

I wasn't thinking like a winner at that point in my career. Given my inability to think more than one or two moves ahead, I was still an amateur. As a result, I was petrified. Driving home, I felt as though I'd made the worst decision of my life. My coworkers started calling me to ask what the hell I'd been thinking. My family couldn't believe it, either.

By the time I got into bed that night, most of the emotion had worn off, and I was left wondering what I was going to do next. Later in my career, I learned how to process while in the heat of the moment. Thankfully, that night I was able to calm down just enough to think about my next moves. When I think back on it now, I realize that it was a defining moment in my life.

I had to look inward and get clear about who I wanted to be—and where I wanted to go. The list I made looked something like this:

1. I want to make the name Bet-David mean something, so much so that my parents will be proud of the decision they made to leave Iran.
2. I want to work with people who keep their commitments—especially leaders with whom I work and who impact my career path.
3. I want a clear formula for how to get to the top based purely on my results. I can't stand surprises or the moving of goalposts.
4. I want to build a team that has bought into the same vision I have to see how far we can go collectively. This includes running mates whom I can trust 100 percent.

5. I want to make enough money that I'm no longer controlled by other people's politics and agendas.
6. I want to get my hands on every single strategy book out there to see the game from a broader point of view so I can learn how to minimize corporate bullying.

Once I was clear about who I wanted to be, I could see my next moves. The first step was finding a sales job with merit-based pay and clear expectations. Twenty years later, I can tell you that clarity comes from making decisions that are aligned with your core beliefs and values.

Use Your Haters and Doubters to Drive You

I shared that story about being denied the promotion because I want you to tap into your own pain. It's those moments of feeling powerless, angry, or sad that clue you in to your deepest drive. Don't underestimate the power of shame to motivate you. When Elon Musk left South Africa for Canada at age seventeen, his father had nothing but disdain for his eldest son. In Neil Strauss's November 2017 *Rolling Stone* profile, he quoted Musk's description of his dad's send-off: "He said rather contentiously that I'd be back in three months, that I'm never going to make it, that I'm never going to make anything of myself. He called me an idiot all the time. That's the tip of the iceberg, by the way."

Barbara Corcoran, the real estate mogul whom you may have seen on *Shark Tank*, was one of ten children growing up in a blue-collar New Jersey town. In 1973, she was twenty-three and working as a waitress in a diner. While there, she met a man who lent her a thousand dollars to start a real estate company. They fell in love and were set to live happily ever after. Had the script played out, my guess is that Corcoran would have built a decent real estate business. But in

1978, the man dumped her and married Corcoran's assistant. To rub salt into the wound, he said to her, "You'll never succeed without me."

In a November 2016 interview with *Inc.* magazine, Corcoran said that she had turned fury into her best friend. "The minute a man talked down to me, I was my best self," she said. "I was going to get from that person what I wanted, come hell or high water. . . . He was not going to dismiss me. I would not tolerate it. I would say quietly to myself, 'F@#& you.'"

That type of rejection, that type of shame, can be one hell of a motivator. I want you to think back to the teachers, coaches, bosses, parents, or relatives who have put you down over the years. This doesn't mean you have to carry their negativity around with you. Instead, you can use it as rocket fuel. Corcoran channeled her rejection into resolve. As a result, she built the most successful residential real estate firm in New York and sold it for $66 million. Then she wrote a best-selling book and became a TV star on *Shark Tank*.

As an investor in entrepreneurs, Corcoran actually looks for people who are fueled by pain. She sees growing up poor as an asset. She said, "A bad childhood? Yes! I love it like an insurance policy. An abusive father? Fabulous! Never had a father? Better! My most successful entrepreneurs didn't all have miserable childhoods, but somebody said they couldn't, and they are still pissed."

I'm not making light of your pain. Believe me, I experienced enough shame as a child to last a lifetime. It hurt then, and it still hurts now. Put-downs, insults, and abuse can be either your excuse or your fuel. And it's damn powerful fuel.

Michal Jordan's late father said, "If you want to get the best out of Michael Jordan, you tell him he can't do something." Five years after he retired from the NBA, when Jordan gave his Hall of Fame induction speech, guess what he talked about most? All of his haters and doubters. He still hadn't gotten over those who had put him down. Leroy Smith Jr. was the guy who had taken his roster spot when Jordan had gotten cut from the high school team. To show you just how much Jordan used pain as fuel, he went so far as to invite Leroy to the ceremony. Jordan said, "When he made the team and I didn't, I wanted to prove not just to Leroy Smith, not just to myself, but to the coach that picked Leroy over me, I wanted to make sure you understood: you made a mistake, dude."

Musk, Corcoran, and Jordan all used pain as fuel. You can do the same. Think back to your toughest moments when you declared, "Never again!" Recalling those experiences will be your fuel.

■ ■ ■ ■ ■

I still feel as though I have enough haters in my life to fill Madison Square Garden. When I was twenty-six, I was invited to my alma mater, Glendale High School, to give a speech. I ran into a guidance counselor, Dotty, who asked, "Why are you here, Patrick? To see the motivational speaker?" She went on to tell me that she had always felt sorry for my parents. Here I was, twenty-six years old, being invited back to my high school to tell my success story, and Dotty was showering me with pity, reminding me that a decade earlier, she had felt sorry for my parents because I had been such a lost kid with no motivation or direction.

Dotty ended up escorting me to the auditorium, where six hundred students were waiting to hear from the motivational speaker, when suddenly the vice principal got up and started to introduce me as the speaker. The look on her face was priceless.

I didn't say a word back to Dotty. Instead, I just filed her away as another hater who keeps popping up in my life. And those people keep driving me. As a matter of fact, I have a list of statements that people have made to me over the years. Most people read positive affirmations to produce confidence in themselves, but I have a completely different set of "affirmations" by people who doubted me or tried to put me down. Reading and rereading the list creates a level of fire inside me that all the money in the world can't match.

Maybe the most important hater in my life was a stranger. When I was twenty-three, my dad had his thirteenth heart attack. I rushed to Los Angeles County Medical Center, a public hospital. The people there were treating him like dirt. I completely lost it—lashing out, throwing things. "You don't mess with my dad! You crossed the line!" I was so out of control that security had to escort me out of the hospital. During my tantrum, a guy said to me, "Hey, listen. If you had *money*, you could get better insurance and get better doctors to take care of your dad. But you didn't pay for this. Taxpayers are paying for this. This is called public health insurance."

After they threw me out of the hospital, I sat in my Ford Focus, and the tears poured out of me. The anger was replaced by shame. The guy was right. My dad was getting lousy care because I didn't have the money to provide him with better care. And I didn't have the money because I spent more time in nightclubs than I did in front of customers. I was at a low point in my life. The woman whom I'd thought I was going to marry had just dumped me. I had $49,000 in credit card debt. For thirty minutes, I cried like a baby.

After all that crying, all the self-pity and shame, I finally got it. That night, the old Patrick died.

Everything about me changed. I used that pain to remember every slight I had heard in my life: "1.8 GPA. Loser. Hanging out with gangsters. Poor Patrick, he's got no shot. Divorced parents. Mom's on welfare. Had to join the army because he had no other choice. Never going to be anybody."

I swore that my dad would never again work at the ninety-nine-cent store on the corner of Eucalyptus and Manchester in Inglewood, where he was regularly held up at gunpoint. He was never going to get lousy health care for the rest of his life. Neither he nor I was ever going to feel ashamed again.

I said to myself, "*Bet-David*. The world's going to know this last name. I know the pain we went through. I know the challenges we went through as a family when we came to America from Iran. I remember how embarrassed Mom would get from speaking broken English. I remember the look on Dad's face at family gatherings when he was looked down upon by people. Before long, you're going to be so proud of your last name. You're going to be so proud you came to America. You're going to be so proud of the sacrifices you made."

A funny thing happened the next day. No one recognized me. I got the best compliments of all time: "Pat, you've changed. We don't even recognize you. We miss the old Pat. We want him back." Back then, I was famous for going to all the nightclubs in LA from Thursday night to Sunday night. I used to go to Vegas twenty-six times a year. I told all my friends to stop inviting me. They didn't listen. They figured it was only a matter of time before their old buddy was leading the charge to the clubs again.

Little did they know that they would never get back the old hard-partying, undisciplined Pat. I had shifted 180 degrees. It was game over. From that day forward, no one, including me, ever saw the old Pat again. I used all those haters as fuel, and it's provided me with a steady flow of energy ever since, a reserve that I can call upon at any moment.

I want you to channel all your fury and pain into fuel. This is your show. If you change yourself and focus on who you want to be, nothing can stop you.

I'm getting worked up remembering these stories. They don't hurt like they once did, but at the drop of a hat, I can go back to any of the scenes to produce the same fuel. Something tells me there will be many new ones to add to the list. And although the pain never vanishes, I now view all those haters and doubters as gift givers. Ultimately, they led me to a point of clarity about exactly who I want to be. They led me to say "never again" and to create a list of my non-negotiables (things you are not willing to compromise no matter the circumstances). I encourage you to try to do the same.

In doing so, don't compromise your quirks or other things that may seem weird to others—these idiosyncrasies are important because of what you have experienced and the way you are wired. You really need to get clear about what you can sacrifice and what you absolutely will not sacrifice. It will lead you to create your own list of nonnegotiables.

Discover What Role Suits You Best

All the discovery questions I'm asking are to lead you to find out which path suits you best. The key is to find the best position that highlights your talents. Founder? CEO? Chief strategy officer? Sales leader? Number two? Business developer? Intrapreneur? The list goes on. We're living in an era in which entrepreneurs get the headlines, but that life may not be for you. That doesn't mean there won't be a place for you to build wealth and find fulfillment.

The only way to choose is by first understanding: Who do you want to be?

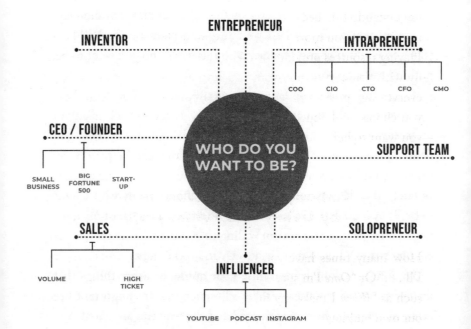

Being an entrepreneur is high risk and high return, both personally and financially. Most people only pay attention to the final product of a successful entrepreneur. People don't see what he or she has overcome—all the struggles, the betrayals, the empty bank accounts. Being home at six o'clock to have dinner with your family is not always going to happen when you are an entrepreneur. Depending on the size of your vision, maybe you can pull it off most nights. But if you're going to be a disruptor and build a multinational conglomerate, you're going to have to make a lot of sacrifices. This is all a part of owning your next moves and having others, including your family, buy into them.

The busier you are, the more organized you'll need to be. There's this notion that you can't win at the highest level and also have a great family life. It won't be easy, but you can find a way to make it work if it matters to you. It's a choice only you can make. For me, being an example to my kids of fighting to fulfill my vision is more important than being home for dinner every night. My family understands this because we've planned for it. Plus, having more money gives you more choices. You may have to work on holidays. Having resources provides you with the flexibility to take your family with you and turn a work trip into a family vacation. As with everything, there are risks and rewards, costs and payoffs. The route you choose will depend on your answer to the question: Who do you want to be?

Embody Who You Want to Be by Living Your Future Truth

How many times have you heard a person say, "*When* I make it, I'll . . ." Or "*Once* I'm successful, I'll . . ." You hear people say things such as "*When* I make my first million . . ." or "*Once* we move into our own building . . ."

I understand the chicken-and-egg conundrum. You can't build a world-class headquarters or license the slickest software until you have cash flow. What you can do—regardless of your income—is position yourself in the best way possible by making the right moves.

A phrase I use all the time is *future truth*. **It means to live in the present as if your future truth has already become a reality.**

I'm inspired by this quote from IBM founder Thomas J. Watson:

IBM is what it is today for three special reasons. The first reason is that, at the very beginning, I had a very clear picture of what the company would look like when it was finally done. You might say I had a model in my mind of what it would look like when the dream—my vision—was in place.

The second reason was that once I had that picture, I then asked myself how a company that looked like that would have to act. I then created a picture of how IBM would act when it was finally done.

The third reason IBM has been so successful was that once I had a picture of how IBM would look when the dream was in place and how such a company would have to act, I then realized that, unless we began to act that way from the very beginning, we would never get there.

In other words, I realized that for IBM to become a great company it would have to act like a great company long before it ever became one.

Did you get that last sentence? You must act like a great company (or a great entrepreneur/intrapreneur) long before you ever become one. Are you following? Let me explain.

A visionary is somebody who is not living in the here and now. He or she has already seen at least five moves ahead and is living in that reality. Explaining your future truth to others, however, may come across as unrealistic, boastful, or even delusional. Not long after we started our company in 2009, I gave a speech at the JW Marriott in

Palm Desert, California, to a group of four hundred people. I said, "One day, the best comedians, athletes, thinkers, and US presidents will attend and speak at our convention." Nine years later, Kevin Hart performed at our annual convention. Before our agency turned ten, I interviewed former president George W. Bush and the late Kobe Bryant in front of our entire company.

People want to follow someone who is driven by his or her future truth. It's the reason we're enamored with visionaries. As long as the person speaking has 100 percent conviction, he or she will get others fired up.

The best leaders have the ability not only to believe in future truths but also to inspire others to believe and execute their vision. On May 25, 1961, President John F. Kennedy delivered a Special Message on Urgent National Needs to a joint session of Congress. JFK's goal was clear: "before this decade is out . . . landing a man on the Moon and returning him safely to the Earth." With five months to spare, that future truth became reality when, on July 20, 1969, Neil Armstrong became the first person to walk on the Moon.

Do you know who you want to be? Do you have a clear vision of what that looks like? At this very moment, is the way you are acting consistent with your future truth?

Use Your Heroes and Visuals to Remind Yourself Who You Want to Be

To take things to the next level and set the bar even higher, aspire to be *heroic*. Think about your heroes, and ask yourself how they would act in such situations. It's no coincidence that there is an entire cottage industry of books asking "What would [name] do?"

You want to be wealthy? There's a book titled *What Would the Rockefellers Do? How the Wealthy Get and Stay That Way, and How You*

Can Too. Want to be more like the founders of America? Reference the book *What Would the Founders Do? Our Questions, Their Answers.*

Asking what someone else would do forces you to take a time-out and consider your next sequence of moves. The second thing it does is challenge you to embrace greatness. I believe so strongly in challenging myself to reach another level that I hired an artist to create a unique visual for my office.

It's an unusual painting with an unusual name: *Dead Mentors.* It stops people in their tracks as soon as they see it. In the painting, I'm surrounded by a number of people who could never have been in the same room together.

Whenever I'm in my office, I turn to them constantly for counsel. They are people with whom I like to process issues on all levels: economics, competition, strategy, politics, and my personal life. Seeing these ten luminaries together is a constant reminder to me to embody ten heroic traits.

From left to right: Albert Einstein, John F. Kennedy, bust of Marcus Aurelius, Abraham Lincoln, Tupac Shakur, Patrick Bet-David (the student trying to soak up wisdom), Mohammad Reza Pahlavi, Ayrton Senna, Milton Friedman, Martin Luther King, Jr., bust of Aristotle.

I chose individuals who differed in their philosophies yet were in the same field.

John F. Kennedy and **Abraham Lincoln**. One was a Democrat, while the other was a Republican. Both were great presidents, yet each took a different approach to getting things done. Both were eventually assassinated, for different reasons (which I won't go into now).

Albert Einstein and **Milton Friedman** both had a way of viewing the world through the eyes of a mathematician, but they disagreed on the economy and taxes.

Tupac Shakur and **Dr. Martin Luther King, Jr.**, both wanted similar outcomes but took different approaches. They were also both killed for having strong views.

Mohammad Reza Pahlavi, the shah of Iran from 1941 to 1979, changed his country's direction until his inability to handle too much power led to the fall of an empire. He's a reminder to never get so confident as to underestimate an opponent such as Ayatollah Ruhollah Khomeini, who led the revolt that exiled him.

Ayrton Senna, the greatest Formula One driver in history, tested his limits to take his craft to the very edge of perfection. He reminds me to push boundaries and hone my power of concentration (I named my daughter Senna).

Marcus Aurelius was a leader who never put himself above the people. He didn't let power get to his head. A practitioner of stoicism, he reminds me to stay both centered and humble.

Aristotle was the voice of reason in Alexander the Great's ear when he was on his way to becoming king. The ability of the Greek philosopher to think and reason reminds me of the importance of slowing down and taking the time to process issues.

In the back, I am whispering something in Tupac's ear while listening to the discussion being led by Abraham Lincoln.

On the far right, there's an **empty seat** for someone, who one day may be revealed.

Together, the people in this painting have become a personal assembly of mentors whom I turn to daily. Who do you have in your mentoring vault, whether dead or alive, that offers perspective and counsel?

Creating a visual of your heroes will challenge you to live up to the ideals of those you seek to emulate.

■ ■ ■ ■ ■

Every time I walk into my office, this painting moves me. I've continued to up the ante. I also have a custom bookshelf that's fifteen feet long and spells out READ. All the images in my office push me to think and make clearer decisions. I often plot my next five moves in this room because it's filled with a spirit that makes me think big.

My office is bizarre, and it was expensive to create. The key is to start somewhere. I started off with pictures from magazines that I taped to my bathroom mirror and now have my entire office as a reminder of what inspires me. I challenge you to find a way to create a visual that reminds you to be heroic. Start with something small. You don't need to hire an artist; Photoshop will do.

If you're a visionary, blow up a picture of Walt Disney or Steve Jobs and put it in a prominent place. Have a little fun with it. If looking at Walt Disney doesn't inspire you, keep a picture of Mickey Mouse or a stuffed Mickey in your office.

If you're building an e-commerce company, ask, "What would Jeff Bezos do?"

If you're running an investment firm, ask, "What would Warren Buffett do?"

If you're running a media company, ask, "What would Oprah Winfrey do?"

Our heroes inspire us. That's why it's so powerful to surround yourself with them. The more we see them and the more we see them looking at us, the greater our chances of acting heroically.

■ ■ ■ ■ ■

Who do you want to be?

That's the question we started with, and it's the one we'll end with. The only way to answer it is by becoming clear about the life you want to live. In doing so, you will immediately embody that person and act as if you are already there.

It's a lifelong practice. I hope the tools in this chapter will lead to some breakthroughs and get you onto the path to knowing who you truly want to be.

2

Study the Most Important Product: You

Become who you are by learning who you are.

—Pindar, ancient Greek poet

It's only in the movies that someone gets hit by a lightning bolt of inspiration and suddenly knows exactly what to do with his or her life. The reality is that knowing who you want to be is a process that requires *effort*.

Let's look at what some of the great philosophers have said about knowing ourselves.

The most difficult thing in life is to know yourself.

—Thales of Miletus

There are three things extremely hard: steel, a diamond, and to know one's self.

—Benjamin Franklin

And you? When will you begin that long journey into yourself?

—Rumi

Thales, Franklin, and Rumi are warning us that this process is hard. For me, making three hundred cold calls a day wasn't hard. Working eighteen-hour days, six days a week was something I could handle. Knowing myself, on the other hand, was the toughest thing I had to do. I did it because I knew there was a payoff. Three sages explained why better than I can.

Knowing yourself is the beginning of all wisdom.

—Aristotle

When I discover who I am, I'll be free.

—Ralph Ellison

At the center of your being, you have the answer; you know who you are and you know what you want.

—Lao Tzu

We read books about studying other people. We focus on how to read, persuade, and influence them. That's certainly valuable. But imagine if you were to spend as much time studying something more important. Studying others gives us knowledge, but studying yourself ultimately leads to an incredible amount of freedom. Studying yourself helps you reach self-acceptance, which liberates you from self-judgment. Instead of beating yourself up all the time, you learn to accept yourself and—as I did—realize that what you thought were shortcomings can actually be assets. I'm going to continue to remind you that the most important person to study is the only person you're going to have to live with for the rest of your life: you.

Align Your Career with Your True Self

My friend Shawn had more than a dozen jobs before he turned thirty. Eventually, he worked for me as an insurance agent. It shouldn't have surprised me when he called one day to say he didn't want to sell insurance anymore. I met with him and asked what was going on. I listened for a while; then I said, "Let me be very honest with you, but it's going to sting. Are you okay with that?"

He paused for a moment, but eventually he said yes.

"Every single job you ever quit, it was your boss's fault. I can name all the bosses you've bad-mouthed over the years. It's always someone else's fault, but you know whose fault it never is? Yours. Why do you think this is?"

It took a little bit of nudging, and to Shawn's credit, he started taking responsibility. He understood that the only way to make our conversation productive was to look inward rather than point fingers outward.

We started processing. He began digging beneath his surface anger, talking about a guy he had hired who had now surpassed his own income. He admitted to feeling upset and even humiliated that someone he had hired was now doing better than he was. We boiled his feelings down to a combination of bitterness and envy.

I suggested that he and that guy might have different dreams; that perhaps that young star wanted to make millions of dollars and he didn't. I said, "Put everything aside for a moment and let me ask you a question: What type of life do you want?"

Shawn was quiet for a moment, and I could tell he was taking the question seriously. Finally he said, "Pat, if I made $150,000 a year, I would live a very good life. I want to coach Little League. I want to be there for all my kids' big moments. And to be honest, I want to be able to sleep in some days. Maybe I need to be honest that I'm not all that driven."

Shawn's candid self-reflection gave him direction. He started to see that he didn't have to compare himself with colleagues or friends. He didn't have to try to be the richest person in his office. Once he realized what would make him truly happy and satisfied—a $150,000 yearly income and plenty of family and leisure time—everything started to fall into place.

As we talked about it, he asked, "But isn't this thinking too small?"

"To someone else, maybe it is," I said. "But are you comfortable knowing that you may never find out your true potential in business but can still make a comfortable living and be a phenomenal dad?"

Shawn became quiet again, and I gave him time to reflect. He started to see that this discussion wasn't about *other* people; it was strictly about him. He needed to be honest about who he was and what he wanted out of life. Maybe as a way to distract himself from how uncomfortable this type of reflection can be, he asked me what I wanted.

"This has nothing to do with me or anyone else," I said. "When you've decided what your best life looks like and execute that vision, you won't be envious."

"I hear you, Pat," he said. "But I'm still curious about what you want."

"I want to take over the freakin' world, but that's me, not you. You can't try to be me, and I can't try to be you. That's the worst thing you can do."

Shawn nodded, relieved. He had a goal, the right goal. He could create a long-term strategy around it, not just a quick fix (i.e., quitting a job). Together we had processed the issue, and after doing so, he was able to make a choice that was ideal for him.

The key for Shawn was to stop comparing himself to others. Being home for dinner every night was important to him. And for the life he wanted, he could coast his way to making $150,000 a year and devote his heart and soul to his kids. Why try to act like Jeff Bezos or Richard Branson when you are wired differently and have different goals?

Studying the most important product requires you to dig deep. Shawn, like many people, had been operating on false assumptions about what motivated him. He hadn't reached down far enough or been honest enough with himself. When he did, suddenly his world made sense and he understood the choices he had to make to be fulfilled. Keep in mind that there still may come a day when he will wake up wanting to give more in order to experience more. As we're about to discuss, your goals will evolve over time. If Shawn notices envy creeping in, it will be a powerful indicator that he should reexamine his goals.

■ ■ ■ ■ ■

In his insightful book *Principles: Life and Work*, Ray Dalio said, "I learned that if you work hard and creatively, you can have just about anything you want, but not everything you want. Maturity is the ability to reject good alternatives in order to pursue even better ones."

When you're honest about who you are, you learn to stop *wanting* everything.

Envy is an indicator that alerts you if you're being honest with yourself. If you can look at someone who has things you don't and say, "You know what. I really don't want that," you know you're in a good place. If you say you don't want something but don't mean it, envy will eat away at you. What it's telling you is that you really do want it but are afraid to work for it.

What will give you peace of mind is being honest enough to know who you are and do what it takes to live the life you want. You'll know you are living the best version of yourself when your reaction to the success of others, including those who have things you don't have, is feeling happy for them. Again, if you feel envy, it's an indicator that either you're lying to yourself about what you want or you lack the discipline to accomplish it.

I've met many unfulfilled, unhappy people. The most dangerous unhappy people I've met are those who are both extremely ambitious and extremely lazy. What this combination produces is envy, which is a deadly sin that will make your life a living hell. These are people who think big and want to do something big, but they're not willing to put in the work to earn it. They'll cheat. They'll throw you under the bus. They're constantly looking for shortcuts. And if someone else has what they want, it eats away at their very soul.

If someone is winning at a higher level than you are, either lower your expectations to match your work ethic or increase your work ethic to exceed your expectations. If you do neither, you'll be miserable.

What it all boils down to is that alignment is the key to fulfillment. Keep these things in mind:

- Your vision must align with who you want to be.
- Your choices must align with your vision.
- Your effort must align with the size of your vision.
- Your behavior must align with your values and principles.

Inquiry Leads to Acceptance, Which Leads to Power

There's only one person you have to spend every second of your life with. Not your parents. Not your spouse. Not your kids. Not your best friend. *You.* The moment you understand who you will have to spend the rest of your life with and learn to accept it, you'll eliminate self-judgment, which will empower you to make more bold moves. It will minimize overthinking and increase execution.

When I read *Power vs. Force* by David R. Hawkins, I was fascinated by his explanation of the different levels of consciousness. Before reading that book, I would have thought that courage would be at the top of the pyramid. Only after doing all of my internal work did it make sense that, as you can see in the chart on the next page, acceptance is even higher than courage.

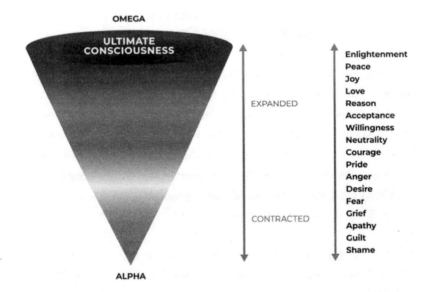

I understand why you may be afraid of self-inquiry. It can hurt to come out of hiding and shine a light on your flaws. All of the hours of introspection I've done have revealed a lot about myself: some things that were good, some things that were bad, and some things that were terrible. Because I did the hard work of examining myself, I started to accept myself. I also learned that it was okay to be vulnerable and to share who I was. In doing so, my friend Byron Udell, who runs a good-sized company out of Chicago, recommended the book *The Hypomanic Edge: The Link Between (a Little) Craziness and (a Lot of) Success in America* by John D. Gartner. That book helped me see that I wasn't alone in my (hypo)mania. I accepted my madness and started using it as an advantage instead of as a crutch. It also made me realize that I was wired to do big things and my personality would be an asset in building a company. Eventually, I learned to start accepting myself, flaws and all.

Four Areas That Drive You

When I was selling gym memberships at Bally Total Fitness, I worked with a guy named Stuart. Like me, Stuart left to sell insurance. Around the same time, we both started our own insurance agencies. We were having lunch one day, discussing our goals, and Stuart said, "Our vision is to be one of the largest insurance agencies in the entire state of California. If I work hard for a few years, the money will be rolling in and I'll be on easy street."

I said to Stuart, "We're going to have half a million licensed agents. We'll be the biggest agency in America." He looked at me as if I were delusional. I looked at him in confusion, wondering how anyone could think so small when the market potential was so big. I was chasing history books; he was chasing a simpler life.

Stuart is driven by the idea of having financial freedom. He makes half a million dollars a year and barely has to work. He knew what drove him, and he got it. He probably looks at my life and feels as though he dodged a bullet. Why would he possibly put up with all the stress and endure the hundred-hour workweeks and constant pressure when he is driven by financial freedom?

Are you seeing where I'm going with this? You have to know what drives *you*. It's going to be different for everybody. Once I realized what drove me, I didn't need an alarm clock. It's the reason that even though I now have financial security, I'm more motivated than ever.

It's why I've endured those hundred-hour workweeks. It's why the minute I feel the smallest amount of self-pity creep in, I stop and remind myself: this is what you signed up for, Patrick. I start to sound like that old Toyota commercial: you asked for it, you got it. The interesting thing is that had I stayed at my former position, I could have coasted my way to a $5-million-a-year income. And even when it looked as though I might go bankrupt and insane (at the same time, no less), I never once regretted my decision.

Why? Because I had taken the time to learn what drives me.

Now it's your turn. You can start by breaking down drive into four categories: advancement, madness, individuality, and purpose.

ADVANCEMENT

- Next promotion
- Completing a task
- Meeting a deadline
- Reaching a goal as a team

INDIVIDUALITY

- Lifestyle
- Recognition
- Security

MADNESS

- Opposition
- Competition
- Control
- Power and fame
- Proving others wrong
- The need to avoid embarrassment
- Mastery
- Desire to be the best (break records)

PURPOSE

- History
- Helping others
- Change
- Impact
- Enlightenment/self-actualization

It's normal to have more than one motivation. It's also normal for your priorities to shift. Take a careful look at the list above, and think long and hard about what drives you. Most of the time, it requires some catalyst to examine what motivates you. There are four reasons that may trigger you to reassess what drives you:

- Boredom
- Declining results
- A plateau or stagnancy
- A feeling that your talent is declining

If you're feeling any of those, now is the perfect time to dig deeper and determine what you really want.

Graduate to Your Next Why

Another way of thinking about drive is by asking, "What's my why?" When someone asks you this, you may say, "I don't really know my why" or "I think I'm doing this for my family" or "I want to be financially free." Everybody has a why. The challenge is that the majority of people never graduate from their initial why.

You may be familiar with the psychologist Abraham Maslow's Hierarchy of Needs. In the 1943 paper "A Theory of Human Motivation" in *Psychological Review*, Maslow described how your needs evolve. If you're facing death, you're not going to be thinking about your purpose. If you're struggling to feed your family, you won't have any bandwidth to think about your legacy. It makes sense. It also makes sense that once you meet your core needs, you naturally move up the pyramid and covet things such as belonging, esteem, and growth.

I view the desire for growth as "graduating to your next why" and see it as being on four levels.

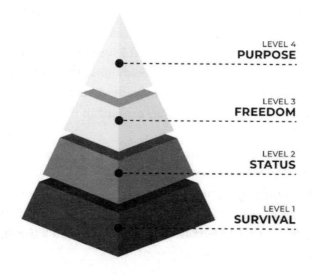

Four Levels of Why

LEVEL 1: SURVIVAL

Everyone who has a job to make money is focused on paying his or her bills. Some people stop here.

LEVEL 2: STATUS

You'll hear people say things such as "You know, I want to make seven figures." Why? Status. They may want to have a nice car or house or send their kids to a prestigious school. They want to be able to talk about having this or that. This is all about keeping up with the Joneses. Status is still lightweight, but it's higher than survival. When most people reach this level, they slow down and settle.

LEVEL 3: FREEDOM

Some people may say, "You know what? I'm so sick and tired of six figures. I want to be free. I want to make the kind of money that gives me breathing room, where I don't have to be in the office every day." They may want to live in a community where their kids can play outside without their having to worry about them. Or they may want to be a digital nomad so they can surf in the summer and ski in the winter.

Freedom as a why is somewhat selfish. There's nothing wrong with wanting freedom, but it may feel empty once you've attained it. If that's the case for you and your feeling of contentment turns to frustration, you now have the luxury of going deeper and focusing on aspects of life that will provide you with a true sense of fulfillment.

LEVEL 4: PURPOSE

Defining your purpose is asking the questions: How do I want to be remembered? How do I want to make an impact on other people's lives? It's about realizing why you were put on this earth and pushing the limits of the greatest version of yourself. Operating at the highest level of the pyramid is driven by:

- History
- Helping others
- Change
- Impact
- Enlightenment/self-actualization

Very few people reach the purpose level. Why? Some of it is fear. Some of it is spending their entire lives stuck in survival mode without any time to think. Some of it is being caught up in too many distractions, whether they are social media, sports, or entertainment. In truth, nobody really gets caught up in these distractions. They choose them to escape reality and avoid the difficult work of self-inquiry. What it comes down to is not spending enough time asking the right questions.

If you want to make a big impact, it will happen only if you're willing to sit down and ask yourself some important questions about life. Unfortunately, so many times people are just going, going, going, and they die never having asked themselves the questions that matter most.

My challenge to you is: no matter what level you're at now, get clear on your purpose.

Personal Identity Audit

Of all the tools I offer you in this book, the Personal Identity Audit may be the most important. We tend to overuse the expression "This will change your life." In this case, I'm speaking from experience when I say that conducting a Personal Identity Audit (a series of questions that lead to self-discovery) changed my life radically and exponentially.

All the disruptors, founders, leaders, and athletes you admire didn't get there by luck. There was a moment (or many moments) when they were brutally honest with themselves. It's a private time when they face their vices, their fears, and their limiting beliefs that have been stored in their hearts and minds and have been holding them back. This usually happens after adversity strikes.

The reality is that very few people are willing to take a time-out in life to experience a breakthrough. Life is going faster today than ever before. Think about how many different apps we have to check on our smartphones that we didn't worry about ten years ago. How often do we check Instagram, Facebook, Twitter, YouTube, email, LinkedIn, and news apps? The list of all the things we check outside our own selves goes on and on.

In August 2003, a wise friend of mine could sense that I was struggling. At age twenty-four, I had begun to show signs of talent and perseverance. I could sell, and I was hungry for knowledge. I was also angry and confused. Rather than lecturing me or sending me to a shrink, that wise friend gave me a list of eighty-three questions. His only instructions were, "Go somewhere quiet, keep asking questions, and don't leave until you find some answers."

I did exactly as he said. I would sit alone on a beach for seven or eight hours and answer these questions. I was so emotional. It was intense. I had moments of frustration and disappointment. I kept asking myself, "Why are so many people experiencing success and not me?" By being alone, I could actually see what was going on and start to notice trends and patterns. Ultimately, I felt a sense of relief because I realized that all the problems and the answers resided within me. With that knowledge, I knew I was in control of fixing it.

That exercise was so valuable that I've condensed the most important questions to create what I call the Personal Identity Audit.

When you study the most important person (you), you will begin to learn how to conquer the most important person who is holding you back (you).

These questions—along with the reflection that resulted—completely changed my life. They took me from being an average person to realizing my potential in life. I came out feeling free. I came out accepting my limitations and challenges. Now when I advise entrepreneurs, I ask them to conduct a Personal Identity Audit.

The key with this exercise is to treat it with the utmost respect. You don't need to finish fast or aim for a perfect score; the only right answer is the honest answer. The idea is to have a breakthrough. The more emotional it is for you, the more the likelihood of it creating a breakthrough. Once you go through the audit, encourage others to take it as well. There's nothing like having a breakthrough in life and inviting others to do the same.

The Personal Identity Audit can be found in the appendix on page 282.

Since I posted the Personal Identity Audit on my website, more than 200,000 people from 130 countries have taken it. The results have been transformational. Please take your time with it. I hope the experience is as profound for you as it has been for countless others.

The Benefits of Self-Discovery and Conducting a Personal Audit

1. Awareness shows you that you are at the center of all your problems (and solutions).
2. You realize that your problems can be fixed.

3. You crack your limiting beliefs.
4. By spotting patterns, you can end detrimental habits.
5. Your anger at others dies out once you see that no one but you controls your fate.

Study Your Blind Spots by Actively Looking for Them

No matter how much you study yourself, you can't help having blind spots. The first step in recognizing them is *wanting* to recognize them. That desire will grow out of understanding that discovering your blind spots ultimately makes you better. That's your why for seeing your blind spots.

I wasn't born with self-awareness. In fact, early in my career, I had hardly any. When I first started my insurance company, I came across as arrogant in meetings. I'd meet with major insurance carriers and start off by telling them "We're going to have half a million licensed insurance agents. We're going to write more insurance than anyone in history."

In their 1994 book *Built to Last: Successful Habits of Visionary Companies*, Jim Collins and Jerry I. Porras coined the term "Big Hairy Audacious Goal (BHAG)." They define it as "an audacious 10-to-30-year goal to progress towards an envisioned future."

After I declared my BHAG to people at those big insurance carriers, they would invariably respond by asking me, "How long have you been in business?"

"Two weeks," I would say.

My blind spot wasn't having a BHAG. My blind spot was failing to understand my audience. The financial markets crashed at the end of 2008. The damage was so bad that AIG, the industry behemoth, nearly went out of business. The entire industry had no choice but to play defense. Here I was in 2009, this thirty-year-old Middle Eastern guy, proclaiming that he was going to have half a million agents. The last thing other insurance companies wanted to bet on was a risky start-up when their focus was on survival, compliance, and risk management.

Cathy Larson was an executive with Allianz, a $400 billion company. When I gave her my bold pitch, she said, "You're full of it. You know how many people say this kind of stuff? You better have more of a track record before you start making these outlandish proclamations."

Her advice hit home. Even though I was certain about my future truth—in my mind, I had already seen it happen—I needed to adapt my approach to meet the needs of my audience. My vision didn't change, but my approach needed serious work.

I began thinking about how I could adjust my pitch. I thought deeply about who I was. With more self-awareness, I came up with a plan that reflected what I wanted to achieve. I learned to translate my BHAG into my next moves and, more important, to understand the *sequence* of those moves against the backdrop of a new awareness about the audience.

Knowing Yourself Is an Effortful Process and Rarely an Epiphany

You need to understand who you are, what makes you tick, how much risk you can handle, and what type of family you want to create. The key element behind all the stories and exercises in this Move is honesty. Looking in the mirror can be painful at times. I shared with you how much I cried when I took the Personal Identity Audit. The pain was worth it.

Once you become clear about the most important product (you), your decisions will flow naturally and lead you to accomplish your goals.

3

Your Path to Creating Wealth: Intrapreneur or Entrepreneur?

> Money is only a tool. It will take you wherever you wish, but
> it will not replace you as the driver.
>
> —Ayn Rand

E ric Drache was one of the most talented poker players in the world. Over a span of thirty-six years, from 1973 to 2009, he finished second in World Series of Poker stud events three times. Many regarded Drache as the seventh best poker player in the world. The running joke was that he only played against the best six! Despite his talent, he was often broke. Let him be your example of how *not* to choose a business.

You want to choose a path that puts the odds of winning in your favor; in poker, it's called game selection. What determines if you win in any game (or business) isn't how good you are; it's how good you are *relative to your competition*. That's why it's so important to know your own strengths and weaknesses and find a market in which you have an inherent advantage.

The first two chapters of this book were about self-awareness. Now that you've defined who you want to be and studied the most important product (you), it's time to get more specific about selecting a career that aligns with your vision.

I don't think everyone wants to build the next Apple. I don't think everyone wants to be the next Elon Musk. I don't think everyone wants to have a life working eighty to a hundred hours a week for twenty-plus years to build a massive empire. Some people simply want to build a small business that will give them control without having to deal with the day-to-day politics of working for a Fortune 500 company. Others want to build an online business that they can run while traveling the world.

Self-awareness is critical to forging your path. When you are honest with yourself, you may realize that being an entrepreneur isn't the right path for you. If that's the case, as you'll see in this chapter, there are still many options to living a fulfilling and lucrative life.

Take Control by Climbing Your Own Ladder

Whenever I give a talk, I ask everyone in the room: Who is the richest person you know?

Most people can answer this question in a heartbeat. We're all aware of that one uncle or cousin or family friend, the one who hosts the extended family for Thanksgiving in his big house, the one who is always posting pictures from exotic locales.

Question two for the audience: Did that person accumulate all that wealth as an employee or as an owner?

When I ask that second question, the room lights up with understanding. I can see it in their faces. "Holy cow!"

Yet, from the time we learn to talk, we are trained to believe in climbing other people's ladders. First you climb the school ladder: get good grades, get into a good college, and then try to get into an even better law, business, or medical school. If you excel on the school ladder, you get to start climbing the corporate ladder: work for a comfortable salary, do work with no personal meaning so you can climb your way up to middle management. Then you've reached "security."

That's a lie, as those who have climbed the ladder can attest. Robert Kiyosaki's book *Rich Dad, Poor Dad* debunked the myth that education is the path to riches. Wealth and success are not waiting for most of us at the top of anyone else's ladder. A richer life—financially, emotionally, intellectually—is possible only when you take responsibility for your own success.

There is more than one way to take responsibility for your own success: you can work on commission for a company; or, as you'll see in a moment, you can carve out a role as an intrapreneur within a big company.

One thing I can tell you with certainty is that becoming an entrepreneur cannot be about the money. I know that sounds odd to say when you're focused on becoming a millionaire or billionaire. If your motivation is only money, you'll stop at some point. You'll become lazy or complacent. If you want to be an entrepreneur, your reason has to go beyond wealth.

The pain of owning a business is too great to tolerate just for money. By no means am I saying that vanity isn't an important motivator for many people. Recognition, power, fame, prestige, and respect (proving your haters wrong) often play a big role in choosing this path. But the ones who keep fighting are driven by something much bigger than just money.

As we just discussed, there are many ways to accumulate wealth and live a fulfilling life. Entrepreneurship may have the biggest financial upside, but it also has the most casualties. I'm showing you different viewpoints and highlighting different people's paths in order to provide more insight into you.

59.1 Billion Reasons to Be an Intrapreneur

I received a message on LinkedIn from an IBM executive who wrote, "Pat, I've been at IBM for a while and I have been following your content for a few years. I make good money, but I really want to be an entrepreneur. However, I have a wife and three kids and I'm kind of worried about them. What should I do?"

We emailed back and forth for a while, and I asked him questions about who he wanted to be. He began to see that intrapreneurship looked like the ideal choice for him. This is when you're part of a company and create a new business unit, lead a new initiative, or work out incentives that reward you for driving growth and innovation. In some cases, it might just mean being so indispensable that a company has to pay you equity to retain you.

The average term of both a CFO and CTO is less than three years. They typically stick around long enough to vest their equity. However, some do end up sticking around longer with the company due to new opportunities. Not only do they earn a solid salary, but they have a major upside. You could say it's having your cake and eating it, too.

As of March 2020, $59.1 billion was the net worth of the richest intrapreneur in the world, Steve Ballmer. In 1980, Ballmer dropped out of an MBA program at Stanford to become employee number thirty at Microsoft. After twenty years of thinking and acting like an intrapreneur, he became CEO in 2000 and remained so until 2013. Through stock and bonuses, he amassed a fortune. When the NBA's Los Angeles Clippers came up for sale in 2014, he easily outbid the other suitors. His success as an intrapreneur made the $2 billion price tag seem minuscule.

We all remember that Steve Jobs founded Apple in 1976, but some people forget that he was ousted in 1985. It was only after founding NeXT and Pixar Animation Studios that he returned to

Apple in 1997 as CEO. He negotiated a deal for the company to give him 5.5 million shares, which, of course, were eventually worth billions of dollars. What's the moral of the story? That even Jobs became an intrapreneur.

What are the qualities of intrapreneurs? And how can you identify a company that attracts and breeds them? Let's start by answering the first question.

Five Qualities of a Successful Intrapreneur

1. An intrapreneur thinks like an entrepreneur.
2. An intrapreneur works like an entrepreneur.
3. An intrapreneur possesses the urgency of an entrepreneur.
4. An intrapreneur innovates like an entrepreneur.
5. An intrapreneur protects the brand (and the money) like an entrepreneur.

This list highlights the fact that intrapreneurs don't act or think like regular employees; they act and think like owners. They're not working for a paycheck; they're working to build something that gives them pride and fulfillment. In doing so, they want recognition, autonomy, resources, and ownership.

One way intrapreneurs and entrepreneurs differ is that the former is typically deferential to authority while the latter is defiant. Intrapreneurs have the respect to say, "Look, I think like you, I work like you, I'm the same as you, but you put up the money. You ignited the vision, and you took all the risk." Intrapreneurs work within the system but find ways to improve themselves while also improving the company. If you don't have that degree of respect for the founder or the current CEO, you are not in the right place to build a business within a business.

How Companies Breed Intrapreneurs

Google hires creative people, and to leverage their skills, it created a policy to foster intrapreneurship. In their IPO letter, its founders, Larry Page and Sergey Brin, described their "20 percent" idea:

> We encourage our employees, in addition to their regular projects, to spend 20% of their time working on what they think will most benefit Google. This empowers them to be more creative and innovative. Many of our significant advances have happened in this manner.

Products created during this 20 percent time include Google News, Gmail, and AdSense.

Companies that attract and breed intrapreneurs do so by communicating in a way that appeals to innovators and stars who might be more comfortable working in a "corporate" environment. These companies put forth a vision that any employee can come up through the ranks—without putting up their savings, without having to risk their sanity and sleepless nights—and still have the freedom to innovate, execute, and cash in on their ideas.

When I was in my twenties, I was a big earner for an insurance company. My idea was to grow my wealth by becoming the CEO. I didn't think that I had to quit to make a big impact and the fortune that goes with it. One day I pulled a move straight out of the film *Jerry Maguire* and sent a sixteen-page letter to the higher-ups explaining my vision. Nobody responded. Then I sent it to the parent company. Within thirty minutes a man named Jack responded and set up a meeting. I told several of the executives my ideas and they tried to implement some of them, but a woman named Katie shut down the entire thing.

It was the opposite culture to Google's. The company made it clear that it didn't want me to innovate. Just as the journalist Laura Ingraham told LeBron James to "shut up and dribble," that company basically told me to "shut up and sell."

Katie was a perfect example of an aristocrat and a bureaucrat. In the book *Barbarians to Bureaucrats: Corporate Life Cycle Strategies*, Lawrence M. Miller described how companies go through multiple states—prophet, barbarian, builder, explorer, administrator, bureaucrat, and aristocrat—and once in a while a synergist shows up to save the company from going out of business. At the time, there were many lawsuits against that insurance company, not to mention a reputation for unethical practices that damaged its brand.

Because Katie was stubborn and unwilling to change, she ended up costing the company a few hundred million dollars. That's not a small number. She was arrogant. She was pompous. She reminded me of Cersei Lannister in *Game of Thrones*, the villain who thinks she's above everyone. What may have been worse is that the company tolerated Katie's behavior. This is very common when the original prophet leaves and the existing builders and explorers give way too much power to someone who doesn't deserve it.

Katie forced my hand. She cornered me. At the time, I didn't see my next move as investing all my savings to become an entrepreneur. Before making a decision, I scheduled a meeting with Katie, the executive team, and their attorneys. There were several people in that room whom I respected tremendously. I went there to share my next five moves and see what they had to say.

They didn't say much at the time. It was only later that word got back to me that they'd thought it was all a ploy. They had assumed I was threatening to leave so they would give me cash to stick around. The president of the company at the time was a man I really respected. He said to me, "Patrick, this is very common in this industry. A major player like you comes and makes demands to get money or else he leaves. The company isn't buying your bluff."

I can tell you that no one at that table has a chance in hell of winning the World Series of Poker. They read the situation completely wrong. I was being 100 percent sincere. Rather than viewing my suggestions as an opportunity for growth, they went on the defensive and tried to justify the status quo by claiming that my intention was to shake them down.

Keep in mind that by no means do I see myself as a victim in this story or think they were vengeful. I simply think their corporate culture empowered a person who was driven by ego and self-image rather than profitability and effectiveness. It was on me to make the next move.

At that point in my life, I had no desire to get sued, work hundred-hour weeks for ten years, or deal with IT, HR, CRM, and dozens of other acronyms I didn't yet understand. If Katie had known how to speak to lions (more on this in chapter 9), I would have stayed. But since she did not know how to foster intrapreneurs, I left.

It's worth mentioning a second time that I don't see myself as a victim in this story. Things are going to happen in business that are beyond your control. How you choose to react to them will determine whether you become a master at your craft.

Sometimes you are forced to make your next move sooner than you previously intended to. I was clear about my nonnegotiables, and once they were compromised, I had to return to the chessboard of my career and devise a new plan of attack.

Traits of Companies That Attract Intrapreneurs

1. Their executives are comfortable taking calculated risks and encouraging creativity.
2. Their compensation plan incentivizes innovation and outstanding performers.
3. Their executives play offense (improve) instead of just playing defense (cover their asses).

4. Their executives elevate potential stars rather than hold them back.
5. Their executives actively seek out ideas from all layers of the organization.
6. Their executives actively look for young talent to keep the company vibrant and innovative.

Let me be clear about who this message is for. I'm speaking to you if you're still deciding on your path or contemplating leaving a job to start a business. I want you to see that with the right company, becoming an intrapreneur might make a lot of sense. I'm also speaking to you if you run a company. Knowing how to attract and reward intrapreneurs will have a massive impact on your ability to grow.

One final story about intrapreneurship. Recently I was negotiating with an insurance carrier. The employees didn't hesitate to share their frustration about their boss with me. Since their ideas were constantly being rejected, they were always playing defense. The company's culture—starting with the guy at the top, who was risk averse—forced them to stay in their lane and keep the status quo. Is it any wonder that sales were flat and the most ambitious employees were leaving? Remember that not making a move is also a move. Losing time on the clock will come back to haunt you, whether you're playing chess or the game of business.

Companies must build their compensation structure to reward ideas and innovation. Intrapreneurs want to see that if they work, act, and innovate, their company will reward them like entrepreneurs with bonuses, stock options, or whatever else they have in place to do so. If you're a rising star in an organization and see a path to riches within the organization, you'll likely stay. If not, it will lose you. That's exactly what happened to me.

Like the IBM executive who reached out to me for advice, you may be ambitious and talented and still have sound reasons not to start your own business. Working with (not for) a company that fosters intrapreneurs is a great alternative.

Don't Judge an Entrepreneur
by the Final Product

It doesn't matter how perfect a person's life looks. At some point in his or her career, he or she has struggled.

This tweet is a perfect example of the gap between how entrepreneurs are perceived and their actual reality.

Eric Diepeveen
@EricDiepeveen

Following @elonmusk on Instagram shows an amazing life. I wonder if the ups and down [sic] he had make for a more enjoyable life?

Elon Musk
@ElonMusk

@EricDiepeveen The reality is great highs, terrible lows and unrelenting stress. Don't think people want to hear about the last two.

Too many people judge entrepreneurs by who they are now instead of who they were before. They also fail to see (or don't want to see) the pressure that comes with success. That misconception is a blind spot that may fool you into making the wrong move.

When I meet successful entrepreneurs, I want to know about the period when it felt like they were in hell. I ask questions such as: What did your schedule look like when you weren't sure if you could pay the mortgage? Did you cry yourself to sleep or stay up all night paralyzed with fear? Tell me about the toughest things you had to overcome. Tell me what terrified you. Tell me what helped you get past all your fears and insecurities.

It's the same when I interview personalities and celebrities on Valuetainment. I don't ask the clichéd questions that everyone else does or glorify notoriety, and I especially don't want to highlight the glamorous side of being a CEO. I want to take the conversation deeper because that's where the real value of someone's story lies.

■ ■ ■ ■ ■

I took a number of my colleagues with me on a trip to Dubai in 2015, including Sheena and Matt Sapaula, a recently married couple. After arriving, Sheena and Matt were on an elevator with a few of my friends, but they didn't know one another. During the elevator ride, Sheena and Matt got into a heated fight. They were both feeling the weight of enormous stress, mostly because they had less than a thousand dollars in their bank account.

Later that evening, I had gathered all the people together at dinner, and I introduced Sheena and Matt to some of the other people at the table. I said, "These two are such a power couple. They are going to be killing it." Immediately, Sheena and Matt turned red in the face and a few other people smiled and laughed, finding something amusing. I had no idea what was going on.

After dinner, we were on a yacht; everyone had had a few drinks, and Matt said, "Pat, they [meaning the colleagues with whom we ate dinner] saw Sheena and me get into a terrible fight in the elevator."

They both felt awkward, but as we talked, the conversation turned to marriage and they started asking me about mine.

"Let me tell you something," I said. "My wife and I have awful fights. We had one last week. If you were to eavesdrop, you would think we were ten seconds away from filing for divorce. But then we resolve the issue and move on.

"Things get heated because we're dealing with a lot of stuff. We have two young kids. [In 2015, my youngest child hadn't been born yet.] We have our own families of origin and all the baggage that comes with it. We're running a business. We're trying to exercise and stay in shape. And I could keep going with a list of issues and challenges that would make your head spin."

My wife and I may look as though we have the perfect marriage in which we're always sweet and loving with each other, but the stress of work and life makes perfection impossible. Ask any couple who has been married for twenty or thirty years if there was ever a moment when they considered calling it quits. I'd bet the vast majority will say yes.

What's interesting about this story is that Sheena and Matt had just joined the company in 2015. Four years later, together they were earning more than $1.5 million a year. Everyone sees their success. Few witnessed what they had to endure to get there.

Rather than judging an entrepreneur by the final product, look at the product in development. Accept the reality of all the adversity involved, and be honest with yourself about how hard it's going to be. If this sounds frightening, mission accomplished! I'm here to tell it like it is. And once again, you may realize that entrepreneurship may not be for you, just as others are feeling more strongly than ever that it's the path they must take.

Find Your "Blue Ocean"

I'm not going to get into the nuts and bolts of starting any specific kind of business. There are many books and online resources that will tell you how to open a franchise restaurant or develop an app. Instead, I want you to think more broadly about finding a game you can beat.

Blue Ocean Strategy: How to Create Uncontested Market Space and Make the Competition Irrelevant by W. Chan Kim and Renée Mauborgne, professors at INSEAD in Fontainebleau, France, was published in 2004. This book was the key resource that led me to find a game in which I could win. The premise of the book is that rather than competing in games where you're an underdog, find unexplored new markets in which you can win—and ultimately make the competition irrelevant.

In the late 1950s, when the Haloid Company saw that it couldn't compete with bigger competitors, it changed its focus to an area where they saw a blue ocean: photocopy machines. It even changed its name to Haloid Xerox in 1958. On September 16, 1959, the Xerox 914 was advertised on TV. The product became so successful that the company changed its name again in 1961 to Xerox Corporation.

Businesses need a unique selling proposition. Part of finding a market in which you can win is knowing who you are. Process the competitive landscape: Is this a place where you believe you can do well, given who your competition is? Do you possess the necessary resources to compete? Do you need to acquire specific resources before you can compete?

In the past, I competed against government-backed companies, and I was always at a disadvantage. To win at that game, you need to be a government insider. And as I learned the hard way, if you're not on the inside, you're on the outside. Because those companies possessed clout and other resources that I lacked, I could work hard and still lose.

Have you educated yourself about the competition? Is there some additional benefit your competitor has that you can't beat, no matter what you do? If so, you're in the wrong niche. Don't complain that the game is rigged. Instead, find a game in which you have a differential advantage.

In *Blue Ocean Strategy*, the authors warned against trying to beat competitors at their strengths. They insist that it's a losing position and offer a ton of evidence to support their claim. They believe instead in focusing on blue-ocean marketing, going into areas that are relatively fresh and open to superior growth.

Let's go back to the year 2007. Barack Obama, a newly elected senator, was using social media to build his platform and become the hot presidential candidate. Meanwhile, on December 17, 2007, Ron Paul, at age seventy-two, raised $6.2 million (55,000 donations, more than 24,000 new donors) online in one day. The old establishment brushed it off. How could they make sense of it when they didn't use social media?

I was twenty-nine years old, and I didn't have an Ivy League Rolodex, much less a college degree. I was an immigrant from Iran, an outsider in an industry in which the average insurance agent was a fifty-seven-year-old white male.

If your first instinct is to think that I was at a disadvantage, you may be more prone to see threats than opportunities. Perhaps you are using your lack of education as an excuse for not forging ahead. What I want you to see is how examining both your unique skill set and the competitive landscape will lead you to blue oceans.

Think about what a fifty-seven-year-old white male often *lacks*. For starters, very few speak Spanish. Second, most aren't comfortable enough with social media to use it as a marketing tool. And last but not least, baby boomers often struggle to understand how millennials view the world today, which makes it tough for them to relate.

In 2007, the typical insurance agent was, in fact, an aging white male. But in 2007, the United States no longer looked like *Little House on the Prairie*. The United States was Los Angeles, Chicago, Miami, and New York. It was diverse. I saw that as an opportunity. The baby boomers were no longer the biggest generation of all time. They had been replaced by millennials, who were carrying a computer (aka smartphone) that went everywhere with them.

The financial industry's marketing approach—like that of the old-guard politicians—was outdated. The industry had yet to embrace social media. At the same time, it had changed its policies. Baby boomers had people cold-call them to sell them financial services. In 2003, legislation creating the National Do Not Call Registry made cold calling a crime. As a result, the old guard had no way to reach new customers.

At the same time, there were techies who believed that life insurance could be sold online. Again, it seemed as though I was at a disadvantage. I could barely pronounce "algorithm," much less build a platform to sell insurance over the internet. And again, I saw an advantage. I knew that, unlike car insurance, people don't *buy* life insurance. It must be *sold*, and it must be sold face-to-face. To turn things in our favor even more, Google figured out how valuable insurance referrals were, so it made "insurance" the most expensive keyword to buy ($54.91)—far more expensive than the next three: mortgage ($47.12), attorney ($47.07), and loan ($44.28).

The workforce had shifted. Women were now often the ones making financial decisions for their families. In 2007, the Latino population eclipsed 45 million and was projected to grow to more than 70 million by 2025. Meanwhile, the competition was not looking to hire women or Latinos.

Another trend was that financial services firms were trying to be all things to all people. There was a movement to create a one-stop shop to sell everything from life insurance to mutual funds to loans, and the list goes on. As a result, workers had to pass more tests and be trained much longer before they could make money. My reaction to this was to find the blue ocean. Rather than go broad, I went narrow. I made it so that new agents, instead of having to get four or five different investment licenses, had to get only one. In doing so, I streamlined the training process and eliminated unnecessary scrutiny by the SEC and other regulators.

In 2008, Barack Obama, an African American man, using social media as a key component of his campaign strategy, was elected president. He beat the establishment candidates Hillary Clinton (in the primary) and John McCain (in the general election). Meanwhile, it was business as usual for the old-guard insurance industry. As a result, I found my blue ocean. This gave me confidence that the strategy of focusing on women and minorities, coupled with a strong social media presence, could give us an edge.

Following the example I just shared, I want you to focus on using your unique talent to find your niche in the business you are pursuing.

When you compete against people whose knowledge and skills are inferior to yours, you're likely to win. No business is risk free, but you can decrease the risk by choosing a game in which the odds are in your favor. It's great to have bravado and believe you can beat whatever competitors are in your industry, but it's foolish to believe you can win at somebody else's game.

MOVE 1

Master Knowing Yourself

WHO DO YOU WANT TO BE?

1. Whether it's solitude, talking to a mentor, or using the questions we discussed in chapter 1, set aside time to get clear on who you want to be. It will help if you tap into your pain. Create a visual that is in your face constantly to remind you of your future truth.

STUDY THE MOST IMPORTANT PRODUCT: YOU

2. Don't wait for a crisis to look for clues about the most important person (you). Make the time now to inspect yourself. Become at ease with asking yourself tough questions and become clear about what drives you. The Personal Identity Audit is the perfect place to start.

YOUR PATH TO CREATING WEALTH: INTRAPRENEUR OR ENTREPRENEUR?

3. Find the path that allows you to use your unique talents with the best odds for the highest possible return, and that also fires you up. Whether you want to be an entrepreneur or intrapreneur or hold some other position, be strategic about how you're going to build your wealth. Identify the competitive edge that will differentiate you and allow you to find your blue ocean.

MOVE 2

■ ■ ■ ■ ■

MASTER THE ABILITY TO REASON

4

The Incredible Power
of Processing Issues

You have control over your mind—not outside events. Realize this, and you will find strength.

—Roman emperor Marcus Aurelius, *Meditations*

E very day, all day long, we are faced with issues. Your best customer threatens to walk away if you don't lower your price. Your star employee says she's leaving if you don't give her equity. A pandemic causes the market to crash 30 percent in a single month. A bigger competitor is bullying you and trying to put you out of business. Your kid gets into a fight at school. The issues never stop.

You constantly hear people talk about the keys to success. It may be the most common question of amateur podcasters, probably because it's safe and simple. You'll hear answers ranging from "marry the right person" to "focus on health," "work hard," "have faith," and a host of other things.

You're going to have moments when you feel as though the world is coming to an end. An amateur panics, but a grand master doesn't.

Before he does anything, he must first "process" what's happening. He has to do so while staying on an even keel. This is why stoicism is both so important and so challenging—and why Marcus Aurelius and Seneca are sages who have stood the test of time. Emotion can get the best of all of us and cloud our judgment. Sadly, I've learned this lesson the hard way too many times. It's why my answer about the key to success for people at all levels of business is **"Know how to process issues."** Life is always happening; the way you respond is based on how you process issues.

Most entrepreneurs don't fail because of a flawed business model or an investor who backs out. They fail because they refuse to abandon their preconceived notions about work and life. They refuse to solve (and learn from) any and all kinds of problems as they arise.

Some people say that common sense can't be taught. I can tell you that it *can* be taught, and it can be learned—because once you learn how to become a more strategic thinker, making important decisions is going to seem like second nature to you. Not long ago, I was a high-strung CEO with a horrible temper. In 2013, I had a panic attack that sent me to the hospital—and recurred every day for eighteen months. The main cause of the panic attacks was indecision! What kept me up at night and made my heart beat faster wasn't my workload, which I could handle. The problem was that I could never stop thinking about issues. I would replay every decision and every conversation over and over in my mind. It was eating me alive and damaging both my business and personal life.

I had no peace of mind because I was so worried that I would make a wrong decision.

I know what it's like to work eighteen-hour days and still feel as though you're spinning your wheels. Like most of us, I spent my early career chasing certainty and treating every issue as though it were black or white, as though there were one right solution to every problem—if only I could figure out what that was. It was as unproductive as it was exhausting.

If I could learn how to process issues, you can, too. I'm going to show you how to solve any problem calmly and effectively, no matter

what the stakes. Building a business requires you to slay many drag-
ons. Problems are inevitable; you'd better get a grip on solving them.
To do so, you must be processing issues constantly.

1. Processing is the ability to make effective decisions based on access to information at hand with the highest odds in your favor.
2. Processing is about subjecting every difficult choice, problem, or
   opportunity you face to a rigorous mental analysis.
3. Processing is playing out strategies, seeing the hidden consequences,
   and sequencing a series of moves to permanently solve problems.

The Most Important Trait to
Process Effectively: Taking Responsibility

Great processors use the word "I" and see their role in whatever problem has occurred. They ask questions such as "How did *I* contribute
to this? What did *I* do to cocreate this situation? How can *I* improve
so I'll be better equipped to handle something like this in the future?"

Poor processors play the victim and blame others and external
events rather than seeing how they contributed to the problem. You
know you're witnessing a poor processor when you don't hear the word
"I." You'll hear him or her say things such as "All millennials are lazy.
These kids have no work ethic. *They* are causing my business to suffer."

Expert processors replace the word "they" (or "you" or "it") with
the word "I."

When dealing with the same issue, the expert processor will say,
"I'm doing a poor job managing millennials. I need to see what my
blind spots are. I need to learn how to better understand them so
I know what motivates them. Or I need to hire a different demo-
graphic. No matter what, it's on me to solve this problem."

What differentiates mediocre people from exceptional ones is
how deeply they process. Most people are surface-level processors,

but the best of the best go much deeper. Long-term thinking versus short-term thinking is the difference between a grand master and an amateur. Surface-level processors are looking for a quick fix. They are thinking only one move ahead, and their goal is to make the issue disappear for now. Deep-level processors look beneath the surface for causes. They are thinking several moves ahead and planning a sequence of moves to make sure the issue doesn't happen again.

It's important that you see how most people process issues. Blame and escape are the most common responses, and they may be your initial reaction, too. I get it. We're all human. Reference this list to see which choice you are making.

Three Approaches to Dealing with an Issue

1. Find someone to **blame**. It's much easier to externalize the problem than deal with it. If you can't identify one person, email all your contacts, telling them to go to hell, followed by a row of middle-finger emojis.
2. Find a safe space to which to **escape**. Find a distraction. Check Instagram. Turn on the news, ESPN, or TMZ. Pretend you can multitask by clearing out your inbox. Better yet, call it a day and go home to your warm bed.
3. Find a way to **process by taking responsibility**. Take a deep breath and remind yourself that these are the moments that separate winners from losers.

The Great Ones Own Their Role

"My bad."

These are two simple words that all the great ones use constantly. Winners also use phrases such as "This mistake is on me" and "We have no one to blame but ourselves."

What do victims do? Blame the software. Blame the market. Blame their teammates. Blame their customers. Blame their managers. They point the finger at everyone but themselves. As a result, they keep making the same mistakes and keep losing.

I bet you know some of these people. They're the ones who tell you that it's always somebody else's fault. It's a constant victim story and a bottomless sea of complaints. Blaming others distracts them from seeing themselves as the common factor in all their interactions. The author and relationship coach Mark Manson said, "I always tell men, if every girl you date is unstable and crazy, that's a reflection of *your* emotional maturity level. It's a reflection of *your* confidence or lack of confidence. It's a reflection of *your* neediness."

Contrast victims to winners. They are easy to spot. They're the ones who take ownership of issues.

Kids will say, "It broke." Mature, accountable adults say, "I broke it."

Joe Rogan is a perfect example of a leader who holds himself accountable. Rogan has found success in stand-up comedy, acting, martial arts, commentating on the UFC, and his own podcast. In my view, the key to his success is his ability to process issues and accept responsibility. He doesn't hold back his opinions and thoughts. He simply talks through how his mind operates and, in doing so, gives us a glimpse into how he processes issues.

On one of his podcasts, he was venting about how a guy he had partnered with to sell coffee used his platform in a way that didn't sit right with Rogan. You could hear the frustration in his voice. Rather than blaming the other guy, Rogan took responsibility. Rather than saying that he had been victimized, he *owned* his role in what had happened. His exact words were "I f—in' bought it. Here we have a problem that we've allowed to be created."

He had every right to be angry. Most people would have focused on what the other person did. Rather than saying he had been sold (and was therefore a victim who had been taken advantage of), Rogan owned the fact that he had bought it (and cocreated the problem by being complicit). When you process issues and take responsibility, you stop blaming others. Sure, Rogan started out sounding angry, but as he processed the issue, he said, "I feel bad because I like the guy. . . . I don't even think it's intentional." In other words, it didn't take him long to realize that the root of his frustration was his own actions.

A pro who has been processing issues for decades understands that nobody does anything to him without his allowing it. Rather than becoming bitter, achievers use adversity as a lever to get better. In this case, Rogan directed his frustration to avoid making the same mistake again. When most people would be blasting someone else on social media or threatening a lawsuit, Rogan was educating himself. He said, "I've f—in' read more about coffee over the last three weeks than I've ever wanted to read or thought I would ever have to."

Processing Steps to Take When Someone Ticks You Off

1. Take responsibility for your role in what happened.
2. State specifically what you did to create the problem.
3. Channel your frustration into getting better and preventing future problems.

That's winning processing in action. That's an effective approach by a person who has created a habit of tackling issues and using them for learning and growth. It's not innate and not something you learn overnight. However, it can definitely be learned.

It can also be taught. If you manage people, you need to go beyond processing issues for yourself. You need to transfer the skill to your managers and employees. The best way is by example. When you become a deep-level processor, you set the example for how to tackle issues. This is essential to scaling your business.

I emphasize that processing issues is the most important skill to master because it's something you'll have to do several times a day for the rest of your life. For starters, shifting to someone who takes responsibility rather than blaming others will change everything. You will go from being a victim of circumstances to a person who creates his or her own reality.

How to Deal with a Crisis

I feel strongly about taking responsibility and owning your role in what happens. Acting like a victim is the opposite of being a grand master. At the same time, let's recognize that things do happen outside your control. As we learned from the pandemic that started at the beginning of 2020, you are going to deal with external forces that have nothing to do with your choices.

Many things are not your fault.

Negative events happen that are beyond your control.

10 Types of Crises

1. Health
2. Technology/Cyber
3. Organizational
4. Violence
5. Revenge from a former employee
6. Defamation of character
7. Financial (personal or a market correction)
8. Black swan
9. Personal
10. Natural

Crises have different lifespans. Some last an hour, and others can last a quarter or even a year. Just as the stock market can't stand uncertainty, neither can businesses. The unknown is what creates fear.

When a crisis does happen, the responsibility of a leader increases tenfold. During heightened uncertainty, too many leaders make the mistake of going quiet. In the absence of a plan, they feel that saying nothing is better than saying the wrong thing.

Going silent during a crisis is an example of making the easy choice instead of the effective choice. In fact, the importance of frequent and quality communication magnifies during a crisis. When everyone is freaking out, it's incumbent upon you, the leader, to be the calm in the storm. Decisiveness, resiliency, and calmly processing issues are even more critical at this time.

The way you react either shortens or extends the crisis. Let's put every crisis on a scale from 1 to 10.

What extends or decreases the lifespan of a crisis:

1. Your strategies
2. Your level of poise
3. Your overexaggeration of a crisis: Turning a 3 into a 9
4. Your downplaying of a crisis: Turning a 9 into a 3
5. Your ability to see five moves ahead.

There's no reason to blame yourself for an accident or a pandemic. You didn't create the crisis. It's your *reaction* to the crisis that will determine the life or death of your business.

Embrace Math and Use Investment Time Return (ITR)

If you think I've gone a bit overboard emphasizing the need to accept responsibility, I plead guilty as charged. So much of processing is about perspective. Instead of blaming external events, you have to shift to seeing yourself as both the creator and the solver of issues. This is hardly a "soft" skill, and it's one that I can't emphasize enough. I also can't emphasize enough that expert processors possess both emotional and analytical tools. Now let's put those analytical muscles to work.

Most issues involve time and money. We make bad decisions when we don't factor both into our processing. Amateurs react first and think second. They decide emotionally and rationalize logically: "Oh, I'm not going to spend any money on new hires right now, when things are iffy." Or they may say, "That new software is cool! We've got to get that in place tomorrow."

What you hear in those statements is emotion. A stoic would advise you to take a more measured approach. The software may be cool, but have you calculated how long it will take you to pay back your investment? Have you taken the time to figure out the true cost of a new hire (salary and benefits are only part of the equation) as well as the expected revenue bump that person will create?

You can't make decisions without analyzing properly and thinking several moves ahead. I've probably said "ITR" (Investment Time Return) to my team a million times. Maybe they're tired of hearing me saying it, but they know how valuable it is. Here's the ITR formula:

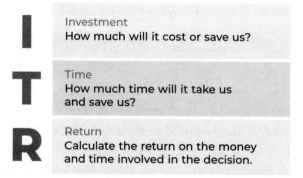

I Investment
How much will it cost or save us?

T Time
How much time will it take us and save us?

R Return
Calculate the return on the money and time involved in the decision.

Before making a decision, start out with the "rule of three" by creating three different proposals for dealing with an issue, each with a different price tag. When people don't know how I work, they come to me with an idea and say, "Here's how much it's going to cost."

If they do that, I'll ask them for two other proposals. Having three different proposals/cost estimates helps stretch the dollar. Having three proposals gives you options for maximizing the value of whatever action you take. And don't tell me that we have only one option. If you think that, you'll inflate rather than stretch your dollars.

Next, figure out your time frame. For instance, if you spend $100,000, you can get something done in six months, but if you spend $200,000, you can finish it in three months. Then you can ask yourself: Is it worth spending twice the money to get the project done in half the time?

Making this determination is a combination of your cash flow and the urgency of the project. If it's heart-attack urgent, you'd better spend the additional money. Then again, if you have to borrow to finance the project, you'd better factor the cost of capital into the equation.

After you have calculated the cost and time, figure out the return. Let's say a project that costs $200,000 and will take a year to complete will lower your risk of losing clients by 8 percent. You are currently writing 30,000 orders a year.

Thirty thousand contracts times 8 percent equals 2,400 contracts. If each contract is worth $200, the total return is $480,000.

POLICIES	CLIENT RENTENTION	CONTRACT VALUE		SAVINGS
30,000	8%	$200	=	$480,000

You don't have to be a math genius to figure out that this investment is worth it. But you need to dig a little deeper into the numbers. Make a list of the blind spots or things that could go wrong with the decision. It's easy to think about what could go right, but it's also important to see the downside.

Take a page from Dale Carnegie's book *How to Stop Worrying and Start Living* and look at the worst-case scenario. In this situation, the worst that can happen is losing $200,000. Can you live with that? Will it put you out of business? Your decision should be based on knowing what your all-in risk will be instead of just winging it or looking solely at the positive potential.

People tend to justify their decisions by running best-case numbers. You need to be realistic with your assumptions. Even if the investment saved only 4 percent of the policies (.04 × 30,000 × 200), you're still looking at a revenue bump of $240,000. If you have to borrow at 12 percent to finance the project (increasing your true expense to $224,000), it's still worth it. In fact, it's a good idea to figure out the breakeven of any project before committing to it.

POLICIES	CLIENT RENTENTION	CONTRACT VALUE		SAVINGS
30,000	4%	$200	=	$240,000

There's no high-level math here. You simply need to think through the Investment Time Return (ITR) formula and make sound projections. It doesn't mean that you need an advanced degree in calculus. It does mean that you can't be lazy with the numbers and you need to think about several different outcomes, which is how you should always think. ITR is a critical skill and one that you'll use time and time again.

Great Processors Rarely Repeat Their Mistakes

Years ago, I had a chance to invest in an apparel company. I like fashion, and I was impressed by both the product and personality of the owner, Ray. Plus I thought I saw an opportunity when Ray was willing to sell 60 percent of his company for only a hundred grand.

My business was on fire at the time. I was patting myself on the back for being liquid enough to buy a big equity stake in that business. Why should I bother doing research when Ray was such a sincere and talented guy?

Right after the deal closed, I became a lot more popular. In fact, my phone didn't stop ringing. As soon as word got out to Ray's creditors that he had an investor with deep pockets, they lined up to get their money back. I fought back. I got stubborn. I ended up wasting far too many hours—hours that took away from my actual business—to fight those people. I blamed the creditors. I blamed Ray. I blamed everybody not named Patrick. And I kept digging a deeper hole for myself.

There's a wise expression that makes perfect sense: when you're in a hole, stop digging. The problem is that when you're in that hole, you're often too angry and too emotional to do anything but fight for your life. Those are the moments when it's important to have smart people around you who aren't afraid to pull you out of the hole. Thankfully, with nudging from my inner circle, I finally relented and threw in the towel on the founder, accepting the loss and getting back to work on my primary business.

I was more upset about my decision-making *process* than about the money itself. I went against my own nonnegotiables—investing in an industry I knew nothing about, looking past the personal issues of a charismatic founder, trying to generalize instead of specialize—and it ended up costing me. My gut told me from the beginning that I shouldn't get involved, but I failed to think more than one move ahead. I was surface-level processing, and I paid a price for it.

When I finally took responsibility, I understood my role in the fiasco. I reflected on all the mistakes I had made. I had not done proper research or performed due diligence. I had invested in an industry outside my sphere of competency. I had been both cocky and greedy. I had failed to remember the simple wisdom: if it seems too good to be true, it probably is.

Once I owned my mistakes, I was left with a closet full of clothes to remind me of a $100,000 mistake, not including all the time I'd wasted. If you're going to lose, don't lose the lesson. Again, you're going to use experiences to become either bitter or better. To get better, you must reflect on your mistakes. I was reminded of how Magnus Carlsen, after a loss, would analyze every decision he had made to see exactly where and how things had gone wrong. *Every master, both in chess and in business, learns more from studying the moves that led to defeat than the ones that led to victory.*

The Eight Traits of a Great Processor

The people I know who are expert processors have very different personalities and business strategies, but they share the following eight traits:

1. They ask lots of questions. Having more data leads to making better assumptions. What caused this? How can we solve it? How can we prevent it from happening again?
2. They don't care about being right or wrong. They're interested only in the truth. Great processors want to handle the situation and move on. If someone else has a better idea, great. Ego doesn't become an obstacle to making the right decision.
3. They don't make excuses. Wasting time and effort on why things went wrong isn't their style.
4. They like to be challenged. Their priority is handling a situation quickly and effectively, and if other people have a solution—even if it differs from their own—they want to hear it. They relish people who cause them to consider alternatives or defend their position.

5. They're curious. You can't solve problems without knowledge. Processors are always learning more about their business and how it works. They love critical details as much as big ideas.
6. They prevent more problems than they solve. People who are really good at processing issues are also really good at spotting yellow flags before they turn red.
7. They make great negotiators. Curious problem solvers use logic to find a win for all parties involved.
8. They're more interested in permanently solving a problem than putting a Band-Aid on it.

Expert Processors Look Forward to Confronting Issues (They Treat Them Like a Game)

It's not a coincidence that great processors who possess these qualities become leaders. As they build a track record of processing issues logically and efficiently and meet people's needs, they earn the trust of everyone who works with them.

Expert processors don't fear issues. They welcome them and treat them like a game. If your top sales producer threatens to leave, you start by taking responsibility. This leads you to own the fact that your compensation plan stinks and you have no strategy for retention. Plus, your sales training isn't the best, and you need to find ways to improve it. Rather than panicking, you embrace the situation. You say to yourself, "Not only do we get to figure out how to retain him, we will also develop a strategy to build the most loyal sales force in the business." This doesn't mean that you should linger in your realization of a weakness. Instead, it calls for processing it and planning your next moves.

Your mindset is everything. When you start viewing a crisis as an opportunity, you are winning the game.

The Chinese word for crisis **shares a character with the word for** opportunity.

I've mentored some great young entrepreneurs during my career, and I've had the privilege of watching them become phenomenal at processing issues. I've seen that skill set elevate them above their peers time and again; it's why I put processing at the top of my list for aspiring entrepreneurs, as well as for my own kids.

Once a month, get together in a room with your leadership team—or simply a group of three to five trusted, open-minded peers—and spend an hour focused on the next big problem to solve. What I do in these meetings is bring up issues and let the team have a collaborative debate on the topic. The stronger the debate, the closer we get to the best decision. Listen instead of argue. Remain curious.

This is the key to entrepreneurial success. Make processing best practices part of your company culture, and this ability will seep into the heads of your people, who will get better and better at using it. It will improve the bottom line, sure, but it will also produce better leaders and better human beings. All the world's problems are issues to be processed, and though you may not be in a position to solve world hunger, you can solve issues in the world in which you live and work.

Most of us don't process issues naturally. It's like marriage. Think about the couples you know who have deeper issues that they're unwilling to address. They avoid certain subjects—problems with sex, in-laws, religion—until they blow up the marriage. Perhaps they manage to stay together for a while, often doing so for the sake of the kids. They're not happy; they may live together, but they are psychologically apart. And when they get older, they can't stand it anymore and get divorced. They've wasted so many years being angry because they never addressed their issues.

When you refuse to process issues, you live a lie and pay the consequences. Don't waste your time, personally or professionally.

If you can learn how to face reality and make decisions based on your own compass, you can succeed in business. The hype you read on the internet would have you believe that some are born with the "bug," a natural appetite for risk that leads directly to success. The truth is a lot more basic. Over a lifetime, success in business (whether as an entrepreneur, as an intrapreneur, or in any career choice) requires a particular mindset, an aggressive and unyielding approach to solving problems. The best strategy is to hone your ability to process issues.

5

How to Solve for *X*: A Methodology for Effective Decision Making

In forty hours I shall be in battle, with little information, and on the spur of the moment will have to make the most momentous decisions, but I believe that one's spirit enlarges with responsibility and that, with God's help, I shall make them and make them right. It seems that my whole life has been pointed to this moment. When this job is done, I presume I will be pointed to the next step in the ladder of destiny. If I do my full duty, the rest will take care of itself.

—General George S. Patton

Processing issues is such an important topic that I want to expand on the last chapter—and give you a specific methodology for processing and decision making.

In my view, one of the keys to success is having a system. Those who have a system for making better decisions win. Some decisions are quick, while others take time. You need a specific methodology to attack any issue, the same way a chess master knows how to play any opening or defend against one once the match starts.

I needed to develop a system I could trust to help me sort through exactly what I needed to fix and to help me see all of my options. I needed to develop an organized way of thinking that would enable me to make choices with the highest odds of success, both in the moment and in the long term. The system I eventually developed didn't always yield the perfect choice, but because I was thorough in how I approached and dissected issues, it left me feeling complete. What finally gave me peace of mind and put an end to the panic attacks was having a methodology. For the first time in my life, I could actually put issues to bed and move on without feeling fear and regret flowing through my veins.

The ability to solve problems well is the ability to take a complex issue you're facing and break it down into a step-by-step formula that helps you identify the root of the problem. It's the same for business as it is for algebra. That's why people often hear me use the expression "Solve for X."

Think about X as the unknown variable. In math, once you figure out what X is, you solve the problem. In business and in life, if you identify X, you also solve the problem.

Though X is an unknown, it's not unknowable. Your job is to figure out exactly what you're solving for.

Look at life as a big list of mathematical problems to solve. Many of the decisions you make in your life today are based on a list of formulas you have gathered in your mind. How to cook spaghetti is a formula. How to get to work the fastest is a formula. How to increase your income is a formula.

If you're not fulfilled and happy with the current results in different areas of your life, it's most likely due to your needing to make some adjustments in some of the formulas you've been using for a while. Your way of thinking got you to where you are today. In order for things to change, your way of thinking needs to change. And this may be, by far, the most difficult thing for you to do. It's not easy to admit that many of the decisions you've been making have been based on a broken formula.

You need to be prepared for X—all the unknowns that will emerge during the course of running a business.

Get to the Source by Solving for X

A colleague named Charlie recently said to me, "You know what? I just don't know if I love this anymore."

"What is *this*?" I asked.

He looked confused.

"You said you don't know if you love *this* anymore. What is *this*?"

Charlie said that he was referring to the financial services business.

"Well, that's not what *this* is for me, even though we're in the same field. Think about it. If you're in the real estate business, do you love bricks? If you're in pharmaceutical sales, do you love pills? Redefine what *this* means to you. For me, it's the people. I love people, I'm curious about them. Every day at work, I'm studying people, learning their tendencies, and making moves to bring out the best in them."

"Oh, I never thought about it like that before."

Our conversation motivated him to think differently. He processed what *this* was—the X for which he needed to solve—and tried to get to the root of his frustration.

Solving for X means isolating your problem. It's not enough to say that your problem is your boss. You need to drill down to determine if it's a lack of autonomy, merit-based pay, or intellectual challenge. You can't solve for "your boss." You can solve for a more specific, isolated issue.

Charlie had to become clear about the true source of his dissatisfaction. If he was feeling run-down, maybe what he needed was a break to recharge. In his case, he was feeling run-down because he had put on weight. He realized that he needed to start getting up earlier and get back to his exercise routine. That was step one.

Then he had to process deeper. His self-esteem was down because he was in a sales slump. As a result, each rejection hurt worse. He was in a downward spiral with momentum working against him. Upon more reflection, he realized that he didn't hate selling financial services. What he hated was feeling exhausted all the time and underperforming at selling financial services. He thrived on the achievement and sense of accomplishment.

Processing deeply means going below the surface. Of course you're going to have days when your motivation wavers. It's normal to feel burned out at times. It's your job to probe deeply and isolate the X that's causing your pain.

Charlie decided to take it a step further. He reminded himself *why* he had chosen to become an entrepreneur. He thought about how his former boss had made him feel when he had given a senior position to his underqualified son instead of the guy who had busted his tail for him for five years. He thought about how much he had hated that job and visualized all the things that had driven him to sign up for this crazy life.

By solving for X, he was able to make decisions about his work that improved both his outlook and his income.

How to Solve for X

When we don't have a methodology, we're prone to going in circles, paralyzed by fear. When we do have one, we have an organized approach for processing issues. A methodology will allow you to process any issue in an organized way.

SOLVE FOR *X* WORKSHEET

Issue:

INVESTIGATE	SOLVE	IMPLEMENT
URGENCY 0–10	**WHO'S NEEDED?**	**WHOSE BUY-IN IS NEEDED?**
TOTAL IMPACT POTENTIAL GAIN: POTENTIAL LOSS:	**LIST OF SOLUTIONS**	**ASSIGNED RESPONSIBILITIES**
REAL CAUSE OF ISSUE(S) Why? Why? Why?	**POTENTIAL NEGATIVE CONSEQUENCE(S)**	**NEW PROTOCOLS**

Processing When Your Business Is on the Line

The most crucial issue I faced appeared just when I thought I had realized my dream. I was only thirty, and I had finally made the leap to starting my own agency. Within five weeks of my founding the company, Aegon, a $400 billion industry giant, filed a lawsuit against me. It had one simple goal: to put me out of business before I even began.

Aegon's leaders and lawyers didn't care about how hard I'd worked to save the money to launch my business. They didn't care that I had just gotten married. They certainly didn't care that I had convinced sixty-six loyal agents to give up their careers with established companies to join this crazy dreamer on a mission. For Aegon, suing me was just business (and it was also just business years later when the CEO who had sued me ended up joining my advisory board). I didn't take it personally, even though my entire life savings was on the line.

That lawsuit was the biggest test I had ever faced. Instead of doing what most entrepreneurs do when things go sideways—blame, complain, rage, and spin in circles because of all the doubt—I decided I would no longer wrestle with the things I couldn't control.

What I needed to do was become clear on what I could and could not control. I made two lists, as follows.

What I Can Control

- Plotting my next moves
- My daily effort
- My choice of attorney and other resources
- Keeping our sales force and our leaders focused on slaying the next dragon

What I Can't Control

- Why Aegon chose to sue me
- Whether the lawsuit would put us out of business
- Whether other insurance carriers would drop our contract

Rather than panicking or overreacting, I crafted a strategy for how to weather the storm and achieve my long-term goals. I chose to settle; I cut a huge check and moved on. Even though the expense crippled us, because I had thought about my next five moves, we were able to stay in business. The important thing wasn't getting revenge on Aegon or winning a lawsuit; I made a decision that freed us to focus on growing our licensed sales force and maintaining our momentum.

A funny thing happened after I cut that big check: I was finally able to sleep again. It's not often that you gain peace of mind after suffering such a big loss, but because I had processed the issue thoroughly and thought about my next moves, I was able to put the ordeal behind me, confident in the fact that I had fully analyzed the situation and come to the right decision.

In the past, I might have allowed ego, emotion, and fear to get the best of me and fought the lawsuit, even if it meant losing the company and bankrupting my family. That sure would have felt good—for about three minutes. Instead, I processed the issue by going step by step through my methodology—as you can see in the chart that follows.

SOLVE FOR *X* WORKSHEET

Issue: Aegon Pending Lawsuit

INVESTIGATE	SOLVE	IMPLEMENT
URGENCY 0–10	**WHO'S NEEDED?**	**WHOSE BUY-IN IS NEEDED?**
10	- Attorney - Bankers - Crisis management team	- Sales leaders - One insurance carrier willing to be patient
TOTAL IMPACT POTENTIAL GAIN: POTENTIAL LOSS:	**LIST OF SOLUTIONS**	**ASSIGNED RESPONSIBILITIES**
Entire savings	1. Settle 2. Countersue 3. Win the case	Attorney to settle case ASAP
REAL CAUSE OF ISSUE(S)	**POTENTIAL NEGATIVE CONSEQUENCE(S)**	**NEW PROTOCOLS**

Why? Aegon eliminating a competitor
 	
Why?
 	
Why?
	- Insurance carriers terminating contracts with us
	- Company going out of business
		- Hire compliance officer to prevent potential future lawsuit
		- Hire 2 new law firms
		  1. experts in insurance
		  2. experts in sales organization laws

EXAMPLE

Identifying the Real Issue and the Deepest Why

The best entrepreneurs look past symptoms and get to the heart of a problem. To do so, let's hone in on a critical part of this methodology—identifying the real issue and the deepest why—so you can get even better at solving for X.

X isn't always obvious. In fact, the real issue may be hiding behind a lot of emotion and biased opinions. That's why you've got to cut through the clutter in your mind. What's real and what isn't? Are you focusing on something because it's someone else's opinion or your own false assumption? Are you blowing up something beyond what it is because your ego is hurt? Are you separating emotion from logic?

Once you've eliminated the "nonissue" issues, focus on causes. You're looking to identify "burning platforms" and "golden gates."

Burning platforms:	Hot problems that you have to deal with immediately
Golden gates:	Bright opportunities that you need to enter quickly

Once you've identified the real issues, start asking "Why?" Keep doing so until you reach a point where you can't ask "Why?" anymore—or when you're forced to repeat an explanation you've already discovered. *That* is your deepest why and the real cause of your problem. For example:

- We lost our top customer. Why?
- A competing product costs less. Why?
- Because it has fewer features. Why?
- Because most customers don't need all of the features in our product.
- Aha!

Now you've identified one of the main reasons why you didn't hit your numbers: because your product doesn't fit your customer's need. Solving the problem, then, becomes relatively easy: you need to offer a less expensive version of the product that has fewer features.

Use this iterative, questioning approach for any issue. Let's say your top salesperson has left the company. As you ask why, you discover that the salesperson left because your compensation plan had been designed for mediocre salespeople instead of stars and had been designed that way because your sales director and your CFO hadn't been communicating properly. The first solution is to revisit your compensation plan within the next ten days. The second solution is to have the sales director and the CFO check in with each other quarterly to make sure that each is aware of what the other needs.

If your new product's shipment was delayed, most people are going to be looking for someone to blame. Remember, though, that great processors look for causes—because causes lead to solutions. By asking why, you find that the delay happened because your best engineer quit when her manager told her she couldn't work from home one day a week—for no good reason. The solution: implement a more flexible work arrangement that will lead to improved employee retention.

Five Questions to Ask to Identify the Real Issue

1. Do I know what the real issue is, or am I looking at a symptom?
2. Does the team have the data regarding the real issue?
3. Is the issue real, or is it an assumption or someone else's opinion?
4. Is there a tangible issue, or is it simply a hurt ego?
5. Am I thinking emotionally or logically?

Going Pro at Playing Offense and Defense

As an entrepreneur, you feel as though you're going to have to face a million different types of decisions, right? Actually, only two kinds of events will require you to make decisions:

1. **Offense.** The opportunity to make money or advance your business or career. The choices here often revolve around growth, expansion, marketing, and sales.
2. **Defense.** The opportunity to solve a problem, to stop losing money, or to stop moving backward in some way. The choices here frequently involve legal matters such as compliance and protection against competitors or market corrections.

Once the problem or opportunity you're facing can be categorized as offense or defense, it immediately becomes less intimidating. You've labeled it, and whether it's offense or defense, you've dealt with both types of issues in the past. Decision making then goes from something scary and unfamiliar to something manageable.

Playing offense involves looking for opportunities to make money or advance growth, expansion, marketing, and sales. Playing defense involves solving a problem, preventing the loss of money, or going backward. Issues such as compliance, legal, and financial hedging fall into the defense category.

Doing the Math Is More Art Than Science

I brought in Alice Terlecky to be our chief operating officer. She'd previously been with Pacific Life, a major insurance company, where she had been very successful. After she became our COO, I noticed that it was taking an unusually long time to process policy applications.

I was frustrated and wanted to know what was going on. I sat down with Alice and asked her to walk me through exactly what happens when an application comes in. I asked a lot of questions to help me determine the flow: what each step was, what actions were involved, and how long each took. It was the same kind of analysis a manufacturing consultant would conduct on an assembly line to identify bottlenecks.

Then I asked Alice another question: Which of those steps required a hands-on method, and which could be run automatically by technology that we could buy or create?

We talked about what functions had to be performed by human beings and which ones could be handled by computers. We figured out that if our carriers could handle a certain step via software (only a small number did at that point), it would significantly reduce the application processing time. Alice eventually helped me understand why the process had slowed down. She had implemented a new system to help improve the quality of our insurance policies, which made a world of difference in our possible liability. As pleased as I was to hear about the quality improvement, I still wanted to speed up the processing time.

I had Alice set up a call with all the carriers who weren't using the software and pitched them on it. Then I brought it up during our next board meeting and asked how much it would cost to cut an additional period of time from our internal process. We determined that, best-case scenario, we would need to employ four IT guys at $150,000 a year for twelve months to be able to do so. When we tacked on other expenses, it was easily going to be a million-dollar project.

A million dollars is an eye-popping number. It's also a number that means nothing without more analysis. That's why we took the time to break down the numbers:

- We could save five minutes of processing time per policy.
- Five minutes times 30,000 policies per year is 150,000 minutes (2,500 hours).
- 2,500 hours times $20 an hour (our labor cost savings) is $50,000.

Investment Time Return (ITR) is a tool that becomes more valuable the more you use it. I'm giving you this scenario so that, once again, you can work your analytical muscles. Every issue you face is going to have its own set of challenges. Solving them is not just a matter of "doing the math." It's knowing how to think through an issue so you know which numbers to plug in. ITR is useful only when you make the right assumptions.

In this case, we could see that it would take twenty years to get a return on our investment. If we stopped there (as any amateur thinker would), the math would tell us it wasn't worth it.

Investment: $1 million
Time: 18 months to complete
Return: $50,000 per year (based on current sales)

That was back in 2017. At that point, I had projected our growth for the next decade.

Being a great decision maker is more art than science. Yes, having a methodology helps. You need to be methodical, and you need to understand the numbers. You also have to learn how to *analyze* the numbers. Solving the question of how to process policies faster went beyond determining the labor cost saved. In some cases, doing so might win us business. In others, increasing throughput would improve the satisfaction of both our customers and our agents. But the real missing factor in this analysis was our growth rate.

When I extrapolated our growth rate, the numbers looked like this:

Year 1: 30,000 policies $50,000 in savings
Year 2: 60,000 policies $100,000 in savings
Year 3: 120,000 policies $200,000 in savings
Year 4: 180,000 policies $300,000 in savings
Year 5: 240,000 policies $400,000 in savings

When we factored in our growth rate, we could see that instead of taking twenty years to pay back the million-dollar investment, it would take less than five years. What had looked like a no-go project quickly became a go project.

Here's another thing I learned: *IT projects almost always take longer and cost more money than you expect.* You need to err on the conservative side when making your time and cost assumptions. As it turned out, the cost of the project more than doubled. The reason, however, was more positive than negative. At each stage of the process, we kept digging to see what other processes we could speed up. With each new finding, the cost of the project increased. The good news was that our processing speed more than tripled, and the long-term savings far exceeded the final cost.

With the benefit of hindsight, investing in our process flow seemed like the obvious choice. But go back and think about the potential blind spots. I could have just accepted that Alice, given her extensive experience, was moving the applications along as fast as possible. I could have assumed that for her to be adequately thorough would take additional time. I could have made the assumption that the cost of speeding up the process was not worth the return.

Are you seeing what it takes to be a great decision maker? It's both art and science. The methodology gives you structure. ITR gives you a specific formula. Your projections give you the numbers to plug into the formula. Staying curious means always looking to improve and tweaking your projections. Your mind gives you the ability to put it all together and make the right decision. It took all of these skills, and more, for me to pass my greatest test and survive what could have been a crippling lawsuit.

■ ■ ■ ■ ■

The Latin root of the word "decision" means "to cut off." When you make a decision, you are cut off from taking some other course of action. Now, that may sound limiting, but it's not; it's liberating. Plus, the alternative is indecision and stagnation.

It's human nature to have blind spots. Laziness, fear, and greed all cause us to accept the information we're given and not dig deeper. As a result, we often miss a critical piece of the puzzle and make bad decisions—or fail to make good ones.

Using this methodology along with ITR takes time, and it also takes practice. Don't expect to become a master processor and be able to solve for *X* instantly. And listen: If you always want to be right or always fear that you're wrong, you're going to have trouble processing. Absolute right or wrong act like processing roadblocks. It's okay to make mistakes. It's the willingness to examine your mistakes that will prevent you from making them again.

Be patient. If you keep working at becoming a better processor, the result will be more than worth it—it will make a huge difference in your business and your life.

MOVE 2

Master the Ability to Reason

THE INCREDIBLE POWER OF
PROCESSING ISSUES

1. Moving forward, take 100 percent responsibility for anything that doesn't work out. See your role as the one who created the issue and has the power to solve it. Apply the Investment Time Return (ITR) formula in order to make better decisions and stretch your resources. Reflect on any possible mistakes or weaknesses, and make your next move(s) accordingly.

HOW TO SOLVE FOR X:
A METHODOLOGY FOR EFFECTIVE
DECISION MAKING

2. Share the Solve for X methodology with your leadership team and use it to process three problems you're currently facing. The Solve for X worksheet can be found in Appendix B. Make sure you identify their true causes and the reasons they happened.

MOVE 3

■ ■ ■ ■ ■

MASTER BUILDING THE RIGHT TEAM

6

The Myth of the Solopreneur: How to Build Your Team

> No matter how brilliant your mind or strategy, if you're play-
> ing a solo game, you'll always lose out to a team.
> —Reid Hoffman, cofounder of LinkedIn

No matter what your line of work, staying successful means working well with other people, whether they are clients, customers, employees, investors, partners, or outside vendors.

When you think five moves ahead, you prevent your ego from telling you that you can do it all alone. Don't assume that if you achieved a lot on your own in the past, you'll be able to achieve even more by yourself in the future. At age twenty-seven, I was a star salesman and a mediocre sales manager. I had to learn the hard way how to manage people. Eventually, I improved. At age thirty, I had become a solid sales manager, but I was a struggling founder. Even five years into running the company, I saw myself as an average CEO. It was then that I realized that thinking big alone wouldn't get the job done. I needed the right team to be able to make scaling my business become a reality.

My goal is to spare you much of the misery I experienced by showing you how to build your team. Working effectively with others will mean the difference between enjoying the process and desperately seeking a day job while hiding under your desk. In this chapter, I'll give you a toolbox for:

1. How to choose your business partners and consigliere
2. How to improve employee retention (create "golden handcuffs")
3. How to get your people to perform at peak capacity
4. How to hire and fire team members without creating enemies

What Benefits Program Do You Offer?

To take the next step from solopreneur or side hustler, you'd better have a good answer to this question:

WHY SHOULD SOMEONE WORK WITH YOU?

This question is equally relevant if you're currently a CEO.

Before your company gets big, you don't recruit people to your company; you recruit them to *you*. Initially, because people are buying you—and you likely don't have the resources to offer an extensive 401(k) plan—you'd better be offering an attractive benefits program. Later on, you will recruit people to your business. Even then, you must keep improving the benefits program, or your top people will leave for a company that has a better one.

Ask yourself this question: If people get closer to you, will they win? Will they do better in life? Do you have a résumé—a list of success stories of people whose lives have been enriched from being around you? In other words, think about what benefits program you are offering prospective employees. If you're going to attract good people, they need to believe you have something to offer them.

Instead of being selfish and looking to see what I could take from other people, I learned to focus on what I could give them—and I improved my own worth in the process. That paradigm shift—that one decision—changed my life for the better. I stopped asking how other people could make my life better, and instead, I asked: How can I make everybody else's life better just by the benefits that I offer them?

You'll know you're succeeding in life when others are winning simply because of their association with you. It could be based on the example you set, your contacts, your coaching, your knowledge, or your tough love. Think about these three questions:

1. What benefits are you currently offering to others?
2. In what way do people improve by associating with you?
3. How many lives have you changed positively in the past year?

Once you have a track record of people you have enriched, you can start attracting people to your team. Think about who you need to help you, not just to do well today but also to achieve your deeper, long-term objectives. Take care of them, and they'll back you up.

This advice isn't just for aspiring CEOs; it's equally relevant for established executives.

Some CEOs make the mistake of thinking that recruiting ends once a person joins the company. The reality is that when you recruit top talent, you'll have to constantly re-recruit that talent.

It's naive to think that your team members aren't constantly receiving offers from different companies. There's a reason why there are so many headhunters out there. Their job is to recruit your best people away from you and send them to other companies that need exactly the people you have. Headhunters get paid handsomely to steal your best people; you can bet they're coming after them, so you'd better make sure you know how to retain them. Depending on the size of the business, a headhunter earns between $30,000 and $60,000 to place a CFO. The fee to place a CEO starts at about $80,000 and may go as high as $500,000.

The people you recruit are also watching you closely. They are constantly reevaluating the benefits program, and if it doesn't keep up with their expectations, they will start looking elsewhere. Your top people, especially, are watching you to see if you're constantly developing yourself and finding ways to take the company to the next level. They want to see if you're bringing in other top talent to keep increasing the value of the company. Showing them that you're doing all these things is part of re-recruiting your best people. It can never stop.

Questions That People Will Ask (and You Must Answer) When They Are Deciding to Work for You

1. What makes your company distinct from your competition?
2. What separates your leadership from that of others?
3. Do you have a code of honor? Do you embody it?
4. What benefits program will they get from being associated with you?
5. Do people constantly see you growing? Can they tell that you are evolving?

Everyone Needs a Consigliere: Finding Trusted Advisers

Even the greatest entrepreneurs aren't solo acts. For many reasons, they require help. They only have so many hours in a day. Their knowledge is limited to certain areas. They need other perspectives to help shape their own.

In a Mob family, there is a position specifically designed to provide wise counsel: the consigliere. The same holds true in the business world. Warren Buffett may get the headlines, but Charlie Munger is indispensable to his success. Steve Jobs had Steve Wozniak. Bill Gates had Paul Allen. Mark Zuckerberg had Sean Parker to challenge him to expand the vision and then Sheryl Sandberg to execute that vision.

Patty McCord spent fourteen years at Netflix and is the author of *Powerful: Building a Culture of Freedom and Responsibility*. Her expertise is in human resource management; her title at Netflix was chief talent officer. In my opinion, her greatest value was challenging CEO Reed Hastings. When I interviewed her, she told a story about a time when Hastings had to deliver an important speech the next day. McCord noticed a sheepish look on his face as he hammered away on his computer keyboard.

She suspected that Hastings was doing what had made him successful as an individual, rather than what he needed to do as a leader. She got into his face and said, "You're fixing bugs. Stop being a geek engineer, and be a leader." Keep in mind that Hastings had the authority to fire her. Not only did he keep her for fourteen years, they also used to carpool to work together. Why? Because she was not afraid to challenge him and point out his blind spots.

Insecure leaders surround themselves with "yes people." Effective leaders surround themselves with people who challenge them. They also find and hire people who are much smarter than they are—especially in areas in which they are weak.

In my videos, you constantly hear me talk about Mario. He's one of the guys I depend on most. When I first started making videos, I struggled in front of the camera. Mario had this incredible way of extracting a better delivery from me without making me feel self-conscious. Even though he technically works for me, he wouldn't hesitate to hold me to the higher standard we had set for the content and the brand.

Your future consigliere is likely someone you already know. The key thing to look for is similar values but different temperaments. If you're impatient and hotheaded, you want someone who is calm and deliberate. If you're an introvert, find an extrovert. If your inclination is to be judgmental and unforgiving, find someone who is empathetic and accepting. Regardless of temperament, it's important for him or her to be calm and in control of his or her emotions.

Both in business and in life, I'm very choosy about whom I allow into my inner circle. One of the reasons I married my wife, Jennifer Bet-David, is that she's the only person who can calm my nerves. For different facets of life, I have cultivated a small group of people I can go to for counsel on different topics.

I put so much stock in balance that when I'm in the middle of a big decision, I'll often invite two different personalities into the boardroom to help process an issue. It's most effective when the two people are polar opposites. After I present the issue to them, I simply sit there and watch them go back and forth. Occasionally, I'll ask a question to stoke the fire. I want to make sure I hear the most convincing arguments for all sides of the issue. The clash of two opinions leads me closer to the truth.

I have a friend who creates written content. He's impatient, and his primary belief is that perfection is the enemy of completion. His partner is patient to a fault and believes that urgency is the enemy of professionalism. Their yin-and-yang approach creates the perfect balance. Mario and I have a similar dynamic. We don't need to *pretend* to play good cop/bad cop. Because we have similar values but different temperaments, he naturally balances me and saves me from being my own worst enemy. He would tell you that I have also saved him on many occasions, and we laugh about those stories as we work and travel together. As much as I love numbers, having someone with whom I can reflect and reminisce has value beyond what I could ever begin to quantify.

A Trusted Adviser

1. Is skilled at processing issues, able to think many moves ahead
2. Has values similar to yours but a different temperament (is strong where you are weak)
3. Is calm under pressure
4. Is not afraid to challenge you and point out your blind spots
5. Is loyal, with no personal agenda

Keep Donnie Brasco Out of Your Business

One of the worst mistakes entrepreneurs make is not doing due diligence before making a key hire. You hire someone who comes highly recommended. He does a great job, and everyone likes him. You promote him until he's in a position of influence within your company. You trust him absolutely, sharing information without reservation. It is inconceivable that he would ever do anything to violate your trust.

Until he does.

You may have seen the movie or read the book about Donnie Brasco, the name used by undercover FBI agent Joe Pistone when he infiltrated the Mafia. He worked undercover for six years as part of the Bonanno family, earning the trust of the top people, including crime lord Dominick Napolitano, aka Sonny Black. As a result of Pistone's undercover work, the FBI arrested 212 mobsters.

After six years, the FBI wanted to pull Pistone out, but Pistone insisted that he stay longer in order to become a "made man." FBI agents finally went to Sonny Black and told him that the guy he knew as Donnie Brasco was actually an FBI agent. Sonny responded, "I don't believe you."

Eventually, Sonny Black was murdered and his body was discovered with his hands cut off. The Mafia dons were furious with Sonny for letting a rat into their operation. The fact that the rat had shaken hands with all of them was the ultimate insult.

There probably isn't a more suspicious, distrustful group than the Mafia, but its members trusted the guy they knew as Donnie Brasco. That's the lesson I want you to absorb: you've got to do due diligence no matter how trustworthy people seem. This is especially true if you're going to give them access to sensitive information that you don't want your competitors to have. Spend time with them. Ask them questions. Ask others about them. Observe how they behave. You can never know for sure if people are trustworthy, but you can get a feel for who they are. That may be enough for you to extend trust to them, at least in certain circumstances and in certain areas of the business.

I asked Michael McGowan, a thirty-year FBI undercover agent who worked closely with the Russian mob, three Cosa Nostra families, and the Sinaloa Cartel, an international crime syndicate, why the Bonanno family had allowed Brasco to get that deep into the family. His answer was simple: greed. The story of Donnie Brasco is the perfect cautionary tale to remind you to do research before you allow someone access to insider information about your company.

Entrepreneurs like to think that they know their people better than their therapists or spouses do, but that's just not true. You don't know if your right-hand man has a secret gambling problem. You don't know if your CFO is vulnerable to making bad decisions because of a traumatic event in his life. Instead of thinking you can see into people's souls, start using data and a systematic approach to research your new hires.

Five Questions You Must Answer
Before Making Any Big Hire

1. How many and what type of references did you call? Did you talk to other people who worked with the hire about what type of individual he or she is?

2. Is this person likable (the reason you hired him or her) but lacks a significant skill set?

3. Did you conduct a background check to determine if there's something in his or her past that might be a red flag?

4. Did you question anything iffy on his or her résumé; for instance, if the person was on sabbatical for two years, did you dig deeper to determine why?

5. Does the contract you offered include a 90- to 120-day probationary period? This will give you enough time to evaluate the new hire's performance. It will also give the new hire time to learn what he or she needs to improve and make an effort to do so.

I can't emphasize enough how important it is to be thorough when hiring. Make a bad hire, and you'll pay for it every day. In a January 2014 article in *Harvard Business Review*, Patty McCord explained why:

> If you're careful to hire people who will put the company's interests first, who understand and support the desire for a high-performance workplace, 97% of your employees will do the right thing. Most companies spend endless time and money writing and enforcing HR policies to deal with problems the other 3% might cause. Instead, we tried really hard to not hire those people, and we let them go if it turned out we'd made a hiring mistake.

Give Me a Piece of It: Granting Equity to Build a Team

Why is the United States the immigration leader? Why does it have more than 44 million immigrants, far more than the number two country? The United States doesn't have the largest population or the most land, but it has something that relatively few other countries can offer: the chance to get equity and build wealth. People can come to the United States and start a business and own it; they can buy a piece of land or a building and own it. This is the American dream, the chance to own a piece of the country.

As a result, the United States attracts the best, hardest-working people. Do you want to attract the best, hardest-working people to your company? Give them a piece of it.

Early in my career, I worked for a company where I was one of the top sales earners. I wasn't happy with the way the company was run, and as I mentioned earlier, I wrote a sixteen-page letter to management. One of my requests was that they give their key people a chance for equity or profit sharing.

Without ownership or profit sharing, I saw myself as an employee only. In the absence of granting me stock, even as the company's star salesman, I was an adversary rather than a partner. Losing me would reduce the company's revenue by several million dollars. All that would be required to keep me was to give me the tiniest incentive so that I would feel like an owner.

The management said no. Furthermore, they were convinced that I was never going to leave, given that I would lose my renewals and lucrative residual commissions on the several thousand clients I had on the books. My plans were to help grow the company to be the largest insurance agency and go on to one day be the CEO of the firm.

I said, "You think my renewals are enough to keep me from leaving? You believe I think that small? You're out of your minds."

I left. But the need for equity wasn't just true for me. It's true of anyone who is ambitious, dreams big, and possesses talent. I always give people working for entrepreneurs this advice: Go to the top person, and ask what you can do to own a piece of the company. If he or she says, "Nothing," leave. If he or she says, "Something," stick around and hit the goals you set up together as a condition of ownership.

You're not going to get something for nothing. Don't say, "I'm incredibly talented and accomplished, so give me a piece of the company." You have to achieve to get what you want, and as long as the markers are fair, it's a good deal for both the entrepreneur and his high-performing people. It's also not effective to use leaving as a threat. The key is to ask what specific achievements you need to accomplish to earn equity.

If you own a business, you may have reservations about granting equity. You may be thinking, "Well, Pat can do this because he has a huge company with lots of revenue, but I'm not as big, so I can't offer the same kind of deal." You're thinking only one move ahead. Contrast that level of thinking to a grand master, who sees enough moves ahead to identify the upside. Look, I'm not telling you to start throwing around shares in your company. What I am saying is that granting even a few shares of stock is enough to make people feel as though they have skin in the game and are long-term partners.

If you have a scarcity mindset, you're always thinking that there isn't enough or some disaster is just around the corner where you won't have enough.

If you have 100 percent conviction about your future truth, you'll think differently. If conviction isn't enough, do the math. Let's say your company has averaged $10 million in revenue the last five years with a 15 percent profit margin. That's $1.5 million in net income. You decide you want to hire Johnny to help you grow the business, but Johnny is insisting on either an equity stake or a bonus. At first, you balk at that. Johnny tells you that if he helps take the business from $10 million to $15 million, he wants a $250,000 bonus. Your initial response is that you can't afford that large a payout.

You do the math. Your net income will go from $1.5 million to $2.25 million. How can you begrudge Johnny $250,000, given that increase in profit? It's essentially a two-for-one trade in your favor. Johnny's hard work will put $500,000 into the company's coffers. (This example assumes that your company wasn't already growing. If it was, you would structure the incentive based on his ability to outpace current growth. For example, if the company had been growing at 20 percent the last three years and Johnny was able to increase it to 50 percent, that additional 30 percent would be attributed to him.)

The only justification for saying no is that you are thinking short-term. If you're still protesting, thinking that everyone in the company will want the same thing, your short-term thinking is digging you into a logic nightmare. Think about it: What could be better than everyone in your company wanting to generate more profit to increase both their wealth and yours?

Do you think Bill Gates begrudges all the wealth created by those who worked at Microsoft? Gates didn't *give* people equity. Because he was thinking several moves ahead, he *granted* equity to those who earned it. I read one estimate that Microsoft has created three billionaires (let us not forget Steve Ballmer) and 12,000 millionaires.

■ ■ ■ ■ ■

Are you starting to see that the way to build wealth is to give others the opportunity to build it alongside you?

Some people are motivated by equity, some by profit sharing, some by big salaries, some by bonuses, and still others by long-term security. No two are the same. The key is to create the right type of compensation plan that will attract and retain the kind of talent you're looking for.

Personally, I favor equity and profit sharing over bonuses, since it increases the odds that the right people will be with you over the long haul (I'll elaborate more on that in the next section). Plus, just as homeowners treat their houses better than renters do, once you give people ownership in a company, their mindset shifts. All of a sudden, they are working for themselves and have an incentive to increase not only their own income but also the value of the company.

This may all seem like common sense, but it's easy to be penny wise and pound foolish. Take a European company, one of the continent's largest battery cell manufacturers. It came to me because it was growing only 2 percent annually. When I met with the CEO, the first question I asked was "How much do you pay your salespeople?"

"Twenty-five hundred dollars monthly."

"Okay, but how much more than that can they receive?" I asked.

"I don't get it," he said.

"I mean how much in addition to their salary do they receive for performance?"

"Nothing."

"Nothing?"

I couldn't believe it. How hard would you work if all you could expect was $2,500 each month, regardless of your performance?

He changed the compensation plan, focusing on implementing a profit-sharing plan. Shortly after he put it into place, the company's growth rate increased by 25 percent. Sometimes the key to growth is staring you in the face. Change your compensation plan so that people feel as though they've been "given a piece," and they will work harder, longer, and more creatively.

Don't Give Up on the First Date: How to Create Golden Handcuffs

Here's the strategy: Give your key people equity, but don't do so immediately. Let them earn it.

You may be smart and perceptive, but no one is a mind reader. Prospective employees may look great at first glance, but you've got to get to know them before you make an investment in them. By creating a waiting period to grant equity, it gives them time to sell you that they belong there. I'm always selling my people. That's part of my job, to reenlist them continuously in our mission and vision. I'm selling them on the money they can make, the future they can have. I'm selling them on the culture. I believe in the company I created, and I want to make sure they believe in it, too.

When people get hired, they often stop selling themselves. They think they're in, so they can just go about their business. No. I need to feel that my people want to be there, that they're excited about it, that they believe they are uniquely able to help us reach our objectives. I'm paying attention to what they say and do. If their words and actions align with what the company needs, then they've sold me.

Don't make snap judgments about the people you hire. Instead, take a wait-and-see approach. They may seem perfect, and they may have a lot of talent, but they may not be a good fit for the culture you're creating. When they're interviewing for the job and first start working, they're on their best behavior. Don't buy it. Make them sell you.

Granting equity to your team is more art than science. When it's done correctly, you will accomplish three objectives:

1. You'll transform your team members' thinking from an employee mentality to an ownership mentality.
2. You'll incentivize your people to work harder and smarter to increase your company's value.
3. You'll increase employee retention by structuring compensation intelligently.

Only two years into founding my company, I created an equity plan. Keep in mind that the nature of financial services, which includes residuals from renewals, automatically creates a high retention level. I wasn't content to be best in class; I wanted a compensation plan that would redefine the industry.

I approached the question the same way a composer or choreographer would. Creating the right compensation plan is like creating the right melody. What makes the Academy Award–winning composer Hans Zimmer special is that he knows how to take different tunes and bring them together to work perfectly for an entire movie. The same goes for an effective compensation plan: all of the pieces need to be put into place to create the best overall package. You may think I sound dramatic, but something this important requires this degree of detail. Here are the keys to creating the most effective compensation structure:

1. Decide what behavior or final result you want to recognize.
2. Study the current compensation structure within your industry. Even if you're going to disrupt the status quo, you first need to know what the status quo is.
3. Find ways to create three tiers of incentives to strive for. This is much more effective than one all-or-nothing incentive to compete for.

I created a plan that allows agents to begin earning equity within two years of starting. The vesting schedule is complex. When you're ready to do this in your company, you'll need either an expert CFO or an outside consultant to handle the details.

The big picture is that your team will earn shares of the company and vest that ownership over time. As a result, they will feel like owners, be paid like owners (simultaneously enriching you), and know that to maximize their earnings, it makes sense to stay at your company. The term *golden handcuffs*, originated in 1976, means that as long as people stay with your company, they'll continue to get their gold.

Above all, remember: Treat your people right, or someone else will.

What You Must Recognize in Order to Retain Talent

- People want to be compensated properly for their efforts.
- Outstanding performers want to participate in the success of the company.
- People want to know that they're part of an organization that's making an impact.

- People want to be recognized in front of their peers for the work that they do.
- People want to know that there's an opportunity for them to grow within the company.
- People want to be judged based on a clear set of expectations given to them without the goalposts constantly changing.

Communicate Your Expectations Clearly, Early, and Often

We often mistakenly believe that people's character is fixed. As a result, when we see a new hire display bad habits, we think we made a hiring mistake. In reality, we might be able to train that person to succeed. The key is to monitor his or her performance and provide feedback and better communication. Letting people know where they stand accomplishes three important objectives:

1. They know the specific actions they must take to keep their job.
2. If they fail to perform those specific actions, letting them go will seem fair and objective.
3. You can begin the process of finding someone else to complete their tasks. The best-case scenario is the person will improve and you will have deepened your "bench." If that doesn't happen and the person leaves, someone else can step in and take over his or her job seamlessly.

■ ■ ■ ■ ■

Set clear expectations like this: "Bob, you told me you're somebody who shows up on time, but three times in the last two weeks, you've been late."

Bob responds, "But it's only eight minutes."

"Eight minutes is eight minutes too many, and you told us you're reliable. We expect people to be punctual. I just want you to know, if that continues, that's going to be an issue for us."

When you compromise standards at the top, you create an environment in which low standards are accepted. It's all downhill from there.

This direct approach gives Bob the option of quitting before you fire him—an option many people will take. You're not going to bat a thousand on new hires. When you see that people aren't a good fit, you must be clear about your standards and tell them how they're falling short. Oftentimes, they will surprise you by stepping up.

Let's say that Bob's behavior continues to be a problem. When it comes time to let him go, he won't be surprised because you've told him what he needed to improve. You say, "Bob, I don't think this is going to be a surprise to you because you were late three times in two weeks, and I told you that's an issue. Even so, you continued to be late. I'm afraid we have no choice but to let you go."

Straight to the point.

For those of you who run a successful business that isn't dependent on people showing up on time, it's an entirely different story. You may be in the creative field and be okay if your editors and developers show up when they feel like it—as long as their work gets done. That's fine if it works for your industry. However, if it's necessary for employees to show up on time, you can't compromise or the bad behavior will spread.

I tell this story to emphasize that the way you both hire new people and manage them will lessen how often you have to fire people, and it will lessen the bad feelings when you do have to let someone go. For specific strategies on firing effectively, let's dig in more deeply.

Fire Gently. Again, Fire Gently

One of the toughest things for entrepreneurs to do right is fire people, and doing it wrong can poison the company culture. Once you accept some responsibility for an employee not working out, you'll approach this unpleasant task with a more empathic mindset. Don't take it out on your employee. Instead, learn how to fire well.

As you're about to discover, this is an important but much-neglected entrepreneurial skill. Show me someone who burns bridges every time he terminates people, and I'll show you someone who lacks empathy at best or is a sadist or bully at worst. The same is true of entrepreneurs who can't pull the trigger, who warn problem employees constantly but lack the gumption to let them go. If you have one bad employee, his or her attitude and actions can affect other employees negatively.

■ ■ ■ ■ ■

Let's draw a parallel between firing someone and breaking up a relationship. To avoid the unpleasantness of a breakup, perhaps you have relied on classic lines:

"It's really not you; it's me."

"Given the direction of our relationship, we both knew this day was coming."

"I'm the problem."

You've tried to be amicable in order to minimize the anger, sadness, shame, and other strong emotions that can arise in such a situation. As an entrepreneur firing someone, you're going to want to resort to similar lines: "I'm sure you'll do great elsewhere; we just have philosophical differences" or "You've got a lot of talent; I'm sure you'll get another job soon, and I'll be glad to give you a good reference."

Generally, though, relying on classic breakup lines won't work. People aren't stupid. They are human, and that means you need to treat them with respect. This isn't just the decent thing to do. It's not just you who is going to be giving them a reference. They're the ones who will be using social media to talk about you, and you don't want them hurting your reputation.

Don't drag the firing out, but don't go nuclear, either. Time does not heal all wounds, nor does it make someone who is incompetent suddenly, magically competent. If you've given that person fair warning and he or she hasn't responded, don't keep giving him or her repeated chances to improve. The odds are that he or she won't. Have your exit meeting and make a clean break. At the same time, let me warn you against employing a scorched-earth strategy. If you lose your temper and decide to get rid of everyone who has ever made a mistake or displeased you in some way, you'll be left with an office of one. Remember, too, that you may be firing them because you should never have hired them in the first place.

That reminds me of Houtan Sarraf, better known as Hoot. I love Hoot, who was one of my favorite assistants. But he wasn't one of my favorites because he was good at his job. In fact, he was probably the worst assistant in the world's history of assistants. He was disorganized and failed to follow through on tasks. He was a great guy, though, and I loved to hang around with him.

After a certain point, I couldn't tolerate his ineffectiveness, and I called him into my office. "Hoot," I said, "I've good news and bad news. Which do you want to hear first?" He said the bad news. "Okay. You're terrible at being an assistant, and that's why I'm letting you go."

"And the good news?" he asked.

"I trust you. You're a kind, wonderful human being who will do well, just not in an assistant position." We talked about what he wanted to do in his life—who he truly wanted to be—and he confided that he had always wanted to surf the best waves all over the world. I encouraged him to follow his dream, and for the next ten years, he did just that. By teaching surfing on the beaches he frequented and working in restaurants, he funded his adventure, traveling to China, New Zealand, and Australia in search of great waves. When he returned from his trip, I heard endless stories about his adventures. I consider him like a younger brother. I also trust that he'll never apply for an assistant's job again.

Patty McCord summed up my philosophy perfectly: "If we wanted only 'A' players on our team, we had to be willing to let go of people whose skills no longer fit, no matter how valuable their contributions had once been."

Six Techniques for Becoming an Effective Terminator

I've compiled this list from a great deal of experience. Please understand that you may be subject to legal action when you fire someone. Therefore, prior to any employment termination, you should consult the company's lawyer or HR department, if there is one.

1. **Fire gently.** When it comes time to tell people they're through, you want to do it without histrionics. You don't have to blame. You don't have to retaliate when your employee blames you. If you bash the employee, no one will want to work for you, and if the employee bashes you, you're not going to give him the type of referral that will help him get hired elsewhere.

2. **Get right to the point.** When you're firing somebody, don't drag it out. Though people may be shocked that they're being fired and emerge from that shock to protest, don't let the process become protracted. Don't waste time trying to justify your actions or prove that they deserve to be fired. There's no point, and you'll end up wasting time and emotional energy.

3. **Be firm yet gentle.** Yes, I'm reminding you to be gentle again because I don't want you to become so firm that you turn into a

rock and start battering people. Being firm means getting to the point quickly and not wavering. Remind yourself that this is not a debate but a decision. It didn't work out. Both of you have to move on. Period.

4. **Acknowledge the other person's feelings.** Say something such as "Listen, I understand that this may be a bit of a frustrating and disappointing moment for you. I've been let go before, and I can tell you, it's upsetting. However, I just want to make sure I totally understand your feelings and what you're thinking." Listen to what the other person says and then communicate that you "get" the emotion he or she is expressing: "I know you're angry . . ."

5. **Have a good exit strategy.** A bad exit strategy is having one of your people fire the employee you personally hired. This is a guaranteed method to create one pissed-off former employee. But what if you hired John and he worked for Sue? Then you and Sue should be in the room together when you tell John the bad news. And make the exit an interview rather than a summary dismissal. Don't kick the person out the door but ease him or her out with information and compassion. If you're firing a supplier who works outside your office, that's a different story and you may be able to do it through a phone call. But if someone has worked in your office, you need to conduct an in-person interview before he or she leaves.

6. **Talk about the person's strengths.** This builds on the last point. Include suggestions about how he or she can leverage his or her strengths to succeed in his or her next job: "You're really good at X, which means you'd be well suited to do Y." Turn into an empathetic coach who wants to help the person find his or her next position based on what he or she does well. If you take that approach, even your former employees will be fans of your company.

■ ■ ■ ■ ■

Hire slowly; fire quickly. Take your time to be sure you hire the right people, but when you're convinced that someone is the wrong person, don't let the individual linger and hurt productivity and morale.

I hope that by now you are thinking beyond being a solopreneur. A company of one has a limited impact. No one builds a billion-dollar company on his or her own.

7

Create a Principles-Based Culture

Leadership is about making others better as a result of your presence and making sure that impact lasts in your absence.
—Sheryl Sandberg, COO of Facebook
and founder of LeanIn.org

It doesn't matter if you're an atheist or an agnostic, elements of religion have a place in your business. Before you dismiss this idea, let's look a little closer. I actually believe there's a lot to be learned from studying the religions of the world. What two things do all religions have in common? True believers and rituals.

What business can succeed without people believing in it? And what business doesn't have particular symbols, sayings, and credos that are part of its culture?

Google is a religion. So is Apple. So are Southwest Airlines and Walmart. Their CEOs won't acknowledge it, but each company follows "commandments," evangelizes through social and other media, and believes passionately in its business strategy and cultural norms.

I believe in the same things, and this belief energizes my company. It helps sustain us when things are tough, and it emboldens us when things are going well. True believers are formidable, so whatever entrepreneurial venture you create, make sure that you and your people are united by a common belief.

Having a great business idea and talented people isn't enough. As an entrepreneur who knows the importance of strategy and talent, you might disagree. I guarantee you, though, if your team doesn't have similar principles and values, it will never come close to reaching its full potential. It doesn't matter if you've invented a better mousetrap or if you employ the best and the brightest. Without shared values, you can't sustain what you've built.

It's one thing to know who you want to be; it's another thing to mold an entire organization to a set of core beliefs that will remain in place with or without you. In this chapter, you will learn how you can achieve this.

Build the Principles

Right after I started my company, I was in Hawaii with my then girlfriend and now wife, and we went upstairs to our room. Hawaii is a romantic place, so naturally, we did what young couples do. You know where this is going, right? As I put the DO NOT DISTURB sign on the door, I couldn't help but think of that '80s hit by The System and started to sing, "Hang a sign up on the door. Say don't disturb this groove." I secured the dead bolt and promptly got down to business. And when I say "got down to business," I mean that I grabbed a pen and piece of paper and said, "Let's make a list of values and principles that we want to live by. Let's see how many we come up with."

We came up with forty-three right off the bat. Then we narrowed the list down to ten.

You might think this is a weird thing to do when you're in Hawaii with your girlfriend, but as everyone who knows me will tell you, I'm obsessed with principles. When we decided to have kids, my wife,

Jennifer, and I took another piece of paper and did the same exercise. As a result, our family has a culture. We stand for something. We have principles along with clear values that we repeat over and over.

What We Stand For as a Family

- Lead—because it will be necessary in every situation you face
- Respect—because everyone has something to teach you
- Improve—because that's how you know everything will work out
- Love—because everyone is dealing with a challenge in life

What We Don't Tolerate

- Bullying and being bullied

Our Core Values

- **Courage.** Not being afraid to challenge others
- **Wisdom.** Making the right choices
- **Tolerance.** Knowing that we're dealing with human beings, who change all the time
- **Understanding.** Appreciating and respecting that everyone has different ideas and values

We repeat these over and over. My kids get sick of hearing them. When it comes to our company, my team is always making fun of me because I repeat these beliefs so often. The way I see it, unless your people are mocking you, you have not repeated your message enough.

Why am I so relentless, in both my personal and business family, about repeating our principles? Because I believe in the power of reminding and re-reminding. I want these values and principles to be top of mind at all times for my team and family.

I've observed other entrepreneurs who have problems in their businesses: people surfing porn sites when they should be working, doing unethical things to get business, and working just hard enough to get by but not hard enough to excel. Some of them have failed to clarify what they value. And some may have been clear about their beliefs but haven't repeated them enough—and *demonstrated* them enough—for them to sink in.

Prove What You Stand For

I was at Nordstrom shopping with my son Dylan, who is six. He was horsing around and climbing on my back when a lady looked at him and started to smile. She said that her kids are now older but she remembers that phase. I asked her the same question I always ask parents who are older than I am: "What are three things you did as a parent that worked?"

Her first two answers were the common ones: love your children, and give them plenty of attention. The last one was about credibility. She said, "If you threaten to punish them or take something away from them, do it or else your word loses value."

In 2010, only one year after starting my company, I hired some "rogue" agents. As I soon learned, they were willing to cut corners and engage in unethical practices in order to get business. Obviously, I didn't know they were rogue agents when I hired them. In fact, they seemed like great hires because they were killing it—each making more than $100,000 during their first three months with us.

Then I started hearing about their shady methods. At that point in the business, I couldn't justify the expense of hiring a full-time compliance officer, but I soon realized that to balance our explosive offense (rapid growth), we also needed to play defense. The reason I hired Amour Noubarentz—he'd been my branch office manager back in 2002—was that I knew he shared my principles. I asked him to look into the allegations about those new hires. Amour warned me that I had to let him do his job and I might not like what I heard. There was a chance that those big earners might be guilty of behaviors that didn't align with the principles that I was pounding into our company's culture. I promised him free rein.

Three months later, he presented me with evidence that our number one producer had generated business in a way that was not only unethical but also possibly illegal.

"You have to terminate him," Amour said.

Despite our earlier conversation, I was reluctant to do so. Like many entrepreneurs, I value people who can produce, and that rogue agent was producing like crazy. As Amour shared his evidence, which included a history of problems with the FBI (didn't I tell you I've learned the hard way about hiring?), I had no choice. Firing people is always difficult, and in that case, when I met with the agent and his business partner/wife, she was crying and telling me they had kids and didn't know how they could support them. I ended up taking care of them as best I could, but I still had to let him go. You simply can't tolerate people who violate your principles.

After that incident, I started our company's book-of-the-month club. I initially assigned two books for the employees to read: Jon Huntsman's *Winners Never Cheat: Everyday Values That We Learned as Children (but May Have Forgotten)* and Ken Blanchard and Norman Vincent Peale's *The Power of Ethical Management*. I wanted to communicate to everyone that we had zero tolerance for unethical behavior.

Everyone started talking about the principles and values in the books. A few people left the company because they didn't want to work in a place where they couldn't bend the rules. For all my talk about principles, I needed to prove by my actions that I was committed to them. Firing our top producer and pushing millions of dollars of revenue out the door was all the evidence my team needed to see where I stood.

As Dad and Dalio Say,
Never Be Afraid of the Truth

Speaking of books, the one that really mirrored my philosophy about business and life was Ray Dalio's *Principles*. (Yes, I'm aware this is the third mention of it. Are you starting to see how my repetitive nature drives people crazy?) Dalio, founder of Bridgewater Associates, the world's largest hedge fund, wrote the book to share the guiding principles that served him in his personal and professional life. I made it mandatory reading for my entire company. I was so impressed by the book that I reached out to Dalio to have him as a guest on Valuetainment. We had an extensive conversation about his culture and approach to business at his headquarters in Connecticut.

As I expected, some people were uncomfortable with the book's concepts, especially "radical transparency." As part of this principle, people are obligated to call each other out when they believe someone is making a mistake or crossing a line. Though our company was also founded on this principle, not everyone was comfortable with it. Ultimately, the book did what I wanted it to, which was to create productive (and often heated) discussions about Dalio's ideas and our culture.

Even Alice, our COO, confronted me and said, "This is too radical. You can't run the home office like you do the sales force."

When someone I respect talks, I listen. But when we processed the issue, there was no data or real evidence to convince me not to be radically transparent. All Alice had to fall back on was that it was too different. Even so, I understood where she was coming from. Because Alice had been at Pacific Life for twenty-two years, she had developed an idea of what an insurance agent *should* be like. Radical transparency was way too different from what she imagined.

Being radically transparent was a nonnegotiable for me. I told Alice I wanted to be different. I'm extremely comfortable being radically transparent; it's being normal that I can't stand. Alice and Ian Benedict, our CFO, got together and strategized with the entire team. They brought up the team's concerns and shared a game plan with me. Ultimately, we decided that we needed to find the balance of respect and honesty—while staying committed to being radically transparent.

■ ■ ■ ■ ■

As I was growing up, I can't tell you how many times my dad said, "Never be afraid of the truth." It stuck with me, and I instilled that value in our company. I had studied many other organizations and felt strongly that being direct and painfully truthful were important.

One of the most famous case studies from Harvard Business School is about Morgan Stanley and Rob Parson. When John Mack became president of Morgan Stanley in 1993, he wanted to change Morgan Stanley's culture and embrace teamwork in order to cross-sell, broaden the firm's reach, and decrease all the internal fighting. The mantra that expressed his vision was "One-firm firm." Employees would be judged based on a 360-degree performance evaluation by superiors, colleagues, and subordinates.

Parson was the classic example of a kick-ass producer and an abrasive teammate. He expanded Morgan Stanley's market share in his line of business from 2 percent to 12.5 percent in a short time and took Morgan Stanley from tenth to second in his market. His colleagues found him to be arrogant and walked on eggshells around him—which was a major issue given Mack's directive to change the company's culture.

Many people who read that case study thought that firing Parson would be a no-brainer. If Morgan Stanley was going to be true to its culture, it needed to put team players first. Though Parson was a big-time producer, his behavior was not consistent with the organization's new mission.

I saw it differently. What I saw was a manager who was afraid to communicate directly. The case study described how the manager would "suggest" things and hope that Parson would get the hint. What Parson's boss failed to do was state directly and specifically what Parson had done wrong and what he needed to change in order to keep his job. The problem wasn't Morgan Stanley's culture; it was the lack of direct communication from one of its senior leaders.

As is often the case, managers are afraid to honestly tell people how they feel. I can understand being fearful of hurting the feelings of a star salesman. But it beats the alternative. Without direct feedback and radical transparency, Parson continued treating his co-workers poorly.

In my view, justice was ultimately served when his manager, not Parson, was terminated.

My Business Principles

- Never compromise our nonnegotiables.
- Micromanage until there is trust.
- What brought us here won't take us to the next level.
- No one has 100 percent job security, including the founder or CEO.
- Create positive peer pressure by challenging one another.
- Beat your prior best.
- Treat the company's money like it's your own.
- Be radically open-minded but not easily persuaded.
- Fight any temptation to lower expectations and standards.
- Create an environment where our team is taken care of financially and professionally.

In addition to these principles, I share with my employees things that don't sit well with me: feeling entitled, complaining, being negative, being pessimistic, leaking secrets, not taking care of one's health, gossiping, and taking advice from the wrong people.

Establish a Company Code

Establishing a company code is crucial if you want to run a thriving business. We hear so much about building a large network. As a result, we may forget that our most important network is within our own business. People need boundaries; they need to know what lines can't be crossed. Part of the code may be that you can't poach business from one of your colleagues. Or it's forbidden to be disrespectful to your boss when he makes a request. Or, in the case of our company and Dalio's Bridgewater Associates, that you call out people—even those who are above you in title and seniority—when they violate the company's core principles.

When I managed my first sales office at age twenty-five, all of us there worked long, hard, and late. You know what happens in a sales office filled with a lot of energy and testosterone. That was fine, except that we established a code: If you're going to date someone's relative, direct report, or anyone else where sensitivities might exist, you had to clear it with the affected individual first. Now, it wasn't as though you'd go up to someone and say, "Hey, I'm going to sleep with your sister tonight." But you owed your colleagues the courtesy of requesting permission to date someone who was meaningful to them. By adhering to that code, we avoided creating blood enemies and the kind of animosity that would poison the work environment.

I'm a man with high testosterone. I'm extremely driven, so I can't sit here and tell you I was an angel. I partied hard from age eighteen to twenty-five, but I had one code: my private life was private, and my choices didn't have a negative impact on the business. I wasn't perfect, but I did my best to stick to that code.

I share this story from a period of my life when the biggest challenge we faced was the team partying together on the weekends and things getting out of control. Fifteen years later, now that I am the founder and CEO of my own company, the code has only gotten deeper and more technical. Especially when people have kids and spouses who depend on their income, the need for integrity becomes even greater.

If you're going to establish a culture, you have to let people know what you stand for. Have a clear code, a guiding set of principles, and make sure everyone knows, without any ambiguity, what the consequences will be for violating it.

Create a Replacement Game Plan

One of the reasons you create a culture is that it elevates everyone. It also allows you to scale up faster.

The less your business depends on you, the more valuable it is. The more your business depends on you, the less valuable it is. There's no exit opportunity if the business relies on your personality.

A company that rarely makes headlines is Microsoft. Yet in September 2019, it was the only public company with a market cap of more than a trillion dollars (at various times, Apple, Amazon, and Google have had valuations north of a trillion dollars). Are you starting to notice a trend here? If your mind didn't immediately go to cultivating intrapreneurs and offering equity, you're not reading carefully enough. Now consider that thirteen years prior to the company's reaching a trillion-dollar valuation, on June 15, 2006, Bill Gates announced his decision to leave his full-time position at the company in order to focus more on philanthropy.

At the time, Microsoft was trading at $23 a share, putting its market cap at $176 billion. In other words, the value of Microsoft has increased by *more than a trillion dollars* since Gates left! Still think organizations can't create a culture that is more powerful than a visionary leader? As highlighted in a December 31, 2019, story in *Barron's*, since Satya Nadella took over as CEO on February 4, 2014, Microsoft's valuation has increased by $930 million. Not to be outdone, since Tim Cook replaced Steve Jobs as CEO of Apple on August 24, 2011, the company's stock has increased by more than a trillion dollars.

(Keep the dates in mind when processing these examples. Because these companies are public, their valuations constantly fluctuate.)

Contingency planning sounds simple, right? But lots of entrepreneurs fail to do it. They are often overconfident, convinced that they are irreplaceable. Many are so egocentric that they can't fathom the idea of anyone but themselves running the company. If you have that mentality, it will keep you in control and prevent you from scaling the business.

Another pitfall is thinking that your key people won't ever leave. Or you believe that if someone does leave, someone else can just slide into his or her role. Neither belief is true. Ideally, you'll have your existing employees training their potential replacements. If you don't, you'll need to have your own eye on potential replacements with the right areas of competence, either inside or outside the company.

If you have a plan in place for how to replace every key member of your team, you can handle an unexpected exit without missing a beat. Plus you'll sleep better at night, knowing your next several moves are already planned out.

Six Strategies for Replacement and Skill Transfer

1. **List your tasks and skills.** Make a list of all your tasks and skills and determine which ones you are the best at and which ones you are not. Focus on your strengths, and replace yourself on all the other tasks.

2. **Identify who's seasonal and who's not.** You can't assume that everybody is going to work for you forever. You need to identify who is there to fill a six-year role and who a six-month role. If you determine that now, you won't be surprised when someone needs to be replaced.

3. **Know the different languages spoken by your sales, support, technical, and executive teams.** Sales leaders generate revenue and build a company through their efforts. Employees are hired to support those efforts. You need to know the difference between them. Executives require empowering language that makes them feel autonomous and respected.

4. **Know who can maintain the company culture.** It is very important that whoever replaces you will fit the culture you established so that the business can keep growing after you leave.

5. **Know your company's practices and procedures.** You need to put pen to paper and write down each department's practices and procedures. Replacements will then have a manual to follow, regardless of their level, making the transfer of specific skills quick and painless.

6. **Develop leaders to help spread the right mindset.** Have one-on-one conversations with your future leaders to inject the company's mindset into them now, before they need to replace someone. Your having a mindset of leadership development will also increase the value of your company.

Entrepreneurs need to play a continuous replacement game, replacing parts of themselves. At the beginning of the business, you did all the paperwork; now you can hire someone to take over that task. You handled all the financials; now you can hire a CFO to do so. This gives you time to devote yourself to the tasks that matter most to the business.

Media.net founder Divyank Turakhia, a thirty-eight-year-old with a net worth of $1.76 billion, once said, "Keep figuring out how to replace yourself because your time is most valuable in this process. Once you figure out what you're passionate about and as long as you're doing it, you'll be successful in doing that one thing and you keep doubling down yourself learning more."

Friction Is Good

There's a misconception that the best company cultures include everyone joining hands and singing "Kumbaya," that everyone gets along great, and that no one ever argues or gets upset.

Going back to personal relationships: Show me a marriage in which the couple never argues, and I'll show you a marriage that's headed for a blowup. If you and your spouse don't argue, one of you has probably found someone else to argue with.

We need friction in all areas of our lives. It's healthy, and it stimulates growth, creativity, and learning.

That's why I create friction when there is none and encourage you to do the same. When I was still working as a sales manager, before I founded my company, I implemented a policy of calling people out. I gave a speech in which I said, "Some of you guys are going to tell me you're upset with this guy, you don't like what he did, you don't like what she said. Stop it! Here are the values and principles we've established. This is our code. If someone violates these values and principles, you call them out. But don't come to me. I'm giving you permission to do it, even if they're senior to you. Values and principles transcend titles and seniority."

You know what happened after I made that speech? Immediately, the office started growing, and the friction between people stimulated the growth. Positive peer pressure is another way to describe the environment that we created. Everyone was pressuring everyone else to give their best and become better team players. We were all holding one another accountable.

I'm not saying that people started chewing one another out vindictively or cruelly. That's not it at all. It's more like the way siblings argue with love in their hearts but an edge in their voices and words that cut deep. And just as sometimes a son or a daughter can call out a parent for a bad decision, the same needs to happen in a company environment.

The key word in the expression "tough love" is "love." You have to love someone enough to put you both through the discomfort of such conversations.

■ ■ ■ ■ ■

There are two books that will help you find both the courage and the technique to navigate these types of discussions: *The Five Dysfunctions of a Team* by Patrick Lencioni and *Difficult Conversations: How to Discuss What Matters Most* by Douglas Stone, Bruce Patton, and Sheila Heen. Lencioni's book focuses on how organization politics can lead to team failure. *Difficult Conversations* guides you through how to deal with conflict and offers specific strategies for how to tackle disputes and talk through challenging issues.

If you want to see an example of tough love in action, watch the YouTube clip titled "Joe Rogan Breaks Down Brendan Schaub." Schaub, a top UFC fighter who is close friends with Rogan, was critiquing his own performance of a recent fight. There was some back-and-forth: two experts talking about the fundamentals of fighting. Rogan said, "A lot of things looked bad about the fight. . . . You looked very stiff. You didn't look fluid. . . . You didn't look like you were well prepared. . . . Your movement just didn't look like an elite fighter's movement."

You can see that at that point in the conversation, nothing was personal. It was more commentary on the mechanics of fighting, which was why Schaub seemed blindsided by Rogan's next comment: "I worry about your commitment to fighting, and I worry about where you stand."

Schaub tried to interrupt. "Really?"

Rogan continued by saying he thought Schaub had one foot out the door.

"I disagree," said Schaub.

"The reality of your skill set, where you're at now," Rogan said. "I don't see you beating the elite guys."

Rogan asked his buddy, "If you had a wrestling match with Cain Velasquez, how well do you think you'd do?"

"I think people would be surprised."

"I think you'd be surprised. I really do. I think he'd f—k you up. . . . There's a bridge between you and the best guys in the world. And I don't know if you can cross that bridge. That's the reality of life."

As rough as his feedback was, it felt to me that Rogan's heart could not have been in a better place. It takes courage to look a friend in the eye and confront him with the cold truth. The exchange continued, and then Rogan said, "I worry more about you than I do about them. . . . What I'm saying, I say with love. A hundred percent. I'm not saying this to hurt your feelings. That's the last thing I want to do. If I didn't love you, I wouldn't be willing to do this. And I wouldn't want to do this."

Such conversations are tough ones. No one ever said radical transparency is easy. No one ever said being direct is comfortable. But what's the alternative to hiding the truth? Watch a loved one self-destruct without doing anything to stop it or, in Rogan's case, watch his friend risk horrible injury—feeling more and more guilty as it all unfolds?

I can't tell you how Brendan Schaub processed that information. By the look on his face, he would have much preferred going to a drug-free dentist to hearing that critique. But as I said earlier, there's the easy choice and there's the effective choice. Rogan chose the latter. How Schaub decided to react was beyond Rogan's control.

Whether in life or business, it takes both courage and skill to be direct with people. Are you willing to go there in life? If not in your personal relationships, in your business, are you going to watch your star employee treat his coworkers poorly (think Rob Parson) and pray that he telepathically catches your drift?

If you want love without conflict, get a dog. I want it so badly that I have two adorable Shih Tzus, Jimbo and Kucci. But if you want to build an effective, principles-based culture, learn not only to embrace friction but also to create it.

Talk Behind People's Backs

Your parents probably told you, "Don't talk behind your friends' backs. It's not nice." Your parents were right. It's not nice. But if you want to produce results, it can be a winning tactic.

In *How to Win Friends and Influence People*, Dale Carnegie talked about giving people a reputation to live up to. Others call it identity building. If you constantly praise a particular skill or character trait, a person will manifest it more often. The praise, in turn, is repeated by that individual and becomes part of his or her character.

Let's say I have an employee named Garrett. I tell another employee, Lois, that Garrett is brilliant at following up on requests, that he never lets things slide and is always accountable for his assigned tasks. Invariably, Lois tells someone that I told her that about Garrett, and someone else tells another employee until it gets back to Garrett.

When Garrett hears what I told Lois, he gets excited about the recognition. I like to think of it as a positive friction. You can compliment someone like Garrett directly, which is fine, but when positive feedback reaches him through other employees, it gains a lot more weight. Garrett knows that others are aware of the boss's flattering remarks about his ability, and it solidifies the connection between Garrett and me and Garrett and the company. He's going to be more confident and motivated going forward.

Process this issue relative to your own employees. Who has talent but lacks aggressiveness or confidence? Have you tried and failed to encourage that person to be a stronger negotiator? What if you were to mention something positive about that person to another employee—what would you say, and how would you say it? Wait a few days, and see what happens. You've been trying to figure out how and when to motivate that employee in an impactful, lasting way. Now you know exactly what you have to do.

Make saying positive things behind your teammates' backs a habit, not just a once-a-year behavior. If you don't do it, your workplace will lack the friction that produces creative problem solving and positive peer pressure. Don't leave friction to chance. Create a culture in which you spread good words about people.

■ ■ ■ ■ ■

We started this chapter by comparing corporate culture to religion. We learned that great ideas and talented people aren't enough, just as in a family, love is not enough. You need principles. You must write them down, repeat them often, and show by example your commitment to honoring them.

I hope that studying Microsoft has provided you with a *trillion* reasons to make culture a priority. It's the key to scaling and the key to your business becoming less dependent on you. If your primary goal is wanting to be loved by everyone, you're in the wrong racket. It takes courage to have difficult conversations. If you believe strongly enough in your principles, you'll find the courage needed to be radically transparent—and, as a result, incredibly effective.

8

Trust = Speed:
The Power of Reliability

The more you know each other, the more you know what each other's thinking, the faster you can accelerate the trust and confidence in one another when you get on the field.

—Tom Brady

I am in the anticipation business. I'm in the life insurance industry, not because people are going to die tomorrow but because when they do, their family is going to suffer for a lack of preparation. Contracts are all about anticipation. After being ripped off and screwed too many times, I've learned the importance of anticipating issues and putting documents and controls into place to guard against the unknown.

I am not pessimistic about human nature. I am, however, a realist about the details of a contract negotiation. It was John McAfee, the eccentric software entrepreneur, who said that when a soldier is captured, he will disclose whatever secrets with which he's been entrusted—that he would give up his own mother under torture. That may not be true of everyone, but I do believe that entrepreneurs need to be cautious about trusting just any team member, especially with information that could hurt or even destroy the business.

Trust is multidimensional, not one-dimensional.

You may trust one of your people to handle sales but not human resources. You may trust someone with information about your current plans but not your future strategy. Trust is nuanced. For instance, I trust my enemies; I trust that they'll spin a story with the intention of trying to drive me out of business.

Since trust is so critical to speed, we also need to ask: Why is speed so important? It almost seems too obvious to have to answer. To say it's everything doesn't feel like an overstatement. Whether you sell a product or a service, speed is required to make it, to deliver it, and to go from the sale to a deposit in your bank account. Time is money. How quickly you do everything impacts every part of your business.

In order for a Boeing 747 jet airliner to leave the ground, it needs to reach a speed of 160 knots (184 miles per hour). Just as an airplane must reach a certain speed to lift off, an entrepreneur must do the same. If a plane doesn't create momentum and sustain it for a long period of time, it will crash. It needs speed, it needs fuel, and it needs the right pilot to guide it to its destination. Here's how the equivalent looks in business.

Speed = momentum
Fuel = money/capital
Pilot = founder, entrepreneur, CEO

Once you understand why speed is so critical, you'll see why trust is so important for speed. Imagine if, before sitting down at a restaurant and placing your order, you had to fill out a lengthy credit application. Imagine having to have a mug shot taken and give your fingerprints before buying a Slurpee at 7-Eleven. Even now, the idea of having to go inside and interact with an individual before buying gas seems like a nuisance. In short, the reason to develop trusting relationships is to speed up every element of conducting business.

I Love You, but Please Sign
the Prenuptial Agreement

I've seen a lot of people get married, and at the start, everything was beautiful. You'd look at those couples and swear that they'd love each other forever. You'd never guess that one day they would grow to hate each other and decide to get divorced.

At that point, each person contacts an attorney, and what was a bad situation becomes immeasurably worse—at least if you measure it in terms of rage, stress, and dollars spent. Attorneys often pit husband against wife, ratcheting up the tension in order to ratchet up their fees; an acrimonious court fight means more money for them. By the end, the couple is drained both emotionally and financially.

It doesn't have to be this way. Before you get married, you can say to your spouse-to-be, "I love you, but we don't know where we'll be five, ten, fifteen years from now. Let's plan for the worst but expect the best. That means we figure out right now what happens in a worst-case scenario—a divorce—in terms of money, the kids, and everything else." In other words, let's plan at least five moves ahead.

After a few dates with Jennifer, the woman who would become my wife (this was long before our Hawaii trip), we went to a bookstore on Third Street Promenade in Santa Monica and bought a book titled *101 Questions to Ask Before You Get Engaged*. One of the questions was: How many children do you want to have? I answered five; my wife answered three. We ended up having three kids, which now feels like the perfect number. We made an agreement on that and other issues, and my wife compromised on some things and I on others.

We talked about all of the key marital issues in advance and hammered out an agreement. Prenups are great for divorce settlements, but they are also valuable for marriages. By discussing key issues in advance, you can navigate the rocky moments that arise in every long-term relationship.

Some entrepreneurs say proudly, "I don't need a contract; we have a handshake deal, and my word is my bond." That's great, assuming the other person is equally honest and forthright. Unfortunately, that's not always the case.

The romantics may argue that by signing a contract, you're planning to fail. The realists see it as something every smart business owner understands: contingency planning. In business, you're going to have relationships with employees, partners, investors, suppliers, and advisers. You might love each and every one of those people, but if you don't have a formal agreement, you're asking for the type of stress and financial loss that comes with the most contentious of divorces.

When you hire someone, document everything: code of conduct, equity ownership, salary, vesting period, probationary period. If it's not documented, there will be no plan in place when you do have a conflict. Before agreeing to any major business deal, you want the following to be agreed upon:

1. Liability cap: What's the most we can lose?
2. Indemnification: You can't sue me.
3. Finite term: Once it's over, it's over.

Let's return to our marriage analogy: people get married emotionally and divorce logically. More specifically, they fall in love and think love will conquer all the problems simmering below the surface; they don't logically weigh the pros and cons of marrying someone. When they divorce, though there's obviously emotion involved, it's a much more logical process: people argue about what they want and what they're willing to give. Lawyers insist on putting a cognitive frame around emotional issues. It's all about numbers: How many weekends will your kids spend with you versus with your spouse? How much support will you provide? What is a logical division of property?

In business, it works the same way: you fall in love with a job applicant or an investor or a supplier or a customer and you think, "This will be forever." I can't tell you how many times I've gotten excited about a hire, and then, a few months or years later, I realized I had screwed up. In every instance, when the relationship arrangement wasn't documented, the breakup was messy and stressful.

One of our investors said to me, "Look, we just gave you ten million dollars. What happens if you die? We'd like to take out a ten-million-dollar life insurance policy on you."

I didn't get upset and protest that I was in great shape and didn't plan on dying. Instead, I loved what he said once I realized that he was telling me, "I love you, but please sign the prenup."

Ask Questions That Go Below the Surface

People tell me I'm demanding. When people describe me, the phrase "tough love" comes up a lot. Before you can care for someone, you have to know him or her. I believe what sets me apart as a leader is my desire to really understand people. I do so by asking the right questions and holding people accountable to their own answers.

I recently got a call from an old colleague named Danny. He said, "You have no idea how reluctant I've been about calling you. It's been a decade." I was curious to know where the conversation was going. When I had been a sales manager, I had been especially tough on Danny. He was one of those guys who had so much raw talent—brains, charisma, street smarts—and who was also so likable that people let him get away with anything. As a result, he was a pushover who was constantly underperforming.

I had asked Danny, as I ask everyone else, "Who do you want to be?"

Danny had big aspirations. He constantly talked about wanting to "retire" his parents by providing for them financially. He may have acted like the life of the party, but when we got real together, he talked about wanting a big life.

Not only did Danny want the big life, I knew he had what it took to live it. And I accepted nothing less than his best. If, in his eyes, that made me a hard-ass, so be it.

We caught up on our lives, and then I could tell he was getting emotional. Danny said, "I remember how you always used to say, 'You will temporarily hate me, but you will permanently love me—because no one will push you like me.'"

"Of course I remember," I said. "I didn't just say that to you. I've said it thousands of times."

Danny and I reminisced about how tough I had been on him and how much he couldn't stand me back then. He confessed that he had even printed out a picture of me and put it on his dartboard.

I remember everything about the people who have worked for me. I remember their stories because I care about them.

Danny said, "Pat, I have to tell you something." He got quiet, and I could hear that he was crying. He continued, "I'm now the president of the bank. I am married. I am so happy I can't even tell you. I'm making a multi-six-figure-a-year income. And I'm here to tell you, everything I'm putting into this leadership position is the stuff I learned when I was working with you."

He wasn't the only one with tears in his eyes. It was one of those moments that is hard to describe, though now that I'm a parent, I've begun to recognize the feeling.

Talk about delayed gratification! It took ten years for me to find out that pushing Danny, and not accepting anything but his best, had paid off for him. It reminded me again why I'm willing to be hated temporarily—even if it lasts a decade.

Smart compensation packages and incentive trips go only so far. When you touch people's hearts, they will move mountains for you. And to touch their hearts, you have to take the time to understand them and know their deepest beliefs and desires.

This means going beyond surface knowledge: your employee Joe likes fishing; your customer Becky is obsessed with *Game of Thrones*.

What you want to know is what makes them tick. I do everything I can to get to know my team members. Mainly, I ask a lot of questions to get to the root of who they are. In this way, I avoid jumping to false conclusions about them and can understand what drives them, what their goals are, and how they like to work.

When you push people with questions, you may touch a raw nerve. That's fine. This is how you get to know them. When they become emotional, they reveal the parts of themselves that they might be hiding.

I can't lead people if I don't know who they are. I need to know their upbringing and what influenced them as they were growing up. In the same way, my people need to know who I am. I want people to know the truth of my story, that I'm a guy from Iran who went through hell, that my drive comes from all those F-you people who are still loud voices inside my head.

It all boils down to the willingness to ask questions—not just the expected ones such as "How did you like your last job?" but ones that poke and probe and encourage people to reveal a deeper part of themselves. You've got to ask dig-deep questions that help you discover who a person really is. That knowledge is gold, because it will allow you to think several moves ahead in terms of how the person fits into your game plan. It's what will help you form a productive, long-lasting relationship. In doing so, the trust you develop grows stronger, and speed follows.

Trust Is a Pendulum

Typically, entrepreneurs move from trust to distrust and back again in a predictable pattern. It pays to be aware of this pattern, since it's going to govern how much leeway you give your people.

When you hire people, your willingness to trust them is low and your desire to micromanage their work is high. After they've been on the job for a while and they've done good work, your trust is high and you are much less likely to micromanage them.

To a certain extent, this pendulum-like pattern makes sense, but you need to be aware of which direction you're swinging. If you're not, you might elicit the following reaction from an employee who feels suffocated: "If you don't trust me to do the work, why don't you just hire someone else?" Or you may wrongly trust a veteran employee, someone who misses deadlines frequently and fails to hit his numbers. After the fact, you get upset with him, but you really should be upset with yourself. Why? Because you failed to hire the right person or didn't properly hold him accountable.

Reliability is the key to trust. After a while, people establish a track record. Once that track record demonstrates that they will consistently deliver what they promise, you can leave them alone more. You have established trust.

Four Levels of Trust

Typically, entrepreneurs feel victimized when people betray their trust. They may think they can trust someone, but then something happens: a customer doesn't come through with the big order he insisted was coming, or a business partner reneges on a deal. Entrepreneurs blame those individuals for lying or deceiving them, saying something to the effect of "That's why we aren't growing as fast as we should" or "We're in a hole because Joe didn't do what he said he would."

No. Don't play the victim. The world of business is tough. People don't always play fair. Some of them are flat-out crooks. Some have no problem telling you what you want to hear while doing the opposite.

The onus is on you for allowing yourself to be hustled. You're smarter than that. In fact, you should be able to figure out the level of trust you should have with anyone, be it customer, employee, business partner, or supplier.

Here's how to do it. First, recognize that you can categorize people according to the following four trust levels:

- Stranger
- Endorsed
- Trusted
- Running Mate

Categorize people as **Strangers** when you have zero experience with them. They may *seem* trustworthy; they're charming, friendly, and talk a good game. Instinctively, you may like and trust them. Remember, though, that even homicidal sociopaths can gain people's trust. Experience is the best teacher. If you don't have personal knowledge of someone or know an individual who worked with him, put him into the category of Stranger and don't trust him until you know more about him.

The **Endorsed** category is for people who arrive with a track record. They are recommended by people you trust or possess a résumé that demonstrates their ability to deliver what they promise. You still need to be wary because résumés can be fudged and recommendations may reflect bias or an unwillingness to be completely honest. Still, this category should provide a somewhat greater possibility that an individual is worthy of your trust.

Individuals who are **Trusted** are those with whom you possess personal experience. One way or another, they've demonstrated their loyalty, honesty, and reliability. They are more trustworthy than those in the Endorsed category because you've witnessed their positive traits, not just heard about them secondhand.

The fourth category, **Running Mate**, is the highest category, and you're not likely to have more than one individual who fits this description. This is the professional equivalent of your best friend. This is someone whom you can call when you have a problem or an opportunity and who will immediately ask, "What can I do?" If you need someone to help you out of a jam, he or she will move mountains to assist.

Before you despair that you lack a Running Mate or start searching for one, recognize that finding one can take time and experience. It took me a lot of battles to discover my Running Mate. I had to learn the hard way who could be trusted—and who was to be trusted absolutely. My trust had to be betrayed before I developed a mental measuring system.

Recognize, too, that the more successful you become, the fewer people you'll be able to trust. If you've read motivational books or heard motivational speakers, you've been fed a lot of propaganda about developing large networks of trusted people. Maybe this is true if you're a consultant, but if you're running a business, you will learn the hard way, as I have, that you can't trust everyone, and those you do trust, you can't trust equally. Talk to any savvy entrepreneur, and you'll hear stories about trusted lieutenants who betrayed them, about employees they considered family who bolted as soon as they received a good offer. Remember Donnie Brasco?

Don't expect to build big circles of trust. Forget about working with tons of people with whom you'd trust your life. Instead, your expectations should be that you'll place each person in one of the four levels. Once you do, you are much less likely to be burned and will have a good idea of whom you can trust and how much you can trust them.

Learn Each Individual's Love Language

A man can't wait to show his wife how much he loves and appreciates her. It's their tenth wedding anniversary, so he saves every penny to buy her a pair of diamond earrings. He wraps them elegantly, and when she opens the box, he's on pins and needles, waiting for her to light up and thank him for his generosity and caring. When she finally opens the box, she barely reacts.

This is not what he was expecting. Her apathetic response reflects ungratefulness and contempt. How can she be so unappreciative? When he finally asks her what's wrong, she says, "I don't know how many times I have to tell you that I don't care about *things*. Why don't we ever go on a picnic?"

To make better sense of this interaction, I recommend reading *The 5 Love Languages: The Secret to Love That Lasts* by Gary Chapman. It's phenomenal. The five love languages are the ways in which we give and receive love. They are: Quality Time, Words of Affirmation, Gifts, Acts of Service, and Physical Touch. In the above example, the man spoke the language of gifts when, all along, his wife had been telling him that she preferred quality time.

In relationships, forget about the Golden Rule. Replace "Do unto others as you would have them do unto you" with "Do unto others the way *they* want to be treated." It's applicable to business, family, and friends. One of the reasons I chose Greg Dinkin as my book collaborator is that when I interviewed him, he couldn't stop talking about how, as part of a workshop he had given to bank executives, he had required that they take the love language quiz. In fact, I recommend taking the free quiz online, and asking those close to you to do the same.

You need to stop asking what motivates *people* and instead ask: What motivates *a person*? Whether you choose to look at this through the prism of hot buttons or love languages, you'd better take the time to understand what works for each individual. Each of us is motivated by different things.

You have to know what makes people tick. If you're paying attention, you'll find out. I know a CEO whose top salesman makes $825,000 a year. After his biggest month, he said to his boss, "You didn't even call me." That statement makes it obvious that he wants to be appreciated. It also tells you *how* he wants to be appreciated. His love language is words of affirmation. Had he said, "You didn't even take me out to lunch," he would have been indicating that he wanted quality time. Had he asked for a Rolex, he would be indicating that he wanted gifts.

Do you want to excel as a leader? Show people that you take the time and care needed to understand what they want. The mistake most of us make is that we give love and appreciation the way we like to receive it. If you like to receive praise, you're probably good at giving it. If you're more of a "money talks" person, you probably have a great comp plan. The truth that you're going to run into is that everyone on your team is motivated by different things.

People who make broad statements such as "Everybody likes to be appreciated" or "Validation is an important human need" are on the right track. You need to go to the next level by getting specific about *how* you show appreciation and validation. As a CEO, I know who needs one-on-one time and who needs public praise. As a father, I know which of my kids thrives on affection, praise, and quality time.

Even though I know it's the right thing to do, I don't always remember to do it. It's not easy to meet the demands and speak the specific languages of all your loved ones—especially if you're already running a good-sized business and have a family to take care of. It can sound overwhelming sometimes, because, after all, we are human.

I read a book titled *Thank God It's Monday: How to Prevent Success from Ruining Your Marriage* that made a lot of sense to me. The author, Pierre Mornell, was a marriage counselor, and after twenty years, he finally found the best solution that worked for him and the families he was counseling: give each of the people closest to you five to fifteen minutes of undivided attention every day. I'm not suggesting you do this with everyone, but your key leaders and rising stars need more one-on-one time with you than you may think. It's easy to try to develop leaders just by conference calls or Zoom calls, but nothing is more effective than giving them your undivided attention.

Questions to Ask Yourself to Reach Each Individual

1. What makes this person tick?
2. How does this person want to be loved?
3. What makes this person feel appreciated?
4. What's the most effective way to show that I care?
5. What action will best "land" on this person?

The Nine Love Languages of Entrepreneurs

Remember that trust equals speed. The higher the level of trust, the faster the speed. Showing people that you care about them brings out their best. As a result, they become more dependable, and all elements of the business move faster.

Just as there are five love languages in a relationship, there are nine love languages that great entrepreneurs learn how to speak with their teammates.

1. WE NEED YOU

Giving people responsibility is one way to show them that you need them. There are people who need to feel needed. In sports, a coach may go to a player who isn't performing and say, "We can't win a championship without you. We need you to come through. We *need* you."

There are also people who don't care to be needed. The more they feel needed, the more they may abuse the relationship. They may say, "Oh, you need me. Without me you can't do anything."

When Steve Kerr took over as coach of the Golden State Warriors, Andre Iguodala had started 758 consecutive games. Kerr wanted Iguodala, an All-Star–caliber player, to come off the bench. Most players would see that as a demotion, but Kerr sold Iguodala on how much he was needed: there was a *need* for a spark off the bench, a *need* to lead the second unit, a *need* to bring in fresh legs to defend the other team's best player. Not only did the Warriors win the NBA championship in Kerr's first season, but Iguodala became the first player in NBA history to be named MVP of the NBA finals without starting every game. This demonstrates what we talked about earlier: When you give people a reputation to live up to, they often do just that.

2. RECOGNITION

If you look at companies that are stagnant, you'll find that recognition is not part of their culture. It's all about pressure, pressure, pressure. Dan Ariely, a professor of behavioral economics and psychology at Duke University, has done significant research to show that companies overvalue money as a motivator. Relying on cash bonuses to motivate people makes them feel as though they need to be bribed to do their work. According to Ariely, "What it says is, 'you know the right thing to do, but you're not interested.'" Giving a bonus is the opposite of getting specific about what makes a person tick.

You can have a lot of fun with team members, especially the intrapreneurs who thrive on recognition. When you recognize one, add your own personal touch. For example, I gave a 1984 Olympic torch to one of our senior vice presidents. I gave an Ayrton Senna helmet to a VP during a time when our company was studying Ayrton Senna's mindset. It could be signed Michael Jordan shoes. It could be a custom Louis Vuitton bag. Sometimes it's a plaque for their wall. If they like words of affirmation, what's written on the plaque is what matters most.

Some people may say, "I don't need any recognition." The ones who say they don't need it actually need double the recognition. Their denial of needing recognition is really a disguise. They're afraid to put in the effort because they may not get the recognition they expect. I don't care how confident a person may seem, everybody needs recognition.

3. PRAISE: THREE DIFFERENT TYPES

There are three different ways to praise someone. Knowing which to choose has to do with knowing that individual. I'll keep reminding you that everyone has different hot buttons.

1. **Private:** The first type of praise is given privately. It could be over a meal or during a casual interaction. It can also be done using text, email, or Slack. It may look something like this: "Listen, I just want you to know that you've grown a lot, and I want to recognize you. I see the work you're putting in and the way you've been improving. None of it goes unnoticed. Thank you."

2. **Public:** The next is public. This plays on recognition and works best with people who like to be in the limelight. You want to call special attention to their contributions in meetings.

3. **Behind their back:** The last type of praise is given behind a person's back. You recognize people behind their backs when you praise them to others when they're not present. I talked about the power of back talk earlier. Again, know the individual to use this effectively.

4. CLEAR DIRECTION

Your team needs clear direction from you. When you say things such as "You can do it. Go get it," it's not effective. They need you to say, "I need you to do this, this, and this by this time. Can you do that?" Typically, you don't want to give people more than a list of three things to do at a time or they'll be overwhelmed, but the point is that there are plenty of people who like to be told what to do.

For these workers, you need to state the exact deliverable and the exact timeline. Make a verbal agreement: "Are we clear, John, that you'll send me a text by 4:45 p.m. EST today with the names and numbers of three different vendors?" That's much more effective than "Do some research and get back to me."

5. VISION

Most people are not visionaries. It doesn't come naturally to think ahead when they're busy putting out fires. But they need to hear you talk about vision and the future. Great leaders are always selling the future of where the team is going and what things are going to happen. They talk about what's next. Great leaders say things such as "Our greatest days are ahead of us." Employees need to know that their leader is like a grand master who is guiding them in the right direction.

You need to paint pictures for people about the future. Especially when they're in the grind, you have to tap into their senses and create a picture of what they are working for.

6. DREAMS

People want to know how their dreams are going to become a reality. They need to see how doing the work today will allow them to accomplish their dreams. If you want to inspire people, you must speak the dream language constantly to those who need to hear it.

These last three are more directives and less about targeting a person's love language. I included them in this list because they still fall under the category of understanding people and speaking to them in such a way that brings out the best in them and ultimately creates trust.

7. INVOLVEMENT

Constantly ask people their opinion and solicit feedback. Constantly ask people what they think you need to do next. People want to be involved in what you're doing, and they want to be heard. If you ask people for their ideas and you never implement them, they will say (most likely to themselves), "Why do I even give them to you? You never do them anyway. You are just wasting time for us both." There's a danger in asking if you're not going to actually listen.

8. CHALLENGE

Great leaders challenge people all the time: privately, publicly, and behind their backs. If I see somebody who is making progress after slipping up, I'm going to pull him or her aside and say, "Listen, I want to let you know that I see it. You're making a lot of progress. I'm excited for you. But I hope you don't slip again. I hope you stay focused."

The things I say publicly are to address complacency: "I was under the impression that you had bigger dreams. I thought you wanted something much bigger. If you can make $20,000 in a month, why can't you make $40,000? Are you getting comfortable? Is your stomach full? Since when are you financially free already? Since when are we there already? Why are we behaving this way? Why are we acting this way? Why are we doing this?"

9. LISTENING

The last language is actually not a language. The last language is when you just zip your mouth and listen, since many people like to talk about themselves or what they are going through. This is not always easy, especially for an impatient CEO, but listening is a critical skill. Sometimes it just means sitting there and hearing a person out. Some of the leaders I'm mentoring just want to call and talk for forty minutes. I let them. I listen, listen, listen, and take notes. I give them feedback. I don't get on the call and put them on mute and do other things. I'm listening and I'll say, "That comment you made fifteen minutes ago, do you still think it's true given what you've heard from the rest of the team?"

You need to listen and show genuine interest. In fact, with all of these love languages for entrepreneurs, you need to be genuine. People can tell if it's an act. If you're not genuine, people can tell. When you speak people's love languages, they feel appreciated.

■ ■ ■ ■ ■

An expression that you often hear in sports is that you cannot teach speed. You can teach how to exploit it, yes, but speed is something you either have or you don't. Other than incrementally, it can't be improved. In business, however, speed absolutely can be improved. And you must be relentless about improving it. Every part of business—from identifying trends to reaching your customer to delivering your product—relies on speed.

You can use the trust levels to filter your assessments, to understand the nuances of a given person or situation. In doing so, your aim is to speed up all aspects of your business.

Think long and hard about whom to put your faith in and why. Is John at the trust level of Stranger or Running Mate? Given that, are you willing to entrust him with major responsibility for the business, or do you need to keep him on a tight leash when you give him an assignment of any significance? Address these and other questions, and you'll find that you can figure out who to trust—and who not to—with great accuracy.

The point of creating trust is to increase speed. Analytical people often miss this point. They also miss the fact that the key to building trust is to tap into people's humanity. Once they know that you see them as human beings and not simply as employees, trust grows and speed builds. Understanding their love languages and what makes them tick are the keys to showing you care.

MOVE 3

Master Building the Right Team

THE MYTH OF THE SOLOPRENEUR:
HOW TO BUILD YOUR TEAM

1. Identify the types of team members you want to attract. Create the right value proposition (benefits program) to attract and retain the right team members. Be even more selective about whom you allow into your inner circle.

CREATE A PRINCIPLES-BASED CULTURE

2. Establish and communicate your values and principles—both for your business and as an individual. Don't compromise your nonnegotiables, or else they will be only words on a piece of paper.

TRUST = SPEED:
THE POWER OF RELIABILITY

3. Inspect every skill needed in each department to make it transferable to any new hire in order to develop new leaders. Inspect the language you use to communicate with your teammates and leaders. Is it one that creates trust or doubt? Ask questions to understand what people care about most, and speak the language that moves them. Make a list of your top five team members, and identify their key motivators.

MOVE 4

■ ■ ■ ■ ■

MASTER STRATEGY TO SCALE

9

Scaling for Exponential Growth

> I am not afraid of an army of lions led by a sheep; I am afraid
> of an army of sheep led by a lion.
>
> —Alexander the Great

In the United States, you can register any business for less than
$200. You can then call yourself a CEO. You can even order busi-
ness cards with the letters "CEO" in big, bold print. You can call
yourself whatever you want. It's when hundreds of other people call
you a CEO that you've earned the title.

In October 2009, I launched a business with sixty-six agents. In
our first full calendar year, we did less than $2 million in revenue.
There was one small problem: as the CEO, I had no idea in hell what
I was doing. I had yet to learn what it takes to scale.

For my entire professional career, I had been either a salesperson
or a sales manager. I had never been the chief executive officer of a
company. I knew nothing about vision or strategy, much less all the
logistics and paperwork that are required to turn a sale into a contract. I basically faked it at first, trying to figure things out. I started
searching, thinking what moves I had to make to succeed as CEO.
The first move was joining Vistage, an organization for entrepreneurs in which Vistage essentially becomes your personal board of

directors, providing you with advice. I also attended a program at Harvard for company owners/presidents that enabled me to interact with other CEOs and learn about management.

I tracked down every resource that could help me, including every case study I could get my hands on. I ordered every book that could shed light on the day-to-day of running a company. In addition to buying every book by Patrick Lencioni, I bought:

Scaling Up: How a Few Companies Make It . . . and Why the Rest Don't
by Verne Harnish

Traction: Get a Grip on Your Business
by Gino Wickman

Built to Sell: Creating a Business That Can Thrive Without You
by John Warrillow

The Lean Startup: How Today's Entrepreneurs Use Continuous Innovation to Create Radically Successful Businesses
by Eric Ries

Zero to One: Notes on Startups, or How to Build the Future
by Peter Thiel

Mastering the Rockefeller Habits: What You Must Do to Increase the Value of Your Growing Firm
by Verne Harnish

Growing Pains: Transitioning from an Entrepreneurship to a Professionally Managed Firm
by Eric G. Flamholtz and Yvonne Randle

The Toyota Way: 14 Management Principles from the World's Greatest Manufacturer
by Jeffrey Liker

At the time, I made a firm commitment to myself: either I was going to decide that I had what it took to be a CEO whom I would personally trust to run a Fortune 500 company, or I was going to fire myself.

The transition to leading a company nearly crushed me. It ultimately required both knowledge and tremendous stamina to survive. Eventually, I got a grasp of not only the everyday moves of a CEO but, more important, what moves were essential for me to produce the type of company I envisioned.

This may be the section you've been waiting for. Everything prior to this point has been foundational: knowing yourself, knowing how to reason, and knowing how to build your team were all about preparing you for the rigors of running a company. Now is when you take the leap to becoming a CEO who operates like a grand master. We're going to talk about the four strategic areas that every CEO needs to focus on. As we do so, you're going to get a clear picture of how to create exponential growth for your business. Ultimately, we'll answer the question: How does a CEO scale to achieve and maintain growth?

The Four Phases of Every Start-Up

1. Formulation
2. Survival
3. Momentum
4. Plateau

As you read this, you need to ask yourself what phase you're in. Formulation phase? Survival phase? If you haven't reached the momentum phase, it's because you have yet to figure out what leads to exponential growth. You'll soon discover the two things that will lead to your business catching fire.

Capitalizing Your Business

No matter what stage your business is in, you need a plan for capitalizing it. When you're starting out, will you borrow from family? Should you find an angel investor and give up equity? Once you start crushing it, should you look to exit or will you leverage your success to raise funds and grow even faster?

This topic could be a book in and of itself. It's also very industry specific. If you're building a tech company that doesn't have a measurable method of making money but can attract tens of millions of eyeballs, such as Twitter, Instagram, and other such companies, you need to raise as much capital as possible up front. In other industries, you are better off growing organically.

In April 1999, Jack Ma started Alibaba in his apartment. It wasn't until January 2000 that the company received a $20 million investment from a group of investors led by Softbank Corporation. The *Wall Street Journal* reported that Ma's meeting with CEO Masayoshi Son was atypical of most investment pitches. Ma said, "We didn't talk about revenues; we didn't even talk about a business model. We just talked about a shared vision. Both of us make quick decisions."

In an interview with Charlie Rose that aired on a *60 Minutes Segment Extra*, Jeff Bezos reflected back to 1995 when he was raising seed capital to start Amazon. "A lot of people did very well on that deal [laughs]. But they also took a risk, so they deserve to do very well on that deal. But I had to take sixty meetings to raise $1 million, and I raised it from twenty-two people at approximately $50,000 a person. And it was nip and tuck whether I was going to be able to raise that money. So, the whole thing could have ended before the whole thing started. That was 1995, and the first question every investor asked me was: 'What's the internet?'"

During an interview at the George W. Bush Presidential Center's Forum on Leadership in 2018, Bezos also talked about raising money to start Amazon. He said, "And that was in 1995. But just two years later, a Stanford MBA with no business experience could raise twenty-five million dollars with a single phone call if they had an internet business plan."

There are many avenues to creating a well-capitalized company. I'm going to give you ten questions to ask before you start to raise money. If you're serious about doing so, don't just read them; answer them.

Ten Questions to Ask Before Raising Money

1. Should You Even Raise Money?

Is your company at the point where you should even be considering raising money? Your idea could be small enough that you could bootstrap it with your own money and get it started today.

2. If You Were Not Able to Raise Money, How Would You Make Your Business Idea Work?

If you can answer this question, Angels and VCs will be more interested in your business. By demonstrating that you don't *need* capital and gaining momentum before you try to raise money, you will become a more attractive investment.

3. How Will the Money You Raise Be Used?

When raising money, you need to put yourself into investors' shoes. Investors want to know how you will use the money. You need to show them how you will convert cash into growth. Whether the money will be used to make a key hire, ramp up production, or secure intellectual property, they need to see your plan for putting it to use.

4. What Does an Ideal Investor in Your Business Look Like?

Is it somebody who's involved? You need to think about not only who a prospective investor is as a person but also what type of relationship you want with him or her. Do you need someone to make key introductions that open up distribution channels? Or do you need someone who has specific experience you lack and can act as an adviser?

5. Do You Want to Keep Total Control of the Business?

Whenever you ask for money, it comes with a lot of expectations. People don't write checks without making demands. Prepare yourself to either retain full control of your business and possibly not be able to raise as much money or cede some control in order to get a bigger cash infusion.

6. Do You Want Accountability?

Most entrepreneurs don't like other people telling them what to do. But venture capitalists want to do just that. They want to work with nimble entrepreneurs who are open to suggestions about their business. Do you view this as guidance or meddling? If the latter, look for a more passive investor, such as a bank.

7. Have You Done Enough Research About Your Industry?

Don't waste investors' time by failing to do your homework. You need to know what your industry looks like before you go out to raise money. It will show potential investors that you are serious and prepared to use their money wisely.

8. What Makes Your Business Model Different?

Investors need to understand why your business stands out. Your company needs to be positioned so that it will have a distinct competitive advantage in the marketplace.

9. Have You Done the Math? What Is the Value of Your Company?

The moment you present bad math, investors are going to walk away. They are expecting you to have real projections and to back up your valuation with sound numbers. Know the industry comparisons, and use "comps" (comparable businesses) for multiples of revenue, sales, or other industry-specific metrics.

10. Are You Building to Sell?

Investors want to know if they will be able to sell their investment for a solid return in five to seven years. Do you have an exit strategy? Some VCs don't want to invest in businesses that are built to sell.

Others are looking for quick returns. You need to do your homework to determine this.

■ ■ ■ ■ ■

It's a huge boost to you and your team's confidence to get venture funding. Look at raising money as buying a longer life span. It's like playing a video game in which you have just scored two more lives in case you die. Having smart and demanding people invest in you creates accountability and can lead to high-level introductions and wise counsel. It makes sense for some people. As with everything else in business and life, you will pay a price for these advantages. Using your own funds, by contrast, often puts you at constant risk of running out of money. The upside is that you get to keep control of your company and your equity in it—which ultimately gives you even more choices.

In terms of connecting with money people, the best way to find investors is through your mentors. Having a person introduce you will go a long way toward legitimizing you.

The best way to gain credibility with your mentors? Answer the ten questions thoughtfully and in great detail. Doing so will prove that you are serious and prepared.

There's no perfect time or method to raise money. You have to do great work while keeping track of your options. It's better to attract than to beg. Now that we've covered raising capital, let's move on to growing your business.

The Strategy Quadrant

Have you ever gone to the gym and seen the same person there every time, but for some reason, you never see him or her making progress? How is it even possible that that person works out so much but continues to look the same? It's possible, all right. In fact, it's normal. Whether in the gym or the office, most people show up and just go through the motions. They work *in* their business but not *on* their business. If you do the same, at best, it will keep you afloat. At worst, your lack of thinking several moves ahead will lead to your company's demise.

Growth is important, but entrepreneurs often treat it as the only function, and that's a mistake. Two types of business growth exist: linear and exponential. The former represents steady but not spectacular gains: you meet deadlines, sell and maintain customers, and expand your network of contacts. The latter represents quantum leaps. It's what happens when entrepreneurs step out of the day-to-day running of the business to do something exceptional. They have a vision and are able to make tough but smart decisions to implement that vision. They don't just want to grow incrementally; they want to conquer the world.

I've boiled down the responsibility of an owner or CEO to these four strategic areas:

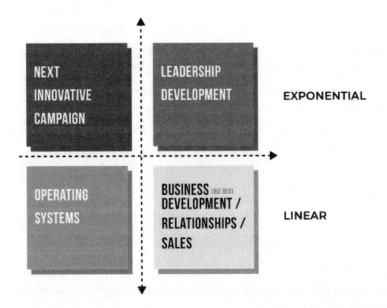

The linear growth side is operating systems and business development/sales.

1. OPERATING SYSTEMS

This is about tightening up your systems, technology, and processes, making them more efficient and effective. To most entrepreneurs, this is the least exciting part of the business. And although it won't create exponential growth, you can still make great strides by improving your operating systems. You saw how my company broke down ITR and how improving operations through technology ultimately saved us millions of dollars.

A business fails for one of two reasons: either it grows too fast, or it doesn't grow at all. Though the former seems like a good problem to have, it can be fatal if you don't have the operating systems in place to support your growth.

2. BIZ DEV AND SALES

Next are business development (biz dev) and sales. This has to do with creating relationships with new vendors and new partnerships and making your sales process better. It's about networking and attending events from your industry. Relationship, relationship, relationship.

Biz dev is linear. You have to close deals and continue to grow your accounts.

The next two areas lead to exponential growth.

3. THE NEXT INNOVATIVE CAMPAIGN

As CEO, you may launch a program or promotion that is potentially game changing. Bally Total Fitness did this when it introduced zero-down-payment gym memberships at a time when its competitors all required a sizable down payment. In 1995 Continental Airlines introduced an incentive program in which each of its 35,000 nonmanagerial employees received $65 in any month that Continental ranked among the top five airlines for on-time departures. That innovative campaign, led by transformational leaders Gordon Bethune and Greg Brenneman, worked like magic. Bethune described it in detail in his book *From Worst to First: Behind the Scenes of Continental's Remarkable Comeback.*

In 2005, when the price of gas was around $3 a gallon, Mitsubishi launched a campaign to pay for its customers' gas for an entire year. Though it was really nothing more than a discount, it was marketed in a way that turned heads. When Hyundai, the Korean car manufacturer, was struggling to gain market share in the United States, it offered the most extensive warranty in the industry: ten years or 100,000 miles. Those were not day-to-day operational decisions that made a small impact; they were choices that led to exponential growth.

In February 2005, Amazon launched Amazon Prime. For $79 a year, members would get free two-day shipping on all purchases. The company later added music, free movies, and free delivery of perishable goods. As of September 2019, there were more than 100 million Prime members. At the present cost of $119 per year, that's $11.9 billion in revenue. Now, that's an innovative campaign.

Making the right move can create a massive surge in your business. You have to synthesize everything you know about your customers' wants and needs, your competition's limitations, and your own strengths to create a campaign that will drive rapid revenue growth.

4. LEADERSHIP DEVELOPMENT

Exponential growth depends on your ability to develop other people into effective leaders.

Identify the next leaders you're going to groom for more responsibility. Make a list of your top three, five, or however many you have.

Then start assessing them. Look at their strengths and weaknesses, and how they respond in different situations. Then look at their level of competitiveness, their ability to come up with ideas, and how solid they are. Also ask them if they believe in the company and want to step into a leadership role.

Next, sit down and identify what they need to do in the next six months, twelve months, and two years. Challenge them to grow. Figuratively speaking, pour water onto them as though they were plants.

As the CEO, you will be judged based on the type of leaders you develop. Finding others who can build the business on their own rather than just following marching orders will lead to exponential growth. This requires finding the right type of people to recruit and making leadership development a high-level priority.

Your Challenge

Most people stay at the linear level. Just because you chose to become an entrepreneur, that doesn't make you a visionary or a CEO. If you spend most of your time in the linear quadrants, you are not going to build much momentum. If, on the other hand, you spend all of your time in the exponential quadrants, you run the risk of not being able to support your growth.

You need to look at the strategy quadrant and ask yourself where you are and are not doing a good job. Where do you need to pivot? Do you need to create an innovative campaign? Maybe you need to look at the next ninety days and prepare for your next innovative campaign.

You'll be amazed by how gratifying putting together a strategy for your business can be. It's exciting when your business grows and money starts coming in. Once that starts, let me tell you, it gets very, very interesting.

To Improve Your Employees' Performance, Apply Pressure to the Point of Desensitization

How can you get your people to perform at peak capacity? How can you motivate them to make significant improvements year after year?

These are tough questions for entrepreneurs. Maybe you try to be your people's best friend. Maybe you provide tough feedback. Maybe you offer support and encouragement. Lots of theories are floating around about this subject, but I know what works for me, and if you can get past your desire to be liked, I bet it will work for you, too.

I have a friend, Chris Hayes, who played defensive back in the NFL for seven years. Chris played for a number of famous coaches, including Herm Edwards and Bill Parcells. One day I asked him, "Who was the most difficult coach you played for?"

Chris didn't hesitate. "Bill Belichick," he said.

At the time, Belichick was an assistant to Parcells for the New York Jets.

"It's not even close," Chris said. "His expectations were so high. It was incredibly annoying. Training and practice were freaking insane. He wanted you to be as close to perfect as possible for everything. He would pick on you for the smallest thing. But you also knew you were going to win because you knew he wanted to win more than anybody else in that room, so you didn't have a problem following him."

Entrepreneurs can learn a lot from Chris's experience with Bill Belichick. I know I have. I apply pressure to my people until they become immune to it. I figure if they can put up with me, they won't have a problem with the grief they get from customers. If they can handle me, they can handle anyone. They don't get rattled. They become better leaders when they've been through my pressure cooker, and they can handle conflict better.

The way I apply pressure is by asking questions—and waiting for the answers. I challenge my people the same way I'm challenging you.

I ask them to become clear on who they want to be and describe their next moves in detail. Once they express what they want, I use their answers to keep them accountable. I don't yell and scream. I don't impose my own goals on them. What I do is repeat what they said they want to accomplish. If they are falling short of their goals, I ask why and shut up. I've found that getting them to self-reflect is much more powerful than telling them what to do. Ultimately, I'm teaching them to be accountable to the high expectations they set for themselves.

Most people don't want this accountability. Being held to the standard of being your best self is not for the faint of heart. That's why, by design, I'm not easy to work for. It takes a few years for people on my team to become desensitized to the pressure, but when that happens, they're golden. Like Belichick's players, they feel the intense pressure of high expectations, and though they resent it at first, they become accustomed to it. They eventually realize that it's elevating their performance, and it results in wins for the team. After a while, the pressure no longer bothers them.

And here's an even bigger bonus: the domino effect. When I apply positive pressure to one person, he applies it to another. When we add more people to the team, we apply the same pressure to them, and they in turn apply it to others. Instead of a management practice, it becomes part of the culture. Remember that you are not doing this to hassle your team, but rather to apply the right kind of positive pressure.

Bill Belichick has won six Super Bowls as head coach of the New England Patriots. Do you think quarterback Tom Brady would describe playing for Belichick as a picnic? Of course not. In fact, *because* Belichick was so hard on Brady, there was a multiplier effect.

When the star is challenged, everyone has to raise his game as well. As pressure is applied and expectations are raised, this becomes the norm. Even though Brady left to join the Tampa Bay Buccaneers after twenty seasons with Belichick and the Patriots, it's fair to say that Brady and Belichick had the best run of any coach-and-quarterback tandem in history. Credit Belichick for applying pressure and Brady for responding to it.

Many options exist for applying pressure: providing constructive criticism, increasing results targets, asking tough questions. Keep the pressure constant by asking questions that create accountability, and you'll see how people will raise their game.

I realize that this might sound a bit tough and could scare some people, so I want to emphasize that it's not something that works for everyone. It has to fit both your personality and your philosophy. It will also depend greatly on your team and culture. Again, I'm just sharing what works for me. By now I trust you to process what I say and use your own approach.

Visionary Leaders Have a Reality Distortion Field

A common theme in Walter Isaacson's biography of Steve Jobs is Jobs's reality distortion field. Rather than accepting others' ideas of reality or "being good enough," he created his own stories and pushed others to make them true. He imposed his will on others to reprogram their expectations of themselves. And because he was not willing to accept the reality of their self-imposed limitations, they ended up surprising themselves.

Being around strong CEOs who are always raising their standards can be uncomfortable. They project a feeling that no matter how hard you are working, it's not enough. People may say, "Every time I get somewhere, you move the marker. When are you going to be fully happy?" That's what makes a strong CEO so effective. That's why Jobs may have been loathed when he was imposing deadlines but is now revered.

Pardon this quick digression, but the misconception about people getting fired is funny to me. Most people think that the day-to-day employee has the highest chance of getting fired, but the reality is that no one is fired more often than the company founder or CEO. Every time an employee quits, for the CEO, it's a form of getting fired. Every time a customer leaves to go to a competitor, it's a form of getting fired. Every time a superstar salesperson leaves, it's a form of getting fired. Every time the company is sued, it's a form of getting fired. My point is that no one is fired more often than the CEO.

When a CEO/founder loses his job, bankruptcy often follows and he or she loses everything, whereas an employee loses only a job and simply needs to find a new one. It's important for your team to know that no one is under more pressure than the CEO. This is not to undermine them but to let them know that the pressure is shared by everyone.

■ ■ ■ ■ ■

Here's an example of how I challenge people. I was meeting with a group of employees, and I asked them, "How many of you want a raise?"

Everyone said they wanted a raise.

"Okay, now do me a favor and write down the most money you ever made in a year. Don't show me; just write it down for yourself."

After they did it, I said, "Now write down how much money you would like to make annually."

Again I waited; then I asked, "Why haven't you made that number yet? Is it the company's fault? Do you want me to give you the kind of answer that makes you feel good? Or do you want the truth?"

They asked for the truth.

"It's because the market determines our value. We can think we're worth more, but if the market isn't willing to pay for it, then maybe you're overvaluing yourself. That number you wrote, you have to go out and get it. It doesn't happen just by luck. Do you want to be a supervisor? Do you want to run a department? Then you have to ask yourself what you need to do to increase your value in the marketplace. The people who stay with us long-term are constantly improving themselves. We encourage improvement. And if you don't improve, others are going to outimprove you and become your boss."

All this ratchets up the pressure, the expectation, and the performance.

The next step is to create the environment that allows employees to self-reflect and chart their own course. I'll ask them to list their next five moves. I'll ask them to email me their moves if they are committed to being held accountable. By doing so, they have set the bar for themselves and given me permission to hold them accountable.

Set Your Lions Free, and Empower Them to Build Empires

The philosopher Ludwig Wittgenstein said, "If a lion could speak, we could not understand him." You have to learn how to deal with lions (standout performers). Lions build empires, and they lead people. They're also going to provide the most revenue and the most headaches. They're demanding and short-fused. At times, it may seem as though they have no feelings. Many are disorganized and seem to be all over the place.

Rob Parson was a lion. He crushed it for Morgan Stanley, and because management didn't know how to handle him, the company almost lost him. You can lose sheep. They're a dime a dozen. But you cannot lose lions.

Great companies are filled with many lions who run their own empires. Before I started my agency, I was a lion working for a big company. I was aggressive. I was brash. Remember that I was the guy who wrote a sixteen-page letter to management and demanded changes. If that leadership team had known how to deal with a lion, they could have harnessed all of my aggression and lined their wallets. I was ripe for becoming an intrapreneur and making a small fortune for myself and a large fortune for the company. But they had no idea how to treat me. So I left.

The key to dealing with lions is challenging them. Even star players, in the heat of the moment, will get annoyed by their coaches. It's not fun to be pushed beyond your pain threshold. Yet these same players ultimately bestow praise on their coaches. Why? Because they are lions, and lions thrive on being pushed beyond their pain threshold.

If you want to be liked, if you find delight only in making people comfortable, you're not cut out to deal with a lion, much less be a CEO. People may hate you in the moment, but the only way for them to thrive and your business to survive is to hold them accountable.

Seven Ways to Hold People Accountable

1. **Don't be afraid to hold people accountable and call them out when they don't keep their word.** Make it very clear that it's not personal; it's their performance you don't like, not their personality. And be gentle.

2. **Ask why, and stay silent long enough to listen to their answers.** When you don't get a good explanation for why an employee has broken a promise or missed a deadline, ask why. Get a specific answer. You need to go deep to find out what's really going on. This is the only way you are going to gain from the conversation.

3. **Make specific quantitative statements, not blanket qualitative ones.** Don't just tell your employees to work harder or get better. Give them specific challenges to meet that can be measured and have deadlines.

4. **Provide clear metrics and specify clear incentives.** Let them know what they will get for hitting (or missing) their metrics. Numbers don't lie. You will avoid future conflicts by being clear about the goalposts.

5. **Coach your people through the workflow.** It's not enough to tell them *what* to work on. You have to coach them through *how* to work on it. Make sure they have the resources and the expertise to complete the task.

6. **Know the role each person plays on the team.** How will accountability affect others on the team? Who else might you also need to hold accountable to make sure that person succeeds?

7. **Finish with heart and empathy.** Know that we are all human beings with feelings. People go through things in their lives that we're not aware of. You can be firm and compassionate.

What's notably missing from this list is who will be keeping *you* accountable. People at your level or lower are not going to be tough on you. Don't look to them to hold you accountable. Find someone you respect who is willing to keep you accountable on a weekly basis. In some cases, it might be your manager. If you're an entrepreneur, it could be an investor or a board member. Organizations such as Vistage and YPO (Young Presidents' Organization) can provide a sounding board and advice. It's up to you to take it to the next level by seeking out people with whom you share your big goals and who will agree to hold you to them.

Make a list of the people who hold you accountable. What's their level of credibility? If those who hold you accountable rank low in credibility, why have you chosen them?

■ ■ ■ ■ ■

You may be ready to make the move to CEO. To do so, you need to have enough capital to run your business. As we discussed, choosing the best option requires you to balance the amount of control (and equity) you're willing to give up with the amount of accountability you're willing to accept.

Once your company is properly funded, your focus will turn to growth. You'll need to execute both linear and exponential strategies to build momentum and maintain it. Your next innovative campaign will be the catalyst for your business to expand. Developing leaders will also create exponential growth, albeit at a more predictable pace.

Let's also not forget that the most important resource you will ever have is the people around you. If you think the world revolves around you as a CEO, you're in deep trouble. Without your people, you have a job, not a business.

You have to really care about your people. They will see through flattery. They will respond to sincerity and authenticity, and the best way to provide them with that is by asking thoughtful questions. Do you think about their dreams, goals, and purpose? If you do, you're going to end up becoming a great CEO one day.

The number one product of all is human capital. You have to know what happens when one person is down, why another is not all in, and why a third is being a little forgetful. Take a person who is having problems out to lunch and talk to them and ask, "Is everything okay? How is your wife doing? Are the kids good?" Good business is about relationships.

If you're reading this and saying "I have a lot of work to do!" know that all of this work is going to take years. Don't expect to become good at this overnight. It's a never-ending process that relies on your never-ending desire to keep improving. One day, you won't just be one of those people who calls himself a CEO just because you registered a business and bought business cards. You'll know you're a CEO when other people start looking at you as one.

10

Make Momentum Your Friend—and Be Prepared for Chaos

The feeling that everything is about to fall apart. That panic is precisely what growth feels like.

You'll want to escape that terrifying feeling as fast as possible. Your brain thinks that your body is in danger, and the most important thing is to get rid of that danger, to end the tension.

You'll want to run away . . . that's the critical moment when most people lose. The key is to recognize when you feel this way, and to lean even deeper into those moments.

—Seth Godin, blogger, entrepreneur, and best-selling author

To accumulate wealth, success, and power, you need to be like a basketball team on a ten-game winning streak. You're rolling and gathering momentum as you roll. Dictionary definitions of "momentum" describe it as the product of the mass and velocity of an object. Translated into entrepreneurial terms, it's the product of who you are and the speed at which you're moving forward.

When you've gathered momentum, you become a force rather than just a business. You may not be unstoppable, but no sane person wants to get in your way. You're barreling forward with increasing confidence, talent, and money.

Get serious about creating momentum. Treat it like a person you're dating who seems like "the one." With every date, the relationship builds. Each time you see him or her, it's better than the previous time. It's not just physical; emotional intimacy and mutual respect develop.

The fastest way to lose momentum is to abuse it. Your "twin flame" keeps telling you that you're the best. And you believe it, get cocky, and start to sleep around—foolishly believing that that person will always be there. Then, boom! Just like that, there goes the momentum, there goes the relationship. You're all alone, feeling humiliated and having to start climbing uphill again, which is even harder now that you've proven you can't be trusted.

I've seen the equivalent of that scenario in business far too many times. It's why, in this chapter, we talk about both the power and the danger of momentum. If you implement the right innovative campaign and develop leaders, you'll gain momentum. The challenge will be maintaining it. Many entrepreneurs have been successful; not so many have stayed that way. The difference is discipline. Just as momentum increases your power, it can blind you to your weaknesses. First we're going to talk about how to create momentum. Then we're going to talk about how to manage it.

If you need further motivation to maintain your momentum, consider this: The average entrepreneur starts to feel godlike when momentum is continued. It can be transformative, so be disciplined and don't let it falter—but don't let it give you a massive ego, either.

If You Overdose on Anything,
Overdose on Speed

If there's one expectation I have of the people with whom I work, it's this: I will not compromise on speed, execution, or efficiency. I don't care how much bigger we get; I want speed, I want execution, I want efficiency. I am greedy in these three areas. I want them all.

Here's a huge question for leaders: How can you reduce the time it takes to get things done? Too often, entrepreneurs don't understand how to increase speed. Instead, they say, "We're going as fast as we can; no way can we do it measurably quicker." Or "Sure, we can reduce our time frame, but that means spending a ton of money on hiring more people or installing better systems."

That's not acceptable.

I would never suggest compromising quality for speed, but I'm going to give you a better way to create speed so that your quality doesn't suffer (and, in fact, should improve). Let's start by talking about Ferraris. Consider three versions of the car produced in different years: 1977, 1997, 2017. Here's how long each of them took to go from 0 to 60 miles per hour:

1977 308
8.1 seconds

1997 F355
4.9 seconds

2017 488 GTB
2.9 seconds

2037 GTX
? seconds

If you look at this trend, what would you project the 2037 Ferrari might be capable of?

It seems impossible to be able to go from 0 to 60 miles per hour in the blink of an eye. No doubt, people in 1977 said, "No way a Ferrari could ever do it in 4.9 seconds." No doubt, people in 1997 said, "No way a Ferrari could ever do it in 2.9 seconds."

When you think about the various functions of your business—sales, hiring, customer service, whatever—what can you do to compress your time frame? It may sound difficult or even impossible, but I guarantee you that there's a way to reduce the time it takes to perform any function.

And before you protest that you've done everything you can, let me tell you another auto-related story. As I read in Jeffrey Liker's book *The Toyota Way*, the catalyst of Toyota's success was the decision to address every problem that arose on the assembly line in no more than fifty-nine seconds. The company gave everyone on the assembly line a bell to ring, and as soon as an employee found a problem, he or she would ring the bell and a supervisor would hurry over to resolve the problem.

That is the major reason Toyota came to dominate its industry. It wasn't that it had better marketing or better prices. It was that it learned how to compress time frames. It could execute faster than its competitors.

Look at the fast-food industry. Why has McDonald's dominated for years? Not because it has better food or service. It's because it is faster at delivering your food. Follow its example. Create a committee of savvy people and task them with figuring out how to make a function faster. Take a sheet of paper and list the steps of any function in your business. Examine how you can eliminate one of the steps. Assess which steps you can shorten. Then beta test your revised steps. Make adjustments based on the test. Implement every tool you can to compress time frames.

Four Ways to Accelerate

Increasing the speed of the following four factors will enable your business to move faster.

1. **Functioning speed.** This is the support system you provide to your team. Examine who your people are and their capabilities. Can you help them improve through training and other means so they might cut some time from a function? Do you need to bring in someone who has the talent to speed things up? Your functioning speed is the core of your business.

2. **Processing speed.** There are a number of functions or processes that make your organization go. How quickly do you get your product from A to Z? Earlier, I suggested that you break down the steps of a given function and analyze each one of them with speed in mind. Let's say you have an online store. The factors contributing to the processing speed of making a sale are as follows: customer finds site through search; visits site; clicks on the page with specific types of products; examines prices and other options; adds product to cart; enters credit card information; chooses type of shipping; confirms purchase. The odds are that you can reduce the time it takes customers to perform at least one of these steps. You don't think so? Ever heard of "one-click" ordering on Amazon? Amazon has come to dominate e-commerce by focusing on processing speed.

3. **Expansion speed.** This is about how quickly you move into new markets, make acquisitions, and introduce new products. What's the average time it takes you to enter a new market if you're a retailer? Again, identify your time frame and dissect your steps. If you're expanding into an overseas market, is there one particular step that always slows you down? You have to identify bottlenecks and find ways to plow through them. If

you're negotiating deals overseas that are constantly blocked by bureaucracy, determine how much they're costing you in terms of time, aggravation, and money. The simple solution may be hiring a well-connected attorney with global experience and the right connections.

4. **Timing speed.** The question "When?" can work magic. Time your moves correctly, and you can beat competitors who have more resources than you do. You know the government is set to release a major study on how a certain vitamin has been found to be effective in moderating the effects of a certain disease. You don't know which vitamin it's going to recommend, but you bet that the high-potency vitamin you've been developing is it. You time your product introduction for the day that the government announces the results of its study.

Timing can involve a variety of actions: when to announce an initiative; when to launch an attack against a competitor; when to fire or hire; when to give people a bonus; when to offer equity. If you get the timing right, you will double your impact. There's a saying that speed kills. That's right; it kills the competition.

A Seven-Step System to Compress Time Frames

1. **Choose a process.** From buying a house to ordering a cab to sharing pictures online with your friends, there is a process to follow. In fact, one of the great ways to identify a potential business is to find a flawed process that you can improve upon.
2. **List the steps of the process.**
3. **Remove a step.** This is where the magic happens. See if you can remove a step. How would the process function without that step? This is where disruption is born. If you're not convinced, turn back a few pages and see why my company spent more than $2 million to accelerate its processing speed.

4. **Minimize the steps.** Take the remaining steps and condense their time frame. Condensing the remaining steps will help streamline the process, which is now missing one of the original steps.

5. **Beta test the new process.** Find a subset of customers to test and see how the new process functions. How does the market respond to it, and where do improvements need to be made?

6. **Adapt the process.** Based on the results of your beta test, adjust your process. This is where you adapt the process to fit a specific need.

7. **Refine.** You've beta tested, and the adjusted process is ready to be unleashed. Sell your product faster to all corners of your market, and don't forget to repeat these steps again and again to create exponential growth.

Plan (Optimistically and Wisely) for Growth

Steve Jobs said, "There's an old Wayne Gretzky quote that I love. 'I skate to where the puck is going to be, not to where it has been.' And we've always tried to do that at Apple." Though this quote has become so overused that it now seems cliché, there is plenty of wisdom in it. Gretzky was the ultimate grand master of hockey. His ability to see more moves ahead than his opponents did is the reason he's still called "The Great One."

You're constantly going to be forced to make decisions while living in the present time, just as your mind and heart live in a future truth. Let's take your office space as an example. If your company is successful, it's going to grow. If it's extremely successful, its growth trajectory will be steep. That means you will need more people, equipment, and space. When the tech hub Built in Chicago announced in September 2019 that VillageMD, a primary care–led medical company, had raised $100 million in Series B funding, its press release said, "The company has raised a total of $216 million to date . . . and has outgrown four headquarters since its launch in 2013."

Rapid growth can cause chaos, but you can control the chaos to some extent by following this simple rule: If you have the capital, lease office space based on what you'll need eighteen months from now. For many companies, *if* is a rather important word. With four moves in six years, the rapidly growing company VillageMD seems to have found the right balance.

If your company grows fast and doesn't have enough space, you'll have people on top of people. When your employees are in too close proximity, some will rub others the wrong way. People will start arguing more often and more loudly. They'll start bickering over who gets to use the conference room. They'll be telling each other to stop listening to their phone conversations. There's no question that not having adequate space can slow your momentum.

■ ■ ■ ■ ■

Romeo raised $750,000 to start a financial marketing firm in Long Beach, California. Like a lot of entrepreneurs, Romeo was a terrific salesperson. A charismatic closer, he was brilliant at getting people, to quote Alec Baldwin's character in *Glengarry Glen Ross*, "to sign on the line which is dotted." Even the best salespeople, however, can be terrible businesspeople.

I went to Long Beach's World Trade Center to see Romeo's operation. He had leased the entire nineteenth floor of the building, nearly 30,000 square feet. At $30 a square foot per year, the monthly rent alone came to $75,000. That was before taking into consideration phones, internet, electricity, or any of the other ongoing expenses of running an office—let alone the support staff. It was apparent that Romeo wasn't thinking more than one or two moves ahead.

Romeo's investor asked me if I thought he'd made a good investment.

"How soon do you expect to see a return on your investment?" I asked.

"Nothing unreasonable," he said. "The next six months would be fine. Hell, even twelve."

I started processing, and it was obvious that the business was headed for a cliff. Do the math: the firm would need to gross $100,000 a month just to cover its office expenses, plus another $62,500 a month over the first year to pay back the investor. Not to mention personal expenses such as food, clothes, and cars for Romeo, who had expensive taste.

I had dinner with Romeo before leaving. He asked for honest feedback, so I told him to minimize his expenses immediately while he still had the chance. I explained that it made no sense to get an office that big for only five full-time agents and thirty part-time agents. With forty empty desks in the offices and cubicles, the place looked like a morgue. As you might expect, he wasn't very happy with my advice.

Romeo had the talent and skills to make the business work. He just wasn't willing to accept that running a successful business requires sound financial decision making. He ended up digging his way into deep debt and had to shut down the business. Do you think Romeo was acting like a grand master? Had he thought even three moves ahead, he could have avoided that catastrophic course.

I understand that managing for both the present and the future is a delicate balance. If you have five full-time employees, your sweet spot may be an office that can accommodate fifteen or twenty. If you're savvy, you will work out an option on adjacent space that you can move into *when* you need it.

Yes, plan for growth. And, yes, plan wisely so you can allocate capital for its most important use. People can talk themselves into anything. Before going crazy on office space, let's play a little game. See if you can match the company with its birthplace.

You probably already know about Apple. For the remaining ones, match the company to its first office.

Company	first office
Apple	Garage in Cupertino, California
Mattel	Home office
Google	Cramped woodshed behind a friend's machine shop
Disney	Own garage
eBay	Uncle's garage
Harley-Davidson	Dorm room
Dell	Rented garage

Regret Minimization

Jeff Bezos, the founder of Amazon, talks a lot about regret minimization—about projecting himself forward in time and then thinking about what, theoretically, he might regret not having done. For Bezos, this is a way to make sure he takes calculated risks, since even if he fails, it can't be worse than not having tried at all.

Turns out that Wayne Gretzky, the leading scorer in NHL history, said one more timeless thing: "You miss one hundred percent of the shots you don't take."

Here's a question that will make this concept clear: at age eighty-nine, Warren Buffett is worth $90 billion (as of January 2020). What do you think he was worth at age forty-seven? Five billion dollars?

Answers: *Mattel: Own garage; Google: Rented garage; Disney: Uncle's garage; eBay: Home office; Harley-Davidson: Cramped woodshed behind a friend's machine shop; Dell: Dorm room*

Twenty billion dollars? If you're like most people, you'd figure it would be at least that much. After all, even though we're talking about a forty-two-year gap, it makes sense that he'd have to have had a lot of money back then to get to $90 billion today.

At age forty-seven, Buffett was worth $67 million.

How is that possible? He had a lot of catching up to do in order to make the leap from $67 million to $90 billion, right? So how did he do it?

Buffett did it because he didn't have bad habits and he minimized his regrets. Now, I don't know Mr. Buffett. Maybe he had other regrets that we don't know about. But I do know from all that I've read about him that he's maintained a consistent record of being a decent, fair-minded person in both his personal and professional lives.

Buffett isn't a drug addict, he doesn't cheat his partners, he doesn't gamble away his money, he doesn't get into legal trouble. On the public record, there's no indication of anything like this. Buffett seems to have minimized his regrets and thus maintained his momentum. That's a big part of what helped him go from $67 million to $90 billion in forty-two years.

Contrast Buffett's path to the path taken by the late talk show host Morton Downey, Jr.

In the late 1980s, Downey's syndicated show was bigger than Phil Donahue's. It was reality TV before reality TV existed, and Downey was on top of the world.

Until he self-destructed.

Allegedly, on April 24, 1989, Downey was in an airport bathroom when he was attacked by three white supremacists. They beat him up, cut his hair, and drew swastikas on his face using a marker. The police administered a lie detector test, which he passed.

Shortly thereafter, Downey admitted that he had made up the entire incident. On July 19, 1989, his show was canceled. In February 1990, Downey filed for bankruptcy.

Now consider a second incident. On one show, Downey had a guest who was a vegetarian talking about her healthy lifestyle. He responded to her by saying, "Let me tell you something, darling. I smoke four packs of cigarettes a day. I drink four glasses of alcohol a day. I eat red meat. I'm fifty-five years old, and I look as good as you do."

Downey died at age sixty-eight of lung cancer after having long since faded from public view. If he were able to look back, do you think he might regret some of his behaviors?

He had everything going for him, but he couldn't sustain momentum. Let him be a cautionary tale for you about what you don't want to regret.

Vice Management

Few people are saints, and many entrepreneurs have vices, but if they can learn to manage them, they can prevent them from derailing their careers. I learned from Pastor Dudley Rutherford that there are four G's that can destroy a business/person.

The Four Hazardous G's

1. Greed
2. Gluttony
3. Girls/guys
4. Gambling

Temptation gets the best of many of us. How many people have destroyed their careers and their lives because of gambling? But it doesn't have to be a common vice such as gambling, drinking, or drugs. Some people have vices attached to money: they are either miserly or they spend like drunken sailors. As a result, they either fail to make the right investments (in technology, people, etc.) or they spend foolishly and can't sustain their operations.

Some people's vice is arrogance: everything is about them. They fail to give other people credit and hog both the spotlight and the money from the business. Sooner rather than later, those around them figure it out, and the top talent leaves.

Cheating is also a vice, and it's one to which some entrepreneurs are particularly vulnerable. Early in my career, I was competing for customers with Larry, and he was kicking my ass, producing three times as much business as I was. It was humiliating for more reasons than one; I had a hypercompetitive girlfriend at the time who was also in our business, and she, too, was losing to him. It drove her crazy.

To calm her down, I said, "Listen, let me put it to you this way: This is a long-term game. Executing our strategy takes time. We're going to keep doing it the way we're doing it because this is a long-term play."

Six months later, the SEC charged Larry with convincing clients to take money out of their mortgages and invest it in variable annuities. He lost his securities license, as did nine other people in his agency who were copying his tactics.

Larry was talented, but he allowed his vice to get the better of him. All the momentum he built when he was selling like crazy was stopped—permanently.

The Five Deadly Sins of Entrepreneurs

The list of vices is endless, but entrepreneurs are especially vulnerable to certain temptations. They are sins that you should do everything in your power to avoid, since they will destroy whatever momentum you've generated for your business. Here are the deadly five:

1. Being too cheap or splurging unwisely
2. Letting the wrong people have influence over you
3. Having a "royalty" mentality
4. Refusing to adapt
5. Obsessively comparing yourself to others

1. BEING TOO CHEAP OR SPLURGING UNWISELY

If you're a sports fan, you've probably witnessed a football coach who plays conservatively when his team has a lead. Without the aggressive play calling that helped build the lead, the other team has an opportunity to mount a comeback. The coach thinks he's being wise and protecting the lead. In reality, his extreme caution makes everyone afraid of making a mistake and allows the other team to gain ground. The "prevent defense" ends up costing them victory.

When entrepreneurs are cheap, they convince themselves that they're being frugal; that they've made a good deal of money (i.e., built a big lead) and need to sit on it. Remember the old saying: You've got to spend money to make money. Fail to spend money to update your software or launch a necessary new product, and you'll pay.

Other entrepreneurs kill their momentum by spending as though they possess a bottomless well of cash. They are convinced that they, unlike everyone else, will never have a down period. They spend too much too fast, often on the wrong things, and when they need the money for something crucial, it's not there. Poof, there goes their momentum.

2. LETTING THE WRONG PEOPLE HAVE INFLUENCE OVER YOU

Your consultant tells you to double the size of your business. Your spouse insists that you have to cut your staff by 50 percent. Your buddy suggests that you merge your company with his. None of this advice is necessarily bad, but you need to analyze the source. Decide who is the wrong person to follow and who is the right one. The wrong person has his or her own agenda. The wrong person is more interested in gaining your favor by being a yes-man than offering objective advice. The wrong person is jealous of your success and secretly wants to see you fail. The wrong person may also be a loved one who doesn't have access to all the intel and data that you have access to.

Process these issues. Don't let people sway you without first analyzing who they are, their character, and their motivations. Remember, too, that just because they've been with you for a long time—as a colleague, a friend, or even a spouse—it doesn't mean that their suggestions are sound.

3. HAVING A "ROYALTY" MENTALITY

You feel entitled, invincible, and infallible. Like a king or queen, you rule and expect your subjects to obey rather than challenge your every proclamation. No doubt you've been successful and feel as though you rule your empire. But stop and think for a moment about what your entitled attitude is doing:

- No one questions your decisions.
- No one ventures an opinion different from your own.
- No one is willing to take a risk (for fear of having his or her proverbial head chopped off).

Leaders who act like royalty lose their thrones. If the peasants don't revolt, a new leader who doesn't have this mentality will take the territory.

4. REFUSING TO ADAPT

Agility is prized in organizations today for a reason. In chapter 12, we'll discuss how quickly companies fall out of the Fortune 500 and the S&P 500. If you can't adapt, you're going to fail quickly. "Pivot" is a useful buzzword; it means the ability to turn quickly as situations shift.

Too many entrepreneurs are convinced that they have to stay the course, that they have to double down on a strategy that isn't working. Just because Strategy A worked and helped your business prosper last year, that doesn't mean it's viable this year.

5. OBSESSIVELY COMPARING YOURSELF TO OTHERS

You can lose sight of the bigger picture if you're constantly envious of a competitor. I'm a highly competitive guy, and if someone in my industry is doing better than I am, my reflex is to find a way to beat him. There's nothing wrong with that. What's wrong is when you obsess about someone else—a competitor, your brother-in-law, your mentor—and don't focus on your strategy and objectives. All you want to do is beat the object of your envy, and if that's all you care about, you're caring about the wrong thing and your business will lose its way. Grand masters possess the incredible ability to focus. They know that if they allow any distraction to seep into their consciousness, they will quickly lose their edge.

The Downside of Speed: Fast Money Temptations

Are you hell-bent on growing your company? Most entrepreneurs are. They're ambitious and map out a strategy that will help them add new products and services, increase their revenues, expand their territory, and grow in other ways.

You're going to be tempted to take shortcuts. Trust me. You're going to be offered ways to make quick money or shortcuts to growth. You may be tempted to partner with someone who has a reputation for being unethical but also has critical contacts. You may try to offer a "gift" to a government official or someone else with the clout to overlook a violation or help your proposal go to the front of the line. You may get into a lucrative business where you see the benefit of violating your moral code.

I'm not saying that you're going to do anything illegal. But you may violate your values and principles for the sake of growth. There are repercussions for doing so.

When my agency started to grow, I received calls from guys who were doing a lot of insurance business with us who were asking for side deals. You have no idea how tempted I was to say yes. I wasn't greedy for money; I was greedy for *momentum*. If a guy offers me a "side deal" that pays $200,000, it's easy to rationalize accepting that money so I can use it to hire more leaders or spend more on our next innovative campaign.

Those types of deals will tempt you, but you have to see five moves ahead to understand that the poison they contain is enough to destroy your business. If I had ever made that kind of side deal and my loyal guys had found out about it, it would have been game over.

Never cross your loyal guys. If they find out that you have made questionable deals, two things will happen. First, they will say, "Hey, I want a side deal, too." Obviously, you can't give everyone one of these deals. And second, when you eventually have a falling-out with one of the side-deal guys, he will tell everyone about it. He may tell you, "Just give me that contract, I won't tell anyone." But he will when he's mad at you, and then everyone will know the games you've been playing.

Maintaining your integrity is always a winning strategy. What happens when you compromise your integrity is that you chase little pockets of growth at the expense of much bigger growth targets. You opt for little scores instead of big, sustainable ones. It's the perfect formula for building a mediocre business and being paralyzed by paranoia. You're better than that.

Mass × Velocity = Momentum

When your business gathers the force of a boulder rolling downhill, it is going to be dangerous. The key is managing its speed. Build on the momentum, and your competitors will be in trouble. Get ahead of yourself, and your creditors will be.

Chaos is to entrepreneurship as dangerous waves are to surfing. It comes with the territory, and if you don't know how to handle it effectively, you're in trouble. You can process information effectively even when your world is topsy-turvy. More than that, you can draw energy from the chaos and use it to redouble your efforts to manage your business. In fact, I deliberately put the Move about systems right after this one. If you're feeling nervous about speed, having the systems to track it and manage it is the perfect antidote.

11

Moneyball: Designing Systems to Track Your Business

It is a capital mistake to theorize before one has data.
—Sherlock Holmes

In business you should be constantly asking yourself: What can I track?

Entrepreneurs love the expression "Move the needle." But you must first figure out *what* the needle is measuring!

If you don't have measurable numbers you look at first thing in the morning when you wake up, you're managing inefficiently. Leaders who are hands on in every aspect of their business have yet to learn the benefits of data. Creating systems and protocols limits the need for you to micromanage. Once you learn to track the key indicators of your business, you will know exactly where to direct your energy and expertise.

A CEO is responsible for getting things done, and in the old days, that may have involved a lot of management by walking around and creating implementation systems. Today, everything depends on data. CEOs often possess strong personalities with distinctive talents. Some of us are brash and bold and use our aggressiveness to get deals done. Some of us are clever and creative and rely heavily on our innovative ideas to sustain our business. As a result, we tend to lean more heavily on our personality than on systems.

If you're not that ambitious, maybe this approach is fine. But if you want to build something big and sustainable, you also have to rely on systems.

I'm a big believer in systems: systems of data; systems of procedures; systems of processes. Systems help you with follow-through and follow-up, and they also help create a culture in which nothing is ever unclear. When you're trying to move to the next level of business growth and you're not sure which option is best, data on different markets can help you make the right choice. When you're trying to figure out how to solve a challenging customer service problem, data can help you implement a system that has made other customers happy.

Knowing how to study data and using it to track your business is a game changer for any CEO. Being a great salesperson or a charismatic networker might make you the life of the party, but at a certain point, you're going to need more than your wonderful personality to make your business boom.

Data-Driven Execution

As a teenager, I used to buy the *Los Angeles Daily News* and devour the sports section. Reading English frustrated me back then, but I could not get enough of numbers. For hours and hours, I pored over box scores like a mad scientist. Of all the sports, on paper at least, baseball presented the most perplexing puzzle.

When I read Michael Lewis's *Moneyball: The Art of Winning an Unfair Game* in 2011, it dawned on me that what I had learned from all those years of studying box scores could be applied to my business.

Though I had always been a strong salesman and had developed into a solid sales manager, adding analytics to my toolbox catapulted me to becoming a bona fide CEO who could scale my business.

Moneyball tells the story of how Billy Beane (played by Brad Pitt in the movie of the same name), the general manager of the Oakland A's, applied predictive analytics to baseball. Among his epiphanies was discovering that on-base percentage was a more important factor in winning than batting average, a statistic that had always been revered by players, managers, and sportswriters. In retrospect it seems so obvious, but for decades, on-base percentage was an undervalued metric. In Little League, coaches say, "A walk is as good as a hit." Even so, the best and the brightest in the game of baseball were analyzing the wrong data simply because that was the way it had always been done.

It is our duty as entrepreneurs to disrupt conventional thinking by considering how our next moves can transform our industry. Just as I was inspired by Billy Beane (whom I interviewed in 2019), I want you to apply analytics to your own business. What is your equivalent of on-base percentage? Are you putting too much weight on revenue and not enough on margin? Does your compensation structure incentivize opening new accounts at the expense of selling more to existing accounts?

As you're about to see, reading all those box scores created the foundation for me to make my biggest leap in scaling my business.

Use Data and Logic (or Make a Key Hire) to Predict the Future

The best entrepreneurs are constantly looking at least five moves ahead. As focused as they are on the here and now, they must also project what might happen in the future. They need to prepare to pivot, matching the velocity of whatever change is sweeping toward them.

Do you see a new competitor on the horizon? If so, what moves can you make now to counteract that competitor? Do you believe your industry is on the verge of fragmentation, of turning into multiple niches? If so, what strategy implemented today will help you dominate your niche next year and in the years to come?

When you prepare for a likely future, your competitors who have not done so will be rattled while you steal their market share. You'll handle trends and other changes calmly while other companies' leaders are flustered.

No one can see the future, but you can make logical deductions about trends if you gather the data and project scenarios. Another Michael Lewis book, *The Big Short: Inside the Doomsday Machine*, illustrates this concept beautifully. It tells the true story of Michael Burry (played in the movie of the same title by Christian Bale), a hedge fund manager who predicted in 2005 that the housing bubble would be the catalyst that would make the entire banking industry collapse. According to Burry, the evidence of the coming crisis was there for anyone to see if he was willing to look, but Burry's peers were too busy raking in money to worry about their next moves. For a while, at least, it was the amateurs who appeared to be the smart ones, because they were doing well in the short term. Meanwhile, Burry, the grand master, plotted his future moves, seeing the larger picture of the chessboard and predicting where the market was ultimately going.

Burry went to all the major banks, including Bear Stearns, Deutsche Bank, and Merrill Lynch, and convinced them to create a new financial product that would allow him to bet against the industry. Both Burry's team and the fund's investors thought he was nuts—after all, it didn't appear that anyone else in the industry was worried about the collapse of the housing bubble. But because Burry had already proven himself so good at seeing the future, his investors had given him the authority to make bold moves.

He bought hundreds of millions of dollars' worth of "credit default swaps." When his initial move appeared to be working against him, his investors almost revolted. Burry, undeterred, held his positions.

When the subprime mortgage market crashed, those swaps brought returns exceeding 500 percent.

Every investor had access to the same data as Michael Burry did, but they were all too busy acting in the moment to think about what the next few years might bring. Because Burry was diligent enough to dissect the data and had the foresight of a grand master, he was able to profit from predicting the future. In your business, it may take this degree of planning and patience to launch an innovative campaign.

I understand that you may not have either the time or the mathematical mind of Michael Burry. This leads me to my next point. I've been asked countless times over the years, "What's the best investment I can make to scale my business?" My answer to that question has changed as I've evolved. Now my answer to this question is always the same: "Spend six figures and hire a predictive analytics expert."

If you have seen *Moneyball*, you may remember that Paul DePodesta (played by Jonah Hill in the film, and now the chief strategy officer for the NFL's Cleveland Browns) became Billy Beane's secret weapon. He was the numbers guy who not only devoured statistical data but also analyzed it with a new frame of thinking. DePodesta was the nerd in the front office, the guy with the economics degree from Harvard. Beane never developed DePodesta's predictive analytics skills. Because he hired him, he didn't have to.

Go find your DePodesta. A critical skill of successful entrepreneurs is hiring people smarter than they are who can make up for their weaknesses. The way the game is played now, predictive analytics is an area in which you'd better excel.

To Scale, Codify Your Knowledge So It's Transferable

Imagine asking Leonardo da Vinci, Michelangelo, or Pablo Picasso to teach you how to paint. They would struggle to explain their methodology, and even if they could, good luck trying to implement it. The gift of an artist—or any other genius—is not transferable. How about that of an entrepreneur, leader, or coach?

We've talked about how the brilliance of Bill Belichick has led to six Super Bowl victories. Thinking that Belichick's genius must be transferable, several NFL teams have hired his assistants as head coaches. Their logic is simple: Who better than coaches who have observed Belichick's genius up close to lead teams of their own? Great idea—except, as has been evidenced by the failures of Romeo Crennel, Eric Mangini, and Josh McDaniels as head coaches, it hasn't worked.

NFL owners so desperately want that Belichick secret sauce that they continue to hire disciples such as Matt Patricia. In Patricia's first two seasons as head coach of the Detroit Lions, the team won only nine out of thirty-two games. Maybe what this is telling us is that the skill of a Super Bowl–winning coach is not transferable. (Belichick's disciples Mike Vrabel, Bill O'Brien, and Brian Flores, however, have shown promise and may reverse this trend.)

Now let's look at Bill Walsh. Walsh led the San Francisco 49ers from 2–14 in 1979 to Super Bowl champions three years later (the first of Walsh's three Super Bowl victories). He had seven assistants on his first staff who became head coaches, including Super Bowl winners George Seifert and Mike Holmgren. Holmgren, in turn, had five assistants who became head coaches. In 2007, nineteen years after Walsh retired from the 49ers, fourteen of the NFL's thirty-two head coaches were either direct descendants or second- or third-generation disciples of Walsh.

What's the main difference between Belichick and Walsh? Belichick is known for secrecy, and Walsh is known for his lists. Yes, *lists*. The reason that Walsh's genius could be transferred to others is that he codified and shared his knowledge.

Some may think that Bill Belichick is even more of a genius for making it hard for his assistants to beat him after they've left. Why in the world would he want to make it easy for his assistants to learn how to beat him? He would gain nothing by making his knowledge available. You, on the other hand, have everything to gain by making yours available. You simply cannot scale your business without creating the systems for it to operate without you.

You have to make lists. You must create manuals (video libraries may be more effective than printed ones). You must codify your knowledge. If it exists only in your head, you have a job to do. If you want to have a sustainable business, codify what you know and make sure it gets transferred to everyone else in your organization.

Make Your Numbers Visible in Order to Identify Leaks and Trends

If you walk through our offices, you'll see screens and data streams everywhere. By displaying our data in the office, we are creating accountability and highlighting radical transparency.

Because everyone sees everything, it's an amazing way of using the carrot and stick simultaneously—without having to say or do anything. Because the numbers are in plain view, performers feel recognized just as nonperformers feel uncomfortable. If the latter feel too uncomfortable, all the better; they will either up their game to avoid further embarrassment or leave the company. Transparency is the ultimate performance-enhancing drug. And when it doesn't work to motivate your poor performers, they will weed themselves out—which is exactly what you want.

You may call this harsh. I call it effective.

Let's go back to analytics. With all the data in front of me, I watch for two things: leaks and trends. Leaks alert me to inefficiencies. If, for example, I see a big spike in submitted policy applications but the processing time from our headquarters to the insurance carrier decreases, I suspect a leak.

The numbers give me clues for where to look. Is the problem the number of people processing the applications, the lack of the right people doing so, or the process itself? If I saw a decrease in processing time tomorrow, I would really be concerned that there's a problem. Right now I'm under the impression that we have hired the right staff and the investment in our technology is working. Why, then, is processing time slower? Though the data won't provide the answer, it will alert me to the fact that there's a problem that needs to be addressed.

I also look at trends. Like a stock analyst, I look at line graphs to see how quickly things are moving. Why did we have a downswing in the first three months of the year? Why did sales skyrocket in May? What are we doing right, and what shouldn't we be doing? Digging down into the numbers helps us tweak our approach and make it more effective.

Most businesses have some degree of seasonality. Retailers depend on Black Friday, just as film studios depend on holiday movies. It's also why retailers have created arbitrary events such as back-to-school sales and why online retailers created Cyber Monday. The problem I often see is *blind acceptance* of these trends. It's long been considered a given in our industry that December to February and June to August are slow months. When I started analyzing data, I saw that 75 percent of policies were sold in six months of the year (March to May and September to November). When I looked deeper, I saw that there wasn't any good reason for this. It wasn't as though we were running a ski slope that depends on weather for traffic.

What that told me was that the agents were mentally checking out in those months. In doing so, they were simply living up to preconceived expectations. Because the industry as a whole, and their peers, slowed down at certain times, they followed suit. And because my competitors accepted this as a given—and as a result tolerated poor results during certain periods—I saw an opportunity.

How did I react to those bits of data?

I ran innovative campaigns specifically targeted to increase sales during the slow months. I also changed the dates of our most prestigious incentive conference to make sales in the summer the most important component.

I then took a page out of Ray Dalio's book and created baseball cards with every agent's statistics for the year. Because the agents were aware that the cards would be going to press on January 15—and their performance would be seen by everyone in the company—sales in December skyrocketed. Within two years of my uncovering and analyzing that data, our sales percentages shifted from 75/25 (peak months/slow months) to 55/45. In other words, we eliminated almost all the seasonality from our business. Data alone didn't solve the problem, but it did alert us to the problem and allowed us to track our progress toward the solution.

With that win under our belt, I started examining the trends for each part of a month. In doing so, I was able to see where we were weak and how to create incentives to avoid the end-of-the-month frenzy to close business. Since we started tracking this, the sales within each month have started to balance.

All CEOs should be looking at their numbers, watching for leaks and trends, and then driving their execution based on what they learn.

Trust Numbers, Not People

When you're running a company, you can't always trust other people to tell you the truth. In fact, you can't always trust yourself. Other people have their own agendas; they want to work on a particular project and are overly optimistic in their projections of its success. Sometimes they aren't even conscious of how they're twisting the truth.

Entrepreneurs can make the same mistakes. You convince yourself that you can make a new product work, but it's your ego talking, not your logic. Or you promote someone because you like him, not because he's earned it.

Numbers help keep everyone honest.

■ ■ ■ ■ ■

Most of your revenue producers have type A personalities. They're aggressive, confident, decisive types, and these qualities are useful in various aspects of business. But type A's are also good self-promoters, and as a CEO, you need to differentiate between self-promotion and achievement.

Here's how to do it. When people tell me how hard they've been working and all the results they've been generating, I start out by asking, "What's your closing ratio?"

Let's say I'm having this conversation with Paul. He responds, "Fifty percent."

"Awesome. Now let me ask, what's your average sale per client?"

"Two thousand dollars."

"So if you make ten proposals and close half of those, that translates into ten thousand dollars."

"That's right."

"So let me ask you: How come your best month last quarter was only six thousand dollars?"

You think you already know the answer. What you may not know is that your trump card is silence. This is not the time to turn into Alec Baldwin's character in *Glengarry Glen Ross* and scream, "Put that coffee down! Coffee's for closers only. . . . 'The leads are weak.' . . . You're weak!"

Rather than stating an assumption or questioning Paul's work ethic, remain silent. Let him answer the question.

At some point, Paul starts talking. Sure enough, he gets angry and protests that he's not lazy.

"Why are you getting upset?" I ask. "I'm just playing back the numbers you gave me."

Paul has already started to reflect. He's protesting that he's not lazy, because he knows the data says otherwise. There's no need to beat him up. Just stick with the process.

Bad managers use qualitative data. They'll analyze such a situation with *words* rather than numbers. They'll say the person is lazy, dishonest, or unmotivated. Those words don't do anything to solve the problem. Data, on the other hand, points to solutions.

By relying on the data, you defuse the emotion from the situation. By focusing on the numbers, you help the other person acknowledge realities. This not only provides the impetus for improvement but preserves your relationship.

Solving for X seems straightforward in this situation. The only variables in Paul's income are number of proposals, closing ratio, and average sale per client. Let's say the last variable is fixed at $2,000. There are only two ways to make more money: make more proposals or improve the closing ratio. When you dig into the numbers, you see that Paul's closing ratio actually is 50 percent. The problem is that he submitted only six proposals.

Just as we had to look into the numbers when performing ITR analysis, we have to go deeper here. The data tells us that Paul isn't making enough proposals. What determines the number of proposals is what gets him to the proposal stage: prospecting. The culprit is that he's not generating enough leads. That's the X you need to solve for.

Has his social media marketing dropped off? Has he dropped out of his networking groups? Has he stopped calling existing customers or making cold calls? You were on the right track when you measured the number of his proposals and his closing percentage. Digging deeper, you see that your next move is to revisit his prospecting strategy and find a way to measure it. For some ideas, let's look at how a major company uses data to manage its sales force.

Analyzing Data Goes Beyond Solving for *X*

Lanier Worldwide (now a subsidiary of Ricoh USA), an office products company based in Atlanta, is well regarded for the quality of its sales training. Its metrics for copier sales reps (when Greg Dinkin worked there in 1994) were simple:

- 20 cold calls per day
- 2 product demonstrations (demos) per day
- 10 percent closing average
- 1 sale per week, $1,200 commission per sale
- Therefore $1,200 commission per week

For recent college graduates, you can see how appealing this pitch is. Sell just one copier a week, and you'll make sixty grand a year. Even better, you had to close only 10 percent of your demos to meet your quota. It's a formula that Lanier figured out based on years of data. The hard part, of course, was that on average you had to make a hundred cold calls a week to make one sale.

Let's pretend that Chris is exceptional and has a closing ratio of 50 percent. When you look at his weekly numbers, you see that he is averaging $2,400 per week. He's absolutely killing it. He's the number one rep in the office. What a stud.

Do you see the problem?

We have to revert back to qualitative data. Being a "stud" doesn't tell us anything.

When we dig into the numbers and see that Chris closes at 50 percent, we start scratching our heads. It's time to solve for *X*. His monthly numbers look like this:

- *X* cold calls per day
- *X* demos per day

- 50 percent closing average
- 2 sales per week, $1,200 commission per sale
- Therefore $2,400 commission per week

Figuring out the number of demos is easy. Since he closes half of them, it's obvious that he does four demos. But how about the cold-call numbers? They're nowhere to be found.

By the way, doesn't this story remind you of the story I just told you about Paul? The reason is that I want you to spot a trend. It is common for your most talented employees to skate by on talent alone. It's human nature that when things come to us easily, we tend to coast. As a leader, it's your job to challenge your most talented people to live up to their talent. Unless you understand the numbers, people such as Chris and Paul are going to earn a nice living. And completely underachieve! But they shouldn't—not on Jobs's watch, not on Belichick's watch, and hopefully not on your watch.

To see what happened with Chris, let's examine the math. If he had been doing ten demos a week, he'd have been making five sales instead of two. That would have been $6,000 a week instead of $2,400. Because he was top dog in the office and his boss didn't have a *Moneyball* mentality, no one bothered to track his activity. As a result, Chris stopped prospecting. When you dig deeper, you see that he did zero cold calls. The demos all came from referrals or existing clients.

The simple answer? Make Chris do more cold calls.

You should have known that that was a trick question. There are no simple answers in business. The data led us to figure out the reason Chris is underachieving: a lack of prospects. Data alone, however, isn't what differentiates the Billy Beanes and Paul DePodestas of the world from other people. It's data combined with analysis. If Chris is that good a closer, my first inclination would be to find him more prospects. Especially if I had people in the firm who were great at prospecting and bad at closing, I'd find a way to combine their talents.

Before I did that, I would ask Chris (you guessed it), "Who do you want to be?"

Great leaders find the intersection of data and human nature. Like a smart doctor who runs blood tests, they use the data to diagnose problems. They then use their expertise to find solutions.

For some entrepreneurs, data is the boring part of the business; they aren't interested in the numbers. But I hope these stories make you see why I am obsessed with data, especially when I can use it to gain a competitive advantage.

As I've said many times, reading about how to solve a problem can do only so much. You need to put this information to use in your own business. I gave you a simple formula for tracking sales success. If you're in the trucking business, your formulas are going to be much different. Before turning the page, come up with three formulas that will allow you to track your business. Ideally, these will become the first numbers you look at before you start each business day.

If You Don't Have a System, You Have a Limited Chance for Exponential Growth

You can see by now that words are not sufficient to tell you what's really happening in your business. Here are four phrases that people with no data or systems use:

"Roughly . . ."
"I think we're at . . ."
"Around . . ."
"I believe we did . . ."

Companies that scale and grow eventually create an effective system. If you believe you are going to grow your business on mere personality, your business will be unpredictable. You need to create systems and protocols that will decrease the need for you to micro-manage.

Five Reasons to Implement Systems

1. What is measured can be scaled and improved.
2. You will know where and to whom to direct your energy and expertise.
3. You can stop micromanaging and empower your employees.
4. Your employees, especially your top performers, won't be able to deceive you with hype.
5. You will simultaneously become more effective and have more freedom.

It's one thing to talk about creating systems; it's another to execute them. When you're sales focused, it's hard to step away from revenue-producing activities. Things such as creating manuals and systems did not come easily to me, and they likely will be hard for you. It's also easier to cash checks than to write them. Both the technology and the people you need to hire won't be cheap. And if you want to be a one-person shop and not grow, you don't have to invest in systems.

How to Increase the Value of Your Business

When you're in the middle of running a business, slowing down and building systems is easier said than done. If you come from a sales background, you likely have a "get the deal now and worry later" mentality. If you want to remain a solopreneur, that may work. If, however, you are interested in creating value rather than just profit, you need to slow down long enough to create systems.

A business that runs on systems, rather than just your know-how, increases in value. You have to document how the system flows.

When new employees come in, what steps do you take to integrate them? You need to document every step. The same is true of everything else in your business, such as the steps to take after someone buys a product, when you need to follow up on a sale, and so on. Businesses built on systems and procedures grow in value because they have a life of their own without being dependent on a certain human being. Obviously, your business needs a driver, but having systems in place will increase its value to a whole new level.

PROFIT SHORT-TERM FOCUS	VALUE LONG-TERM FOCUS
Working in the business to make money now	Working on the business to increase value later
Instant gratification	Delayed gratification
Sales mentality	CEO mentality
Independent contractor mentality	Business owner mentality

■ ■ ■ ■ ■

You can't just measure data; you also have to analyze it. As they say on Wall Street, don't fight the tape. When the numbers paint an unpretty picture, your ego is going to get involved. You're going to start looking for ways to rationalize your dips. Anticipate this happening, and you can avoid it. The data never lies.

It's going to be a lot of work to reach the point of having data to track. I can also say from experience that it's going to feel tedious and painful—especially if you see yourself as a visionary or you are a salesperson who lacks the patience to do work that doesn't produce an immediate return. I fought it for a long time. And whether it was from reading *Moneyball* or suffering from panic attacks, I finally learned that the only way to run a business with scale is to implement systems that track data.

12

Stay Paranoid;
The Grand Master Never
Lets His Guard Down

I attribute Intel's ability to sustain success to being constantly
on the alert for threats, either technological or competitive in
nature. The word "paranoia" is meant to suggest that attitude,
an attitude that constantly looks over the horizon for threats
to your success.

—Andy Grove, former CEO and chairman, Intel

Business is war. Or, to put it another way, for a business, peace
never exists. You can be the market leader, you can be making
record profits, you can *believe* that you can relax and ride the momentum, but . . . someone is always out there preparing to attack
you. You can experience the illusion of peace when things are going
well, but it's just an illusion. If you let down your guard for a second,
you make yourself vulnerable to attack.

History is one of our best teachers. We use the term "Fortune
500" so often that we may have forgotten its origin. In 1955, Edgar P.
Smith, an editor at *Fortune* magazine, published a list of the five

hundred largest US corporations by total annual revenue. Today, the list includes both public companies and private ones (if their revenues are publicly available). Of the original five hundred, guess how many are still on the list. Half? Two hundred? Even if only 20 percent made it, you're still looking at one hundred.

Try fifty-two.

You think it's easy to stay relevant? Boeing, Campbell Soup Company, Colgate-Palmolive, Deere & Company, General Motors, IBM, Kellogg Company, Procter & Gamble, and Whirlpool Corporation represent the minority of firms that were on the list in both 1955 and 2019. You think other businesses aren't out to destroy their competition—especially their biggest competitors? Eighty-nine percent of the original Fortune 500 have either gone bankrupt or fallen off the list (some have been acquired). Business is a bloodbath. The moment you think you're on safe ground is the moment you become the most vulnerable.

Depending on where you are in your business cycle, this next set of data is either going to excite you or frighten you. I found it on the website of the Foundation for Economic Education (FEE).

> According to a 2016 report by *Innosight* ("Corporate Longevity: Turbulence Ahead for Large Organizations"), corporations in the S&P 500 Index in 1965 stayed in the index for an average of 33 years. By 1990, average tenure in the S&P 500 had narrowed to 20 years and is now forecast to shrink to 14 years by 2026. At the current churn rate, about **half of today's S&P 500 firms will be replaced over the next 10 years** as "we enter a period of heightened volatility for leading companies across a range of industries, with the next ten years shaping up to be *the most potentially turbulent in modern history.*"

Technology and social media are great equalizers. As a result, it's even harder to stay relevant. It's also easier to knock off the big boys.

You can't stay relevant by staying the same. Get complacent for one minute, and you're going to be toast.

Every Day Is Urgent: Stay Alert; Stay Alive

A heightened sense of urgency is a trait that the most successful entrepreneurs share. For them, every day is a battle, and they treat it as though it's a matter of life and death. It gives them that urgent energy that translates into a business edge. You don't want to compete against one of those people. It's not that they're smarter or more skilled; it's that they will outwork you. They are obsessed with winning.

In *The 33 Strategies of War*, Robert Greene said:

> You are your own worst enemy. You waste precious time dreaming of the future instead of engaging in the present. Since nothing seems urgent to you, you're only half involved in what you do. . . . Cut your ties to the past; enter unknown territory where you must depend on your wits and energy to see you through. Place yourself on "death ground," where your back is against the wall and you have to fight like hell to get out alive.

I'm not telling you to be crazy paranoid but be cautious paranoid. In the latter condition, you're alert for what can go wrong but you're not obsessive about it. You're conscious of potential dangers and pitfalls, and you keep your antenna up for signs that things are going south.

Think about a common scene in war movies: A squad goes into combat and wins a battle, captures a villain, and settles in for the night. They celebrate their victory, partying with drink and the local women. They pass out, and then what happens in the middle of the night? They get ambushed. They let their guard down, and the enemy takes advantage of it.

When I was in the army, we had a saying: "Stay alert; stay alive."

The same holds true in business. You've got to be alert for what can go wrong. Don't be naive and think all your people are loyal and hard-working and will function perfectly well without supervision. Don't think you've squashed all your competitors and no one can come up with a way to challenge your position. Don't trust that the innovation that paved your way to success will continue to pave your way into the future.

Good generals are paranoid, and they respond to that paranoia by creating one great strategy after another. If you can outstrategize the competition, you can protect yourself from things that will go wrong. Don't wing it. Don't rely on a strategy until it gets stale. Keep mapping out fresh plans based on changing conditions; anticipate trends, and have a strategy in place to capitalize on them.

Every general from Napoleon to Patton mastered this technique, and every business leader needs to do so as well. Why are your numbers always off in February? Why is there always a mad scramble as deadlines approach? Why do a lot of your meetings degenerate into yelling and scapegoating? Why have you lost three major customers in the last six months? These are the types of questions that ought to give you pause. Investigate the deepest cause. See if you can identify the problem that is hidden beneath the surface of things. When paranoia leads to curiosity, which leads to solutions, it is serving its function.

The Better You Do, the More Vulnerable You Are

Success will diminish paranoia. This may seem counterintuitive, but think about what happens when everything is going great. You've probably experienced this: You had one win after another, and then suddenly, out of nowhere, you're dead in the water. What happened?

What happened was that you got complacent. What happened was that you stopped being the hungriest person in your industry. What happened was that you felt you had graduated past the point of having to be paranoid.

I'll tell you what happened to Rick, a good friend who was a criminal defense lawyer in Los Angeles—not just any criminal defense lawyer but one of the best. He ended up representing powerful and wealthy drug dealers in the 1970s and '80s, and they invited Rick to party with them. One line of cocaine led to another, and pretty soon he was doing a lot of it. They introduced him to Playboy playmates, and soon Rick was going out with not one of them but two—and at the same time! After a series of poor decisions and cocaine-related legal transgressions, Rick was sentenced to twenty years in prison. He lost his law license, and when he finally got out of prison, he was earning around $3,000 a month selling ad specialty items such as pens and shirts.

He was in his late sixties when I asked him what kind of guy he had been in high school. He said, "I was a regular guy. I married my high school sweetheart."

As we talked, it became clear that he had been overwhelmed by his success. As his law career took off, people began treating him like the captain of the football team and women threw themselves at him. He was a late-blooming golden boy, and the glamour of the drug scene beckoned. Rick couldn't resist. Like many successful people, he couldn't imagine how anything could derail his career (remember Morton Downey, Jr.?). As a result, he wasn't prepared for the success that ultimately ruined him. I'm sad thinking about Rick, who died in 2019. He was a good friend with a big heart who made one bad move (trying cocaine) that led to a series of moves that put both his life and career into checkmate.

Brené Brown, a research professor and best-selling author, gave a TED Talk called "The Power of Vulnerability" that has been viewed online more than 46 million times. She understands how peer pressure can get the best of us. She said, "Daring to set boundaries is about having the courage to love ourselves even when we risk disappointing others." Loving ourselves often translates into saying no. I wish Rick had been wise enough to heed that advice.

You might remember Robert Shapiro as the lawyer who helped

defend O. J. Simpson. He was and remains a highly successful attorney who maintained his momentum despite his success. He's made the transition from criminal to civil law, and when I interviewed him, I asked him about his criminal defense work and whether he had ever been tempted by clients who could offer him drugs and beautiful women.

Shapiro said, "I never established a relationship, a friendship, with my clients. I always kept them at a distance."

In contrast to Rick, by setting up boundaries, Shapiro maintained his momentum, even after achieving fame and success.

Entrepreneurs need to be prepared for unexpected attention, flattery, and other perks of becoming successful, especially if they're not accustomed to this type of attention. They need to be aware that if they buy their own hype, they'll screech to a halt.

Along those same lines, both Robert Greene and Jordan Peterson offered me similar advice about being careful with whom you share both good news and bad news. Those men understand human nature and know that there are not many people who will be happy for your success. Before sharing anything with anyone, consider who—deep down—wants to see you succeed and who wants to see you fail. Some people whom you consider friends may not give you the best counsel, especially if they are in competition with you.

Staying Centered Despite Uncertainty

Here are three tactics that will allow you to keep your head while all those around you are losing theirs.

1. MAKE FRIENDS WITH MURPHY'S LAW

Savvy entrepreneurs respect Murphy's Law. Before you launch a new product, make an investment, pull the trigger on an acquisition, or make any type of major move, ask yourself this question: What are the very worst events that might happen as a result of my action?

Then take steps to mitigate those potential worst events.

You may be a positive thinker, which is great, but don't be a naive one. This holds true for smaller events and decisions as well as big ones. If you're about to make a major presentation, check the projector, and then check it again. It may have worked a hundred times flawlessly in the past, but something in the universe will make sure it doesn't work when you need to use it to make a PowerPoint pitch to investors. And when it doesn't work, you're going to be dealing with chaos—maybe not all-out, wreck-the-business chaos but the kind that ruins both the presentation and your day. The kind that causes you to chew out and alienate your people. The kind that throws you off your game and raises questions from your potential investors.

Here's an anti–Murphy's Law technique I use all the time. I meet with the best brains on my team—no more than five. We sit and talk about what we should anticipate and prevent from going wrong. And I have to tell you, sometimes as a result of this anti–Murphy's Law meeting, we decide to hold off on a planned launch because we realize we're not ready to proceed or that the odds of something big going wrong are too high. Sometimes, too, we may even trash an idea that seemed like dynamite when we first conceived of it. Having a brain trust provides a valuable check and balance.

2. ADMIT DEFEAT BY ACCEPTING SMALL LOSSES

When Groupon and LivingSocial first became popular, I saw an opportunity to start a competing service. I imagined something like Groupon and Yelp, combined with a gamification component, and put $100,000 into creating and testing early versions. Several investors were willing to go along on the ride with me, but before pulling the trigger I decided to run the idea by several trusted friends. They ranged from the CEO of a large life insurance company to the head of one of the largest transportation companies in the United States.

After I presented my business plan and projections, they pointed out holes I'd missed. After answering their questions, I accepted their concerns that the project would steal focus away from my successful core business. It didn't mean that the idea would fail, but there was a good chance that it would create chaos that might affect my company adversely. Anticipating Murphy's Law, I did the one thing that made sense: I let go of the idea.

Great entrepreneurs accept losses. Rather than throwing money at bad investments, they admit defeat and conserve cash for their next venture. Show me a losing gambler in a casino who is vowing to get even, and I'll show you someone who is a few moves away from losing it all.

3. IDENTIFY YOUR NEXT THREE (OR MORE) STEPS

Once you've entered a chaotic situation, you're vulnerable to decision paralysis. When things get crazy, you might want to hunker down and play it safe. But entrepreneurs don't have the luxury of inaction. You can easily forget this truth when chaos strikes.

To avoid this problem, commit to deciding on your next three steps quickly. I know how much we talk about thinking five moves ahead. But when you have to act quickly, focus on three actions you can take to address whatever problem you're facing right now. These actions can be solutions or temporary measures to stop the bleeding.

For example, a major client tells you that she's ending your relationship. You could:

- Call the sales rep who brought in the client and get the entire story.
- Call the client yourself and let her air her grievances.
- Send the client another shipment of the product, free of charge.

As you can see, these actions don't have to be breakthroughs or complex plans. They will, however, prevent you from doing nothing as you seek the One Perfect Solution (which may not even exist). Don't fall into that trap. Make a plan, and act on it. Things will begin to resolve themselves once you're back in motion.

Manage Your Ego and Build Alliances

Nobody becomes the CEO of a large company who doesn't have a big ego. Nobody. There's nothing wrong with having a big ego—as long as you have built a support system to keep it in check. If you can't control it, it will lead to your demise. When you become very successful and start making a lot of money and have fame and recognition, everyone will be looking for a way to get into your wallet and inner circle. As a result, you will be flooded with compliments.

You'll be inundated with praise because you're surrounded by people who are afraid of the decisions you make. For instance, the members of your team may fear that you will fire them. So they will all tell you how amazing you are. Let me tell you, 90 percent of it is lies. Most people are not going to tell you what you need to hear.

You need a small circle of people around you who will tell you the truth. It's the only thing that will keep your ego in check (though having three kids helps as well). If you don't have a small group of people such as a board of directors or mentors who aren't afraid to tell you off, you're going to be in trouble. I've seen this happen in sales many times. People start making money, and everyone tells them how amazing they are. They're no longer coachable or willing to learn. They don't listen to advice. That's a sign that they have forgotten how to manage their own ego.

Staying paranoid also means staying humble. If you don't have humility, you can't bring people together. Without humility, people who disagree with you won't want to do business with you. How can you generate new ideas or invite fresh perspectives when you don't have diversity or dissenting voices in the room? When you have only people around you who agree with you, you'll naturally get complacent, which is the opposite of being paranoid.

■ ■ ■ ■ ■

Keeping your ego in check means understanding that you can't do everything yourself. If you're overly paranoid, you won't trust anyone. If you're sufficiently paranoid, you'll build strong alliances. It's important to have partners who are also on the lookout for competition. Think of it as a way to increase intelligence.

In *The 48 Laws of Power* by Robert Greene, Law 18 states, "The world is dangerous and enemies are everywhere—everyone has to protect themselves. A fortress seems the safest. But isolation exposes you to more dangers than it protects you from—it cuts you off from valuable information, it makes you conspicuous and an easy target."

Greene makes the point that as hard as it is to trust people, the alternative, working in isolation, is much worse.

You may be surprised at where you will find allies. When Apple was struggling in August 1997, there were few people who would help Steve Jobs. What had once seemed unthinkable—going to an enemy—became possible because he was willing to get past his ego. He bit the bullet and approached none other than his archnemesis, Bill Gates. All he did was ask for a minor favor: an investment by Microsoft of $150 million.

As reported by Stephen Silver at AppleInsider, according to Jobs, "there were too many people at Apple and in the Apple ecosystem playing the game of, for Apple to win, Microsoft has to lose. And it was clear that you didn't have to play that game because Apple wasn't going to beat Microsoft. Apple didn't have to beat Microsoft. Apple had to remember who Apple was because they'd forgotten who Apple was."

In truth, it wasn't really a "favor." Microsoft invested $150 million in Apple stock, and the companies agreed to settle their existing legal disputes, saving both firms time and money.

In addition, Apple agreed to make Microsoft Office compatible with the Mac. In short, rivals became partners.

Imagine what would have happened if Jobs hadn't built that alliance. We're not exactly talking about a guy with a small ego. Yet when it mattered most, he didn't get stubborn and insist that he could do everything himself. Today we can use iPhones and other Apple devices because a paranoid guy with a big ego was man enough and smart enough to build the right alliance.

The next example highlights both the need for alliances and the need for paranoia. In August 2000, Amazon and Toys "R" Us created what the *Wall Street Journal* called a "groundbreaking agreement: For 10 years Amazon would devote part of its Web site to Toys 'R' Us's toy-and-baby-products. The toy retailer would choose the hot products to stock and buy the inventory for the virtual shelves." Keep in mind that the dot-com bubble had burst on March 11, 2000. Amazon was fighting for its life. In my view, if there had not been an alliance, there would be no Amazon. In addition to the revenue the alliance created, partnering with Toys "R" Us helped drive traffic to Amazon, which, in turn, helped sell other products on the site. Amazon could then keep building more partnerships.

Five years later, the two companies were facing off in New Jersey Superior Court. What had started as an alliance had turned into a war. The biggest casualty was Toys "R" Us, which, in 2018, went out of business.

The moral of the story? Even after you build an alliance, stay paranoid!

Seek Wise Counsel

When adversity strikes, you're going to need help. If you've created a wise team—selected them well and treated them right—they can save you when things get tough. You need allies, especially when your business starts to falter. They'll give you the strength to overcome obstacles, to rebound and grow.

I've met many smart entrepreneurs who failed in business, but I've yet to meet a wise one who wasn't able to rebound. The difference between being smart and being wise is that a smart person thinks he knows all the answers while a wise person is comfortable knowing he doesn't. Wisdom is especially valuable during chaotic times.

Here's how I learned this lesson. By age twenty-two, I'd racked up $49,000 in credit card debt and had a credit score that failed to crack 500. My relationship with my girlfriend at the time was headed into the gutter, mostly due to my financial situation. I had an epiphany: if I limited myself to what I already knew, my life would keep going in the same direction.

I decided to seek wisdom. I went from making fun of nerds in school to becoming the biggest nerd of all. All I wanted to do was learn. I devoured books. I became a sponge with my mentors. And, most important, I surrounded myself with the wisest people I could find to teach me about life and business. One of those mentors gave me the questions that became the Personal Identity Audit (which we discussed in chapter 2 and can be found in the appendix).

How do you find wise mentors? Let me share some hard-won lessons. I've worked with lots of coaches and consultants, and I have discovered that many of them offer advice based on their reading rather than their experiences. It struck me that when it comes to mentors or advisers, you can choose from three expertise levels: Theory, Witness, and Application (TWA).

- **Theory.** These are well-read individuals with degrees from prestigious universities. Most consultants and professors fall into this category. They're smart, but they may not be wise. Wisdom comes from practical experience, and these people offer suggestions based on theory. They will teach you how to run a business, but if you ask if they've ever run a business, they will likely answer, "No, I have not. But I've consulted many. I've read all the books." That's a theory-level mentor. There's nothing wrong with that. They can still give you good advice, but they're the lowest-level mentors.

- **Witness.** These advisers have worked directly with successful entrepreneurs and, thanks to that vantage point, can tell you exactly how successful leaders built their business. For example, Guy Kawasaki often shares what he learned working with Steve Jobs on the original Macintosh team.

    Witnesses didn't run the business, but they worked closely with someone who did. For example, if you wanted to be mentored by someone in real estate, you could ask, "Have you ever done real estate before?" If he answers, "I never have, but for ten years I was the assistant for the number one real estate agent in Beverly Hills and learned a lot from her," that's valuable right there. That person can tell you what the person did, how she worked, how she treated her clients, what she did when she almost went out of business, and so on.

- **Application.** Application means that the information is coming directly from the source. These are the people who can tell you what they've done that has worked for them. The most valuable mentors are those who have walked their talk. Fellow entrepreneurs can share what didn't work in their businesses in a way that someone operating from theory or observation simply can't.

Those who possess all three characteristics—theory, witness, and application—are called "trifectas." And by the way, they're tough to find.

A lot of people making YouTube videos are purely Theory and Witness. Very few are Application. So again, do some due diligence to know where a mentor sits on the TWA hierarchy. All three of these levels can be useful, though Application is far and away the best, especially when you're trying to make your way through difficult periods. This is why the grand master Magnus Carlsen hired his former opponent, world champion Garry Kasparov, to be his coach.

■ ■ ■ ■ ■

The game of business can be ugly at times. If you have a warlike mentality, you won't take it personally. Your competitors can make you frustrated, angry, and confused. You can almost guarantee that they're going to hit below the belt. Similarly, one of your top people may leave suddenly—an employee whom you nurtured, helped grow, and supported during his struggles. You will feel the sting of ingratitude. Or you may have a consumer activist group or a government agency on your case; you believe it's singling you out and making you jump through hoops for no reason except that it has a grudge against you.

Recognize how unproductive it is to take things personally. Your ego is your enemy. Building a business is not just ugly; it's messy. It's not just a cognitive effort but an emotional one. When you take things personally, you get drawn into the chaos and can't think clearly. You become furious and vengeful.

As difficult as it may be, step back and view situations analytically. Don't let fury or shame dictate your decisions. I'm not saying to strip yourself of all emotion. You're entitled to whatever feelings you're feeling. Just don't let those feelings cloud your judgment. The best entrepreneurs are able to push their emotional reactions aside and make objective decisions in the midst of chaos.

Show me a successful CEO with decades of longevity, and I'll show you a CEO who has stayed paranoid. Being a CEO means connecting the dots and doing things in ways they haven't been done in the past. Stay alert; stay alive.

MOVE 4

Master Strategy to Scale

SCALING FOR EXPONENTIAL GROWTH

1. Decide how you're going to capitalize your business. Execute strategies for both exponential and linear growth. Lead people by demanding their best and holding them accountable.

MAKE MOMENTUM YOUR FRIEND— AND BE PREPARED FOR CHAOS

2. Create strategies to increase the speed of growth without crashing your business. Look for ways to compress time frames. Keep your ego in check to avoid temptations and being your own worst enemy.

MONEYBALL: DESIGNING SYSTEMS TO TRACK YOUR BUSINESS

3. Decide what are the most important formulas of your business, and track them religiously. Codify what's in your head by creating manuals to transfer knowledge. Determine if new hires are needed to help implement this transfer of knowledge.

STAY PARANOID; THE GRAND MASTER NEVER LETS HIS GUARD DOWN

4. As your company gets bigger, it will become more vulnerable. Know where people can attack you, and stay on guard. Constantly put yourself in your enemies' shoes, and ask how you would put yourself out of business if you were them. Don't take it personally when they try to do just that.

MOVE 5

■ ■ ■ ■ ■

MASTER
POWER PLAYS

13

How to Beat Goliath and Control the Narrative

I'm not a businessman. I'm a business, man.

—Jay-Z

Everyone in business has a Goliath, and it isn't always the biggest company in your industry. Your Goliath could be a company that is taking up market share in a particular region, or it could be more localized, such as another salesperson in your own sales department who has more experience and bigger, more lucrative accounts.

Before you decide to go up against Goliath, you need to know that Goliath is bigger than you are and has more capital, experience, and resources (especially attorneys) than you do. Goliath also has a well-known reputation and brand. As a result, Goliath is more comfortable than you are.

If, knowing all this, you're still dedicated and committed to taking on Goliath, you'd better know the obstacles you face. Hopefully, you also see an opportunity. If Goliath is comfortable, and, as a result, less paranoid, you have an opening to make your move(s).

I want to make one thing very clear: this fight isn't for everyone. The odds of beating a real Goliath are stacked against you. Who would have thought that the small Walmart could practically put Kmart out of business? For every story of Amazon, Microsoft, and Google, there are tens of thousands of stories of individuals and companies that lost everything. Beating Goliath is doable, but it requires being someone who can tolerate pain. If you're still thinking about trying to do it, keep reading.

Things to Know Before Facing a Goliath in Business

1. **You'll be afraid.** As scary as the thought of losing money is, it may be even more painful to your ego to put yourself out there and fail.

2. **You'll have panic attacks and anxiety.** If you don't, it's a sure sign that you haven't put yourself out there. Putting yourself out there means you have to devote everything you've got to delivering. That's going to cause tremendous stress.

3. **You'll be bullied and laughed at.** This will result not only from trying to take on Goliath but also from even thinking it's possible. It will bring a lot of scrutiny, so you'd better brace yourself for negative attention.

4. **You have to be delusional.** In this case, being crazy will actually work in your favor. You'd better be a bit "off" if you think you can dethrone Goliath.

5. **You'll have to work ten times harder than you think.** Just when you think you are at your limit, it will take ten times that to defeat Goliath. Time with your family, of course, will decrease, and you can pretty much forget about hobbies, which is why it isn't for just anyone.

6. **You'll have to stay healthy to have the energy to compete.** I've worked myself into exhaustion and hospitalization multiple times. It's helped me build a tolerance for hard work as each

time I've come roaring back even harder. I'm telling you this not because I want you to fear burning out, but so you can be prepared for doing so when you're in the throes of fighting Goliath.

In Move 2, when we broke down the Solve for X Methodology, I told you the story about how Aegon sued me right when I started my business and how it nearly put us out of business. Goliath had me by the throat and nearly took me down for the count. Once I escaped, I had the confidence to beat Goliath. More important, I understood *why* he could be beaten.

Why Goliaths Can Be Beaten

Are you still not afraid? That's great to hear, because I'm about to hit you with the good news: if you're prepared for the battle, you can win. Here's why: Goliaths tend to get softer the more they win and eventually stop working as hard as they once did. Goliaths typically lose touch with the most current methods of marketing, since they rarely speak directly to customers. Goliath isn't as nimble as you. Goliath has too much to lose to take risks.

Goliath can't recruit the crazy and hungry people because the crazy ones are turned on by underdogs who aspire to take out a Goliath. They would much rather go up against Goliath than join him. This explains why so many people were critical of Kevin Durant when he joined the Golden State Warriors the year after they broke the NBA record with seventy-three wins in a season. It may also explain why Durant left "Goliath" after winning two titles in three seasons.

Even if you are up for the challenge, you must always respect Goliath. One ounce of complacency, and it will knock you out. Goliaths didn't get to where they are by pure luck. They are formidable for a reason. This makes it that much more rewarding when you defeat them. Here's how you can do so.

A Dozen Ways to Beat Goliath

1. **Know your weaknesses.** Knowing your strengths is easy, but knowing your weaknesses will enable you to be nimble and pivot when taking on your Goliath.

2. **Know Goliath's weaknesses.** You cannot fight Goliath where it is strong. You must find its Achilles heel and exploit it.

3. **Master three things you do better.** You set the terms of your battle in the marketplace. Use your strengths to master three things Goliath can't do and do them better than it can.

4. **Don't try to be Goliath.** You can learn moves and information from Goliath, but if you model yourself after it, how are you going to beat it? You have to take advantage of your own strength, not someone else's.

5. **Focus on specializing.** Goliaths tend to generalize in order to spread their influence and power. You must specialize to capture market share from them.

6. **When you're small, make yourself appear bigger.** Walk tall, and don't be intimidated by Goliath's size and strength. Embody your future truth and compete as though you're the one with the advantage.

7. **Keep a low profile initially.** You are going to need a lot of help, and you will need time to get better. Don't waste your early years rubbing people the wrong way and making noise. Work on your business first before looking for a Goliath to fight.

8. **Move quickly.** Use your inherent advantages of strength and speed against Goliath. It can't move as fast as you can.

9. **Partner with competitors that share an enemy.** Goliaths create a lot of enemies. Look for your synergies with those enemies, and build strategic alliances.

10. **Study history.** History can give you context and strategies that you never even thought of in your fight against Goliath. Knowledge is out there for you to harvest and can only help you.

11. **Let other competitors wear your opponents down.** Goliaths must fend off a lot of competitors, and you don't always need to be on the front lines. Standing back and letting someone else take the spotlight can help you focus your resources better and give you an advantage over Goliaths.

12. **Don't disclose every aspect of your strategy.** To a grand master, this should be self-explanatory.

Controlling the Narrative

It's time to think about how and what to broadcast to the world, since all eyes are going to be on you. If you don't talk about what you believe in, what your views are, and who you are as an individual, the world is going to decide who you are. It's up to you to control the narrative and talk about what you're dealing with. If you don't, others will.

Social media is the great equalizer.

When I started my agency, Goliath used every resource it had to bully me. My competitors said horrible things about me and made up nasty rumors that could easily have ruined my reputation. That was when I fully grasped the fact that using social media properly would allow me to control the narrative.

There are many different forms of bullying. It has evolved over the years. When your company is small, people will defame your character and spread rumors. I realized that the way to fight back was by controlling the narrative.

When people heard awful things about me, they would turn to Google to confirm their suspicions. And what did they find? That the monster they had heard about was very different from the guy they were watching online. I was able to control the narrative, and as a result, many of the people who heard negative gossip about me ended up becoming my partners.

Think about how different this was in a pre-internet world. Steve Jobs had to call *Playboy* to ask it to write a story about him that offered his narrative. From the time Jobs did the interview until the time people saw it, two months had elapsed! Now two milliseconds elapse between your writing something online and people reading what you've written.

Goliath can spend millions of dollars on PR. Meanwhile, you can make a video with an iPhone and get more views—and make a bigger impact.

■ ■ ■ ■ ■

When you post, really share yourself. We've been brainwashed that professionalism means only putting our best foot forward. The problem is that people don't connect with perfect robots. They connect with all of who you are. Show your mistakes, and be vulnerable. If you talk only about what you do right, it's a turnoff. There's no way in the world anyone can make it to the top without making mistakes. People identify with you more when you share your down moments.

People will also identify with you if you challenge them to question your views. Ask them to share their thoughts. Ask for specific recommendations to solve problems. One, you'll learn something. Two, you'll increase your viewers' or readers' engagement.

Another key to connecting with your audience is to be consistent. Your audience should know when they are going to hear from you and rely on a regular schedule of content. Two best-selling authors have different approaches. People following Seth Godin know they can expect a short and thoughtful daily blog post. Daniel Pink, on the other hand, sends out his *Pinkcast* every other week. The key to both strategies is that each one's audience has an expectation that is met.

Going hand in hand with consistency is integrity. Especially as you gain a following, you are going to get proposals to promote other people. **Do not prostitute your brand.** If you're going to take on a sponsor, you need to be aligned with that brand. Your followers will appreciate you if you stay solid with your message and don't sell out. This is going to require you to delay gratification and refuse a quick buck in order to play the long game of maintaining your integrity.

Be Shameless About Self-Promotion

The first rule of self-promotion is that you have to be shameless. What holds people back is the fear of being judged. Visionaries have gotten past that. You can't be afraid of judgment when promoting yourself. You *want* people to notice you. Phil Knight of Nike is shameless. Jerry Jones of the Dallas Cowboys is shameless. Dwayne "The Rock" Johnson is shameless. Kevin Hart is shameless. Do you think Hart reached nearly 100 million Instagram followers by being timid? If you're not shameless, no one is going to know who you are.

What holds us back from being shameless is the fear of humiliation. So what if you're humiliated? Do you know anyone who's not been humiliated? The people no one knows anything about—the people hiding in safe corporate jobs. When I say "Be shameless," I don't mean you should brag. I mean that you should do as much as you can (within your narrative and brand) to make sure you get eyeballs. Self-promotion is an art form.

You may feel uncomfortable bragging, but you can do it in subtle ways through the stories you tell. Let's say you're in an attorney's office and he or she has some plaques on the wall. You could say, "You know, these are impressive plaques. Listen, I can tell you that to be recognized as a top attorney takes a lot of work. I respect that because when I got my plaque for being the top broker in our company, I remember the effort it took to get there. What's crazy is that many times people don't see the effort behind closed doors. So I applaud you for what you did."

Another way to self-promote is by making predictions. Make some predictions based on your intuition and research. Why is that important? Because if even some of your predictions come true, you gain credibility and look like a sage.

Now, some people may say, "What dumb advice, Pat. Are you really telling me to put myself out there? What if I'm wrong and end up being humiliated?" Consider the alternative: never being wrong and no one knowing who you are.

Conor McGregor, the former UFC champion, said, "I'm cocky in prediction. I am confident in preparation, but I am always humble in victory or defeat." He shamelessly puts himself out there, and win or lose, McGregor always controls the narrative by making bold predictions.

Great real estate developers also make predictions. So do great stockbrokers. They put themselves into the news. You think Jim Cramer landed a TV show by being timid or never going out on a limb? His show isn't called *Shy Money*; it's called *Mad Money*. He gets people talking about him. Some say he's an idiot; others swear by his advice. I've never met Jim Cramer, but I can bet he's laughing all the way to the bank.

Don't be afraid to make predictions within your industry. Again, think about the framing. Here are some titles of articles by the investment adviser and personality Peter Schiff.

"Peter Schiff: Negative Interest Rates Are Boneheaded"
"Peter Schiff: The Only Winners Will Be the People Who Bought Gold and Silver"
"Peter Schiff: Whatever the Fed Is Going to Do Will Stink to High Heaven"

Schiff has been singing the same tune for decades. Sometimes he's right, and sometimes he's not. But he's always in the news. He self-promotes. He makes bold predictions. And as a result, he has become synonymous with investing in gold. When a financial TV show is looking for an expert on gold, Schiff gets the call.

I realize I've thrown a lot of examples at you. To summarize, the most important tenets of social media are:

- Have a personality.
- Be bold.
- Be brash (if that's who you are).
- Be engaging.
- Trumpet yourself when you're right.
- Poke fun at yourself when you're wrong.
- Accept the loss when you're wrong.

Promotion is something you must constantly be doing. Here's another technique. Instead of name-dropping, book-drop. Let's say you're sitting in a meeting and in response to a comment, you say, "One of the books I read was such and such, and in this book it talks about this, and I feel like this is what's going on here with the company. And I recommend that book to you." If the other people in the meeting are ambitious, they'll write down the name of the book. If you can give two or three book recommendations in a business conversation with somebody, in that person's mind you're a well-read autodidact. Whether you have a college degree or not is irrelevant.

The next way to self-promote is to have strong opinions about subjects within your field of expertise. For instance, you may say you don't agree with where the marketplace is going or talk about one of the mistakes the industry is making. A great place to do this is on your blog, vlog, or podcast. When the topic comes up, you can say, "You know, I recently wrote a blog about this. It created a lot of controversy because my belief was such and such. I'll send it to you so you can read it."

I wrote an article about why home ownership is not the American dream. It blew up. Fox contacted me. CNN contacted me. The *Denver Post* did a feature on it. It wrote about this entrepreneur who doesn't believe in home ownership. That was my opinion. It created so much controversy just because I wrote one article saying what the real American dream is and that it's not home ownership, it's entrepreneurship. So share your thoughts and opinions, and then self-promote the articles you write.

You need to have a level of certainty about what you're talking about. People can tell the difference between certainty and uncertainty. Believe me, it's not that hard to know when somebody is certain about what he or she is talking about. Having certainty alone is a way of self-promoting.

Don't overdo it, and don't make things up. Have an opinion, have evidence for that opinion, and state that opinion with certainty.

My challenge to you is to self-promote. Put your fear of being judged aside, and put yourself out there. Say or do something bold. Let people know who you are and what you stand for.

Align Your Brand with Your Master Vision

When I first started creating content on YouTube, I named the channel Patrick Bet-David and called the segments "Two Minutes with Pat." As I thought more about my vision for its content, I realized that the channel was about education. I wanted to provide value and entertainment that would inspire entrepreneurs around the world.

My *unselfish* reason for creating the content was to give back. I wanted to offer everything I wish I'd had when I transitioned from salesperson to entrepreneur and later to CEO. I made a list of the questions I'd had at every phase of my career when I'd felt powerless and clueless—and I went about answering them. I was also committed to doing it in a way that was interesting. So many of us struggled in school because the approach was so damn boring. I wanted to create content that would make people want to watch it—that they could learn from and be entertained by at the same time.

I also had two *selfish* reasons for creating content. One was for my kids and (future) grandkids to have access to what I thought about life. I visualized my kids one day binge-watching the content—maybe at a time when they think I might not be too happy with them, only to realize that Daddy loves them.

The second reason? You guessed it. To control my narrative.

Getting back to my business reasons for creating Valuetainment, I realized that to scale the brand, I would need to take the focus off me and direct it to the vision.

I imagine you spotted the problem quickly. The title of the weekly segment—"Two Minutes with Pat"—was all about me. It had nothing to do with my vision.

You've heard me talk passionately about how to think like a chess grand master. When it comes to launching a new idea with a massive vision, it's time to put the mindset of a grand master to use and plot fifteen moves ahead. Are some coming to mind? Can you put yourself in my shoes back then and strategize how to go from a struggling solopreneur making videos to a leading educator? I'm guessing that you may even be thinking of some things I missed. And when you see my list, you're probably going to poke holes in my strategy. Yes! Please do.

All right, time to take a look at how I implemented my plan to take my video series to where it is today.

Fifteen Moves to Transform a Weekly Segment into a Channel Focused on Entrepreneurship

1. Spend alone time getting clear on the vision.
2. Consult with our creative team to brainstorm new names for the channel.
3. Buy and study every book on marketing and media that exists.
4. Identify who we don't want to be as much as who we want to be.
5. Make the channel about the mission rather than my personality.

6. Create a new logo, name, and website that embodies a leading educator.

7. Attend social media industry conferences to learn different strategies.

8. Start learning the language of media and what needs to be tracked.

9. Hire people in areas where we are weak. In the next ninety days, hire an expert in SEO (Search Engine Optimization).

10. Gradually increase the rate of posted content.

11. In the next thirty days, hire a full-time editor.

12. Map out a strategy for Instagram, Twitter, Facebook, and YouTube—and be prepared to act quickly if the next social media app overtakes the big four.

13. Present myself as an expert in the marketplace. Write an article as an expert and post it on multiple platforms.

14. Create clear criteria for which guests to invite on the show that match the brand of Valuetainment.

15. I'm keeping this one quiet for now. This next move will be revealed soon enough.

The result of those fifteen moves? We changed the name to Valuetainment, and the rest is history. Today, Valuetainers around the world have watched billions of minutes of content. What's been fascinating is that each time I've chosen to touch on a new topic, a new audience has shown up from that community. It's led to many business deals and contacts that have helped cement the brand and, as a by-product, attract business to my company. As of May 2020, we have more than 2.3 million YouTube subscribers and are the leading channel on entrepreneurship.

Turn Off the Noise and Cut the Fat

In 2005, the National Science Foundation published an article stating that the average person has between twelve thousand and sixty thousand thoughts per day. Of those, 80 percent are negative and 95 percent are exactly the same as those of the day before.

A major power move is turning off the noise. Once you start controlling your own narrative, you also need to reduce the time you spend paying attention to everybody else's noise. Do you think big thinkers are paying attention to celebrity gossip? Do you think they obsess over the news? They do get the bullet points in the morning because they need to stay informed about current events, but they don't waste time with conspiracy theories or clickbait. That's way too much noise.

Also, turn off the noise of negative friends and small thinkers. Turn off the noise of family members who don't support what you want to do. Don't even bring up ideas in front of them if you know you'll hear only negativity. Turn off the noise. Stop any distractions and negativity. Remember, there is a big difference between someone who will give you constructive criticism and someone who is just downright negative.

You also need to cut the fat out of your life. If playing video games isn't how you plan to make money, cut them out. If you have multiple boyfriends or girlfriends or you party at a nightclub three times a week, stop it! If you post twenty selfies a day or check your fantasy football team score every thirty seconds, cut it out! If you have bad habits and vices that no one knows about, find ways to take control of them.

Anything that holds you back from thinking big needs to stop. You know exactly what I'm talking about. I don't need to explain it to you. Think about it. Right now you're thinking about what you need to cut. The thing that you're thinking about? Cut it, right now.

It's holding you back, and it's not worth it. It won't give you as much fulfillment as thinking big and carrying out your vision.

Let me give you an example. I love women. When I was younger and single, if you wanted someone to go clubbing with and have a great time, I was that guy. I was being interviewed on a radio talk show, and I was talking about my plans and goals. One of the hosts asked me, "What's the biggest thing that changed in your life?"

I told them, "When I was in my mid-twenties, I made the decision not to have sex again until I made my first million."

"So you must have made that million really fast."

Unfortunately, no. I "fasted" for seventeen months. It was difficult. But doing so accomplished two things simultaneously. First, it provided me with the discipline and motivation I needed to achieve my goal. Second, it forced me to spend my time on what mattered. Before setting that goal, I was spending so many hours in clubs, not to mention all the mental energy it required to meet and court women. That was nothing but noise. Once I replaced that noise with revenue-producing activities, my productivity skyrocketed—and I eventually met my wife and settled down with her.

There's no margin for error if you want to beat Goliath. You can't afford to waste time if you want to succeed at the highest level. Wasting time also impacts your social media strategy. Thank goodness Instagram didn't exist during my partying days or else you'd find some strange pictures all over social media.

I'm not telling you that you should copy my example. I'm not a typical guy, and what worked for me probably won't work for you. I would tell you that if you are aware what your weakness is—stuffing yourself with desserts, binge-watching TV, obsessively following sports—you can put your focus there. Some people think nothing of spending all day Sunday watching football and another three and a half hours watching *Monday Night Football*. That's more than thirteen hours. So maybe you don't quit your fantasy football league or stop watching your favorite team's games. But if you limit watching football to one game a week, you've just reclaimed ten hours a week. Can you imagine what adding an entire day to your workweek will do?

Self-discipline can take many forms. You can impose limits on how much time you waste surfing the web. You can dedicate five hours daily to working on the most important task for your business. You can assess threats to your business at least once every day. The rigor in such actions will pay off. Exerting self-discipline results in continued excellence.

Future Truth Versus Positive Affirmations

We just saw that you have up to sixty thousand thoughts a day. What runs through your mind matters—a lot.

Given the huge success of the book and film *The Secret*, positive affirmations have become all the rage. People have begun to believe that words are so powerful, we can "speak things into existence." To me, the Law of Attraction is both real and misunderstood. That's why I want you to understand the difference between living your future truth and using positive affirmations.

I'm not against motivational quotes or positive messages, I just find them useless without emotion and conviction behind them. You have to find the right affirmation along with a story of validation that makes it real to you. Instead of "I am great. I am powerful. I am abundant," you want to say, "I am powerful because the time my family needed me to come through for them, I stepped up and handled the situation."

Think about a director trying to coax an emotional performance out of an actor. To do so, he must get him to tap into his feelings. To do the same for yourself, here's what you do:

Do a mental inventory and write down:

1. Your five most painful moments
2. Your five most successful moments
3. Five moments when you felt untouchable

State the affirmations and include the validation:

1. Start with "I will be a great leader" or "I'm going to make the greatest comeback ever."
2. Add the story, drawing on your pain and triumphs. Use the word "because" to provide the evidence: "*Because* I came through"; "*Because* I've been there before"; "*Because* I've overcome more."

People ask me: What gave you confidence to be who you are today? Four things:

1. Fate: I believe I'm destined to do something big.
2. Faith: I believe that a higher power has my back.
3. I became clear about what I wanted. I cast my vision. I told the world who I wanted to be, and the right people showed up.
4. I believe I'm the luckiest man alive.

It's about, in this very moment, embodying your future truth. When you imagine your future truth, you already have what you want and now it's about becoming the person needed for that to become a reality.

There's a great example in the 1996 film *Swingers*, when Vince Vaughn's character, Trent, is coaching Jon Favreau's character, Mikey, on how to meet women. Mikey is scared and timid. He seems light-years away from turning into a confident guy. But he wants to impress a woman *now*—not after years of training. Trent understands this. Instead of telling his buddy to "act as if," he uses emotion to urge Mikey to embody his future truth. Like a coach speaking to a player or a director speaking to an actor, he says:

> When you go up to talk to her, man, I don't want you to be the guy in the PG-13 movie everyone's *really* hoping makes it happen. I want you to be like the guy in the rated-R movie, you know? The guy you're not sure whether or not you like yet. You're not sure where he's coming from, okay? You're a bad man. You're a bad man. You're a bad man.

This is not deep psychology; it's a commonsense power move. If you don't think you are worthy, others won't, either. If you don't believe in your product (or yourself), no one else will, either. If you look like a slob, you're going to act like a slob, and people will perceive you as a slob. As we see in this movie scene, we often need a coach to push us to embody our future truth.

If you're going to "speak your story into existence," you'd better have the right story and the emotions to back it up. And if you're going to broadcast it to the world, you'd better back up the talk by living it. That's how you control your life's narrative.

Incremental Growth:
How Much Can You Bench-Press?

I hope your mind is racing a mile a minute. I want you to be so fired up that you grind your foot into Goliath's throat until he begs for mercy. I hope you have already made a bold prediction on social media and have taken steps to control your narrative. I also understand that all this may seem daunting. Here's where we take a step back and remember that it takes time. Rather than feeling overwhelmed, start breaking down your goals into small steps.

When I was fourteen years old, I was more than six feet tall and weighed only 135 pounds. I mentioned before that our family couldn't afford the monthly membership fee of $13.50 at the YMCA. Probably because I was so skinny, some of the guys took pity on me and opened the back door for me to sneak in. All the people there called me "the Somalian"—not a nice or politically correct term but one that tells you that I looked as though a stiff breeze would knock me over. I was embarrassed by how skinny I was, so I wore sweaters to hide my slight physique.

A guy named Fred who worked out at the Y took an interest in me. When we were in the weight room, he noticed that I was looking at other lifters who had huge muscles. He could tell that I was discouraged by what I saw; they seemed as though they belonged to a different species. Fred watched me struggle to bench-press forty-five pounds. That's right, with just the bar alone, I could manage only one repetition.

"That's okay," Fred said. He pointed to a 2½-pound plate and said, "That's your best friend."

"What do you mean?"

"Moving forward, I want you to improve your press by five pounds [one 2½-pound plate on each side] every week and see what happens."

"That's embarrassing," I said, referring to the small weight increment.

"Don't worry about it, just do it and see what happens."

Reluctantly, I followed Fred's advice. Gradually, I could lift a bit more each week. Gradually, I got bigger and stronger. I persisted. I followed Fred's advice with religious devotion. After eighteen weeks, just as Fred had predicted, I could bench-press 135 pounds. After a few years, I was bench-pressing 385 pounds. I looked like the guys I'd used to envy.

Translate this 2½-pound principle to your business and career. Stop comparing yourself to people and companies that seem light-years ahead of you. Instead, focus on regular, achievable improvement.

I guarantee you that other people and companies will be vulnerable if you follow this regimen. Even Goliaths get lazy. Goliaths can be beaten because they rest on their laurels at some point. Remember how we talked about so many of the Fortune 500 companies from 1955 that were no longer on the list in 2019?

Committing to incremental success will help you outimprove anyone. If you can outimprove others, you will catch up to them and pass them. They may be bigger than you, but eventually they will slow down and start celebrating their victories. While that is happening, those who quietly keep improving themselves and their company will suddenly show up and surprise them. The commitment to constantly beating your prior best is by far the simplest and best-proven formula to eventually find yourself at the top of your game in your industry.

■ ■ ■ ■ ■

We covered a lot of material in this chapter. By now I know you can handle it. We looked at what's required to beat Goliath and what makes Goliath vulnerable, as well as specific steps you can take to beat the giant in your industry.

You have let go of your fear of being judged and seen the importance of self-promotion. Because you understand that social media is the great equalizer, you are on your way to creating a strategy that best suits your skills. In doing so, you will be controlling the narrative.

If you want to achieve greatness, you have zero margin for error. You can't allow negative thoughts, negative people, or negative activities to distract you. It's time to be honest about what's holding you back and cut that fat from your life.

14

Study Mobsters: How to Sell, Negotiate, and Influence

> I'm gonna make him an offer he can't refuse.
> —Marlon Brando as Don Vito Corleone in *The Godfather*

Y ou've read the title of this chapter, and you're thinking that I've taken leave of my senses, right? But hear me out. In a way, mobsters are the ultimate entrepreneurs. They're willing to take big risks for big rewards. And the most successful among them are brilliant at negotiating. They have to think on their feet, and they have to make the right decisions quickly at the same time that lots of information is coming at them.

Let me be clear: I'm not suggesting that you run your business in unethical or criminal ways. I shouldn't have to state the obvious, but I will anyway: I'm against murder, extortion, and drug dealing. I'm against breaking the law, but I'm all for breaking rules. There's a big difference between the two. To disrupt a market or to tap into a market that's extremely competitive, a founder has to be comfortable breaking the rules. This chapter is not an endorsement of bad guys; it's about learning from what they do well.

In September 2012, I asked everyone in my company to read *The*

48 Laws of Power by Robert Greene. The goal was not to become manipulative or learn how to play games. The goal was to understand those laws *so they couldn't be used against us*. At every stage of our growth, others have used every dirty trick in the book to try to take us down. We needed to better understand how such people think in order to combat their tactics.

There's a reason why so many CEOs and leaders consider *The Godfather* (parts I and II) more education than entertainment. Every struggle a CEO or a founder will experience occurs in those movies. Betrayal, loss, recruiting, negotiation, working with family, stealing money, having to get rid of someone with loose lips, and having success get to their head are things mobsters deal with—and you will as well.

It's why I've interviewed so many mobsters for my YouTube channel—guys such as "Sammy the Bull" Gravano, Frank Cullotta, Ralph Natale, and Donnie Brasco himself, Joe Pistone. You may think you're in a competitive field, but consider the fact that mobsters have competitors who literally kill to win. You screw up, you lose your business; they screw up, they lose their lives. Most mobsters aren't operating under any illusions; they know exactly what they're getting into.

Networking, negotiating, and selling are power moves that will have a massive impact on your bottom line. Mobsters are masters at recruiting because they know how to sell the dream of the benefits of joining their team. The ability to attract, influence, and convince people from all walks of life is the special talent every entrepreneur needs.

I have found that former mob members are some of the best teachers. Because the stakes are so high, often life and death, they are experts at communication, preparation, and reading other people. They are also master psychologists and negotiators. These are skills that can be learned by anyone. Studying mobsters is a great place to start. Let's see how.

A Made Man Knows How to Prepare

Michael Franzese was reputedly one of the highest-money-making caporegime (captain, not boss) in the history of organized crime. Michael walked away from "the life" and left his criminal past behind. Still, he's been compared to the fictional Michael Corleone character in the *Godfather* movies for good reason: both Michaels share the ability to process information with lightning-quick speed and thrive in stressful situations.

Years ago, when Michael was still working for the Mob, he was summoned for a meeting with his boss in Brooklyn. He recalled that the short walk from the car to the apartment was the longest walk he had ever taken. His boss confronted him with the rumor that Michael had stolen $2 billion from the government. It wasn't that the mobsters cared about the rumor that he had taken money from the government; they just cared that if it were true, they would get their cut. It was a life-or-death situation; Michael knew that when he walked into the room, he might not walk out if the boss thought he was withholding a tribute.

Because the stakes of a meeting like this were life and death, Michael was obsessive about preparation. He's not big on lists, but I am. Here are seven things you must do before any meeting.

Seven Essential Steps to Prepare for a Meeting

1. Consider the other party's needs, desires, and frustrations. Remember that what motivates most people is fear, greed, and saving face.
2. Anticipate what the other party will say.
3. Develop a script/outline for what you want to say.
4. Role-play the meeting several times in order to be prepared for different reactions.
5. Ask trusted advisers to point out your blind spots.

6. Put yourself into the best possible frame of mind before the meeting.
7. Build a reputation for overdelivering on your product.

Because he had prepared well, Michael didn't cower or quake. He didn't explode. Instead, he addressed the accusation head-on: "When they [the media] write about someone else [other mobsters], it's a lie. When they write about me, all of a sudden, it's the truth? I'm giving you guys all this money [$2 million weekly]; you don't have to do anything, I'm taking care of everything. . . . If anybody goes down, it's me and my crew. What's going on here?"

Michael showed some emotion. It was all part of his plan. During his preparation, he had decided that the best plan of action would be to set his adversary back on his heels. Even a seasoned mobster like Michael has emotions, and there's no doubt that he was upset. He was processing the situation, and he told himself that he would have to watch what he said and did. He remained respectful of his boss.

Once Michael threw his opening punch, he sat back and listened. He learned that the whole situation was a result of his father, John "Sonny" Franzese, throwing him under the bus. Michael's father thought it was possible that Michael was making more money than he was disclosing, and this meeting was designed to determine the truth.

Imagine you're in a life-and-death meeting and you've just learned that a family member, close friend, or a business partner has sold you out. You would probably be seething. Submerged in all that emotion would be your ability to think and process. How can you think about solutions and survival when all you can think about is revenge?

Even though he was hurt by his father's actions, Michael processed the situation like a master. He remained calm in front of the boss and told him he would take care of the issue. He even thanked his boss for bringing the issue to his attention. He could not have done so had he not rehearsed every minute of the meeting beforehand.

Once the meeting was complete, Michael had to process the impact of his father selling him out. He knew not to talk to his father until he had worked through these issues on his own. After much thought, Michael came to terms with his father's actions. He knew that the life could separate a father and son. He refused to let that happen. He never mentioned the incident to his father. He told himself, "In that life, you learn to keep things quiet until the right time. But it really put me on notice that I've got to be careful. I was very disappointed in him, but it didn't change my love for him."

Great processors take responsibility for their actions and redirect their frustration to learning and creating new patterns. When Michael reflected on what his dad had done, he said, "I almost thank him for it now. I met my wife two years after this incident, and that's when I made the decision to walk away. . . . I think that was God's way of separating me from this bond or hold that my dad had on me."

Problem solving isn't easy. In the heat of the moment, Michael had to defend himself credibly but at the same time not appear defensive. A lot of thoughts must have been swirling in his brain, but he processed them under pressure and came up with the right solution. The real brilliance was in what was not seen: his obsessive preparation.

The Art of the Sit-Down: Preparing for a High-Stakes Meeting

The five big Mafia families relied on a business resolution method called the sit-down. In ways, it was similar to what goes on in business, where the top people get together in the boardroom to discuss important matters. In Michael's world, though, the meeting place was often the back room of an Italian restaurant.

I had a sit-down recently in the Cayman Islands with the senior executives of one of the world's largest insurance companies. The CEO was in the room, as were two other senior vice presidents. My purpose in being there was to request an increase in my company's compensation.

The stakes were high. The worst possible scenario was that they would be so offended by my demand that they would drop my account. That would have been catastrophic for my business. Another bad scenario would be if they refused to give me an increase. If that happened, I risked losing many of my agents because I simply wouldn't have enough revenue to pay them as much as my competitors did.

It was a tough request to a tough audience at a tough time in my business. These are the types of meetings that can wreck you emotionally—if you lack the tools to process and prepare for them. Therefore, I followed the first rule of sit-downs: Do not attend a meeting unprepared. As is always the case, I used the "Seven Essential Steps to Prepare for a Meeting" to guide my preparation. Like any grand master, I was planning many moves ahead.

1. Consider the other party's needs, desires, and frustrations. Remember that what motivates most people is fear, greed, and saving face.

Before the meeting, I had assessed what the executives' frustrations were and who wrote the most business for their company, as well as our company's standing with them. I did my homework and found out that, in two years, we had skyrocketed from a small player to the firm that wrote the second highest number of policies of all the companies with which they dealt.

In *The 7 Habits of Highly Effective People*, Stephen Covey said, "Seek first to understand, then to be understood." What that meant for me was getting out of my own head and walking in their shoes to see the situation from their perspective.

- I played on **fear**: Losing my account would have meant their company's losing millions of dollars in revenue.
- I played on **greed**: Keeping my account would potentially bring in even more millions of dollars of revenue and seven-figure bonuses for the executives.

- I played on **helping them save face**: They would look really foolish if I left for a competitor.

2. Anticipate what the other party will say.

Think about how a shrewd attorney crafts an argument: he first has to consider what the other party will say. The more you can anticipate what the other party will say and why, the better you can craft your story or request.

3. Develop a script/outline for what you want to say.

I started out with pages of notes. As I continued to practice, I was able to become more precise about my message. How you prepare depends on your style. Some speakers like to write out their entire speech, and some simply need bullet points. I prefer bullet points.

4. Role-play the meeting several times in order to be prepared for different reactions.

The next step was to assemble a team and ask them to play the roles of the executives I was going to be meeting in the Cayman Islands. Stepping into the shoes of those executives, they asked questions and challenged me. As a result, I modified my script and was prepared for different reactions.

5. Ask trusted advisers to point out your blind spots.

Much of this was handled during role-plays. To take it to another level, I asked the opinion of trusted peers outside my industry to make sure I didn't have any blind spots.

6. Put yourself into the best possible frame of mind before the meeting.

Every detail before I arrived at the meeting mattered. I flew in a day early, so I would be rested and didn't have any fear of a delayed flight making me late. The way I dressed, what I ate, and my exercise routine were all part of putting me into the right frame of mind. Visualizing the success of the meeting—and my business—was also a critical step.

7. Build a reputation for overdelivering on your promises.

None of the above matters if you don't do what you're going to do. The worst thing you want in business is to have a reputation as someone who does a lot of talking but rarely delivers.

Since I was so committed to understanding the situation from *their* viewpoint, I became keenly aware of my company's flaws and the areas in which it needed to improve. To address these flaws and demonstrate how we were going to correct them, I arrived at the meeting with a stack of data to bolster my argument. I had a ten-point plan prepared and ready to go. Six of those points were about the other company, and four were about mine. As I suggested earlier, when you have a sit-down, you want to spend the majority of time focusing on the other party's concerns, not yours.

I went into the room and said, "Listen, here's what you want, based on what you told me the last time we met. This is what makes you unhappy, and this is what we're going to fix. If we do what I'm proposing, you won't have to hire additional people. I've already made a call [to a supplier of systems], and I know you're interested in buying the system, and they'll charge you a fee of $1 million. I give this company a lot of business, and I convinced them to waive the fee."

I was able to deliver the message with confidence and clarity because I had rehearsed it over and over.

"Wait a second," you may be thinking. "I thought you went in there to increase *your* compensation. Why in the world do you start by telling them you're effectively giving them a million dollars?"

A simple rule of business is that in order to get, you have to give. Most amateurs are experts at making demands. What they fail to do is offer value first. When you put yourself into the other party's shoes and lead with how they will win and make money, it will be natural for them to give you what you want.

I then pitched them on providing us with a compensation increase based on the data I had gathered—data that showed why the increase was warranted.

"If you say no to it, no problem. I have another company that I think will give us what we want. Do you have any questions?"

They had many. We went back and forth for two and a half hours. In fact, I had already heard their questions, objections, and challenges. How is this possible? Because I had role-played. Like a grand master CEO who is always several steps ahead, I was able to lead them to where I wanted them to be because I had anticipated their moves.

In *The Godfather*, Don Vito Corleone, played by Marlon Brando, uttered the classic line "I'm gonna make him an offer he can't refuse." In this case, the offer was a win-win agreement that increased the value of both of our businesses. With the data I presented, of course they couldn't refuse. The key to my success? It was the work I had done *before* the sit-down began.

Effective Sales Are About Conviction and a Transference of Feeling

Even though this chapter is about the Mafia, it wouldn't be complete without some wisdom from the legendary Zig Ziglar. Before he died in 2012 at age eighty-six, he may have been the most influential sales trainer in the world. He told a powerful story about one of his cookware sales reps who was in a slump.

When Zig asked him why he wasn't selling, the salesman rattled off a list of reasons: times were tough, and cookware was expensive. Zig then asked him if he owned a set of the cookware that he sold to others. The salesman said no. When Zig asked why, the salesman told him that he couldn't afford it, especially since he was in a slump.

Zig asked questions. He listened. He empathized. In his heart of hearts, Zig believed that the cookware was a worthwhile investment. After all, he owned it himself. He understood that it was expensive, but he had internalized all its benefits. As with any investment, there was an up-front cost. And as with any smart investment, Zig truly believed that it more than paid for itself.

Zig listened to his salesman's objections. And although there were valid reasons for the salesman not to buy the cookware he was trying to sell, Zig truly believed that this man's life would be much better with it. After hearing him out and overcoming every single objection, the salesman eventually bought the cookware. It turned out to be the ultimate power move.

During his next presentation to a potential customer, the salesman heard all the usual excuses. As Zig had done with him a few days earlier, the salesman asked questions, listened, and empathized. The difference, because he had bought the cookware himself, was that he believed so strongly in its value that he would not let those people make a bad decision. He truly felt that they would be better off with the cookware than with the money it cost.

He hadn't learned any fancy sales tricks or manipulative tactics. He had simply changed the way he *felt*. Sure enough, he made the sale that night and went on to become one of the company's top performers. Once he believed in the product enough to buy it himself, his slump was over.

I'll leave it to Zig to tell you the moral of the story: "Have an absolute and total belief that what you're selling is worth more than the price you ask for it. Your belief in your product should be so great that you ought to be using it."

Remember that the "gift of gab" is overrated. What's underrated is conviction. Since emotion and belief are what truly sell, I hire people who believe in both themselves and the company. With that integrity, that passion to be of service, they can get up in front of any audience, large or small, and talk to them with conviction about what we do.

Sales should feel effortless, like a natural extension of who you are. It should excite you to talk about what you do. Estée Lauder, who cofounded the cosmetics company that made her the only woman on *Time* magazine's list of the twenty most influential business titans of the twentieth century, once said, "I have never worked a day in my life without selling. If I believe in something, I sell it, and I sell it hard."

Despite what some people would have you believe, no one is born a salesperson. Stop trying to find "naturals." Rather than looking for salespeople, look for people who believe in your vision and want to build relationships. They may not be social butterflies. In fact, some of the most outgoing, magnetic, and influential people I know are honest-to-goodness introverts.

Having influence isn't about "selling anything to anyone," or convincing people to act against their own best interest. Selling is about believing in yourself, believing in your business, and believing in the value you can offer to the other person, whether a potential customer, a key vendor, or a major industry figure. If you believe in what you're selling, if you're operating from your heart and gut and not your head, if you believe in a win-win outcome for every negotiation, if you believe deep down that you can be of service to that other person, then networking, negotiation, and sales will all become second nature to you.

Negotiation Is About Leverage

Whoever has more leverage in a negotiation should come out on top. However, it's not always obvious who has the leverage. For one, as much as you prepare, you can never know exactly everything that's going on with the other party. Ultimately, the important thing is to understand leverage and know how to gain power from that leverage.

If you use too much leverage and overplay your hand to maximize your profit from a particular deal, you may win the battle but lose the war. The late Amarillo Slim, a gambling legend and 1972 World Series of Poker champion, said, "You can shear a sheep a hundred times, but you can skin it only once." Even a hustler like Slim recognized that the key to a long career is treating people in such a way that they want to keep doing business with you. In any game, the goal is not to make a score; it's to build a partnership in which both parties make scores *in perpetuity*.

Early in my career, I rarely had leverage. What made me an effective negotiator was not pretending otherwise—in other words, I didn't feel a need to bluff. Instead, I would structure deals so that the other party could minimize its risk, thereby making the deal much more enticing to them. In the short term, it often meant I was getting the worst of the deal. Because I was thinking several moves ahead, however, I asked for deal points that would improve the deal if we hit certain markers, while still enriching the other party. Because I was viewed as being fair, I was able to build long-term partnerships.

In the early days of my agency, a guy named David came to me with a proposition for licensing his software. He asked me to negotiate with other insurance companies on his behalf. He knew that the more people who used this product, the more it would ultimately make my business more efficient. Because his software was best in class and something he knew I needed, he pushed the envelope. In addition to asking for my help with other companies, he wanted me to pay $50,000 to license the software. Since the "retail" price was slightly more, he pitched it to me as though he were doing me a favor.

I thought David had a lot of nerve trying to sell me the product *and* leverage my contacts in the business. But just as a grand master doesn't tip off his future moves, I stayed quiet. The reality is that I did need the software, and given our cash position, I was happy to get a discount. Plus, even though David was seemingly asking me for a favor, it would also benefit my business if other companies used the same software we did. David pitched it as a win-win, and there was plenty of validity to that claim. Truth be told, if all our partners adopted the software at that time, we knew we could significantly reduce processing time on contacts (you know how I feel about speed!) and significantly reduce our labor costs.

This is where understanding leverage comes in. For one, I didn't share all my thoughts with David. It would only have hurt my leverage if he'd known what I was thinking. And to David's credit, he had pitched this so smartly that my own president (at the time) told me it was a good opportunity. He may have been partially right, but I was still flabbergasted. Sometimes in an organization, a top executive may not value the cash in the bank as much as the founder does. Fifty grand might not have seemed like much to him, but he wasn't the one writing the check.

I asked my colleague to set up a call with David. The call lasted only four minutes. I simply stated how I viewed David's proposal. "Let me get this straight," I said. "You want me to use my credibility to negotiate on your behalf with carriers, yet you still want to charge me fifty grand for your software?" I stayed quiet for a few beats to let that sink in. Then I said, "That won't happen unless you waive the entire fee. You can let my guy know if you're comfortable with that, and if you're not, I understand. Do you have any questions?"

After a five-second pause, he said, "No."

You might think that I was reckless for taking such a hard line. But because I had followed my own rules of preparation, I had walked in his shoes to see the deal from his perspective. In doing so, I saw how much he had to gain if I used all my contacts to negotiate on his behalf. I figured that he would be smart enough (know your opponents!) to think like a grand master and realize that waiving the fifty grand for me would mean nothing in the long run, since I would be able to help him gain so many new clients. I used that as leverage and made my request.

How did that power play turn out?

I've shared enough of my failures with you by now that I can sit here with a smile on my face and share that success.

Not only did David accept my terms and waive the fee, but he also told the story to his friend Greg, who runs a private equity firm. David told him I had what it took to compete in the marketplace. As a result, Greg invested $10 million in our next round of funding.

How was all that possible?

When you're confident about your delivery and you are committed to coming through, you can push the envelope. If you don't execute, you're just another arrogant loudmouth. The delivery on your promises is what gets you respect in the marketplace.

How to Win:
Let the Other Guy Think He Won

In business, you're going to meet and work with an extraordinary range of people. Some will be brilliant, some will be arrogant, some will be idiosyncratic, and some will be crazy. The ability to work effectively with a range of individuals—customers, employees, business partners, investors—is crucial to success. A lot of that ability involves sizing up people quickly and learning how to forge solid working relationships.

There's a fine line between being crazy and brilliant, mad and madly successful. In addition to John Gartner's *The Hypomanic Edge*, I recommend *A First-Rate Madness: Uncovering the Links Between Leadership and Mental Illness* by Nassir Ghaemi. These books will help you see the way many of the top 1 percent of the 1 percent think differently. Most are wired differently, and you need to understand that wiring to deal with them effectively.

You'll need to learn how to negotiate with these types of people. At first you'll feel as though you're in a room filled with narcissistic jerks who have no feelings. You'll still need to figure out a way to deal with them because they're not going to go away. And the odds are that if you're reading this and you're absolutely determined to get to the highest level, you're probably a little "off" as well.

I'm definitely more than a little "off." And because I want to be prepared to reach the level of the 1 percent of the 1 percent, I study anyone and anything that can help me.

If you can step outside your ego, you'll realize that you often win by letting others also win. It also pays, at times, to let others think that your great ideas are actually theirs. Let's shift from the Mob world to another pressure-packed world, the hedge fund business, to see how it works.

When young Darius was working at a hedge fund, his boss might as well have been John Gotti. He (we'll call him Dale) had a big reputation and an even bigger ego. Darius would spend months researching ideas and looking for arbitrage opportunities in the market. When he finally had an idea with impeccable data to back it up, he would walk into Dale's office and explain the investment from every angle. Both his research and his presentation would be Oscar worthy. He was smart, well prepared, and convincing.

Invariably, his boss would say no.

It drove Darius up a wall. He dissected his pitch from every angle and couldn't, for the life of him, see where he had gone wrong. He was so frustrated that he almost quit. The truth is that Darius had a blind spot, and only because he was determined to see it did he start searching for it. In a team investment meeting, he noticed that one of his colleagues said very little and always deflected praise to Dale. Since Darius knew that the colleague had come up with many of the ideas, he was amazed that they were presented as Dale's.

That was his "Aha! moment."

The next time Darius had an idea, he used a different approach. Instead of walking into Dale's office with recommendations, he walked in with questions. Instead of appearing confident, he appeared confused. "Dale, I noticed that the yield curve is starting to flatten."

"What's your point?" Dale asked.

"I also noticed that ten-year Treasuries are priced higher than their historical average."

"That makes no sense," Dale said.

"I can't figure it out, either," the sheepish Darius replied. "It just seems like something is off."

"You bet your ass something is off. We need to short ten-year Treasuries."

"I guess you're right. Not sure how I missed that."

"I am. I keep telling you young bucks that it takes thirty years to become an overnight success. Now get out of here and short those ten years."

Given what you now know about power plays, this (true) story ought to make sense. Because Darius finally figured out how to think like a grand master, he was able to make a series of moves—and ask a series of questions—that led Dale to where Darius wanted him to go.

■ ■ ■ ■ ■

The Mafia is a fascinating organization. Though I don't advocate much of what it does, I have learned important lessons from how it operates. Though we may like to joke and say, "Make him an offer he can't refuse," I expect you to take this to a different level. By preparing like a mobster, you will understand the stakes of any meeting and do everything you can to succeed before the meeting even starts. An offer that enriches both you and the other party—now, that's an offer no one can refuse.

15

Cultivate Your Power, and Stay Battle Tested

If a man is proud of his wealth, he should not be praised until it is known how he employs it.

—Socrates

Everybody likes you until you're a competitor, especially if you're a formidable one. When I started my business, all the cheerleaders lined up to wish me well. People just love a warm and fuzzy underdog story. Once my company really started growing, enemies appeared from everywhere. People started blocking me on social media. Rumors were spread; they called me Darth Bet-David. People in my industry, as you now know, did everything they could to shut me down.

Staying a successful entrepreneur, year after year, is the ultimate challenge.

In our final chapter, I want you to learn even more about leverage. I want you to see how having options will change your mindset and ultimately take you to a place of power. I want to show you that asking how you can help others before asking for something in return will shift every interaction you have.

We're going to expand on many topics we've already covered. Since you need people to scale your company—and you need fulfilling relationships to enjoy your life—we're going to drill down and explain how you can guide people to becoming their best. Don't mistake "drive" as meaning you're the one who is at the wheel. Rather, you need to understand what drives people, recognize that it's different for everyone, and use your leadership to assist them in steering.

Real Power Is Having Options

Leverage is such an important element of power that we need to dig deeper to understand it better. The person who really has the leverage is *the person who needs the deal the least.* Options give you power. If you can walk away from a deal, you're in the best position to negotiate the best terms. If you must make a deal happen, you're going to be at the mercy of someone else's power, and you're probably going to make a lousy deal.

That's an obvious concept. The question is how to put it into practice. The short answer is: whenever possible, cultivate multiple options. Instead of looking for that one dream home (the same idea applies to a car, an office building, and a key hire), survey the market and find three options you would enjoy. Then when you go to make a deal with your top choice, you'll have the advantage, because you'll have other options that would also make you happy. If you sense that you are the seller's only option, now you really have leverage.

I know entrepreneurs who go after one big client, hoping it will solve all their problems. They think that getting their product into Costco, Target, or Walmart will mean they can stop prospecting. Maybe a deal like that will become your magic bullet—for a month or maybe even a year or two. Eventually, though, that big customer will use its leverage to take away your power.

How much mental anguish do you go through worrying about losing a key customer or a valued employee? Now look for your deepest why. The real reason is that you don't know if you would survive if you lost the customer or employee. As a result, you've already given away your power.

I'm an adviser for Bobby's company, which is doing $8 million in annual revenue. On paper, his business looks great. There's only one problem: $5 million of his revenue comes from one customer. For a while, the customer was satisfied and life was grand. Over time, though, the customer kept pushing for more concessions. And why didn't Bobby push back? Because he had no other options. For all the talk of posturing and bluffing—which can have its place—people know who has the power in a relationship. The customer kept asking for better and better terms, which came with an implied threat: if you don't give us what we want, we'll take our business elsewhere.

We're all supposed to be grand masters in business by now. We should be able to come up with the perfect move to get Bobby out of this jam. That, in fact, was what he asked me to do. The problem, however, was that the moves he had failed to make years before had put him into that bind. When he had stopped prospecting, when he had stopped growing his business, when he had gotten complacent after landing this big customer, that was when his problems had begun.

I had an easy solution for Bobby. I told him to go get more options. His leverage was already gone. There was no move he could make, no posturing he could do, to keep the big customer and make even a cent of profit.

He, of course, didn't want to hear it.

Bobby lost the customer and went from an $8 million to a $3 million business overnight. As if that weren't bad enough, he was forced to sell the company because it was unsustainable without his main customer. You know who bought him? That's right, his old customer, and it cut Bobby out of the business right after making the acquisition. Because Bobby was playing like an amateur, never thinking past one or two moves ahead, he got checkmated right out of business.

The moral of the story? The key to power is having options. If Bobby had spread his revenue over a larger group of customers, he wouldn't have been so vulnerable. If he had grown to the point where the demand for his product exceeded his capacity to produce it, he could have been the one dictating the terms. The power would have shifted, giving Bobby the ability to raise prices or insist on quicker payment terms.

Maybe in your relationships you'll get lucky and find the perfect person and live happily ever after, but in business, the perfect customer doesn't exist, no matter how beautiful or rich she may be. If 30 percent or more of your revenue comes from one place, you're in trouble. It doesn't matter how much money you're making. When your revenue stream is concentrated in one customer, that customer is in control.

Generate options for yourself. This is true regarding customers as well as talent. When you have plenty of both, you won't have to worry constantly that people are going to leave you. You can make yourself more attractive to anyone if you keep yourself in good shape. In business, that means outworking, outimproving, outlasting, and outstrategizing your competitors.

Playing the Long-Term Game of Power: Humility and Service

In 2019, I gave a speech for a group of aspiring entrepreneurs at an event called DRIVEN in Long Beach, California. After I spoke, a guy came up to me while there were forty people around us, five cameras on us, and he started talking. "I've got to tell you, Pat, your content has changed my life. I mean, I'm not the same human being."

I live for such moments. Hearing how my content has helped people is a tremendous source of pride for me. Just as I was enjoying the adulation, he handed me a business card and said, "My name is Ritchie. If you ever want to buy real estate in Vegas, give me a call."

I stopped him right there. "Let me ask you a question," I said. "Do you know what you just did?"

"What did I do?" he asked.

Let's pause for a second so you can think about what he did. In my view, what he did was the equivalent of walking up to a woman at a bar and saying, "Oh, my gosh, you look so good. Oh, my gosh, your hair. I can see you put time into it. Your eyebrows. Perfect. Wow. You're absolutely gorgeous. Listen, if you ever want to go to bed with me, here's my card. Give me a call."

Does that sound like a power move to you?

I liked Ritchie. I appreciated the hustle. I just wanted him to see how his method was going to kill any chance of his building a long-term relationship with me. Sure, a shotgun approach to business or dating will enable you to make a sale every now and then if you play strictly a numbers game. Even amateurs who only think one step ahead close the occasional deal.

I asked him, "What do you want to do here with this relationship? Look at the lens you've got on. Your only lens is to see what you want to get out of this."

We chatted a bit more, and I sensed enough curiosity and humility in Ritchie to tell him a story.

In my early twenties, when I had just started selling insurance, I met a well-connected guy named Eli. He was also Middle Eastern, and we had some mutual friends. It wasn't a business connection; he was more like a friend of the family. We became buddies, and he invited me to his fiftieth birthday party. The party was at his house in an expensive suburb of LA. I arrived in my Ford Focus, and I saw a bunch of nice cars parked near the house. I realized that the party could be an incredible networking opportunity. Even so, I kept a low profile. I didn't talk business or hand out one business card. I even stayed and helped wash the dishes.

Eli and I built a friendship. As we got to know each other better, I asked him, "How can I help you? What can I do to make your life better?"

Eli got emotional and told me that his son had been in prison for nine years. No one was visiting him because it was four hours away, near San Luis Óbispo, and it was a rough prison. "If you're willing to go," Eli said, "it would mean the world to me. I understand if you don't want to, but that'd be a big favor that you could do for me."

I said yes. Before going, I had to do a background check, fingerprints, the whole nine yards. It took thirty days to get clearance. Once I did, I drove there and spent an entire day with Eli's son. He was sitting in the corner and saying things like "That guy just shanked that person. He was in the hole for this. That guy's the king around here." He was pointing out everyone and telling stories as though we were old friends.

We became pen pals, writing letters back and forth. Not email, letters! I made that four-hour drive several more times. After my first visit, Eli called me and said, "You have no idea how important it was what you did for me."

I said, "Brother, anytime."

We met for lunch at his house, and he asked, "How can I help you?"

That's when I told Eli I was a financial adviser and looking for clients.

He gave me a list of six hundred names and told me I could use his name when I called them.

At that point in my career, I had experienced the difference between cold calls (mostly hang-ups) and introductions (which often led to meetings).

One of those people led me to meet somebody who introduced me to somebody who introduced me to somebody who introduced me to somebody who introduced me to somebody who ultimately made me $30 million.

When I finished telling the story, Ritchie had a different look on his face. I said to him, "See, if I would've gone to him on day one and said, 'Can you get me some leads for clients?,' can you imagine what would've happened? He would've said no."

Power plays are all about the long game. Why do you think we've been talking so much about chess masters? If you want referrals, if you want to build long-term relationships, the next time you meet anyone (much less a key influencer), don't go up to him or her and say, "Do you want to go to bed with me? Can you give me what I want?"

The power move is to flip it and instead ask, "What can I do for you? How can I help you?" It's a life-changing move that requires a complete shift in mindset. Not only will you build better relationships, but also, if you are truly committed to the long game, it will make you a boatload of money.

The Formula for Gaining Power

Outwork. It's critical to put in the time. But hard work alone won't be enough.

Outimprove. This constantly gives you new ways to take your business to the next level. It gives you confidence. If there was an area I was always obsessed with competing in, it was improving faster than my peers.

Outstrategize. This means thinking five moves ahead. It means figuring out how to scale and having the patience to plan many moves ahead before they bear fruit.

Outlast. You really learn about people both when you achieve great success and when you suffer tragic failure. It's hard to know who will keep going. To outlast, you need endurance, which comes from making choices that keep you alert and focused on the game.

Shadow Who You Want to Be

Now we're bringing things full circle. The first move was for you to figure out who you want to be. The power play for becoming who you want to be is finding someone who is already experiencing that success.

Warren Buffett enjoyed the good fortune of having Benjamin Graham as his professor at Columbia University. The late Graham was the author of *The Intelligent Investor: The Definitive Book on Value Investing* and is regarded as the father of value investing. Having a front-row seat to one of the greatest minds in investing played a massive role in Buffett's success. Buffett so badly wanted to shadow Graham after business school that he was willing to work for him for free. Graham didn't offer him a job, and Buffett went back to his hometown of Omaha, Nebraska. Graham later hired him, and Buffett said, "I took a job with Ben Graham, my hero. I never asked the salary. I found out at the end of the month when I got my first paycheck what I was earning."

Physical proximity is what differentiates shadowing from finding a mentor, which we discussed in chapter 12. If you can find a person who will let you observe him up close, take advantage of the opportunity. There's a big difference between having a mentor and shadowing someone. A mentor may *tell* you what to do, but a performer you shadow *shows* you what to do. You get to observe firsthand what he does during conflict and intense negotiations. You can also learn how he handles enemies and how he motivates his team.

I can't emphasize enough the power of surrounding yourself with other people who are living your dream life. The key point to remember is that you want to shadow successful people no matter where you are in your career. At every stage of my growth, I've attached myself to the people I admire. As a kid, I tried to go everywhere with my dad. In the army, I stayed close to the best leaders. I also worked out with the strongest guys. As a salesman at Bally, I shadowed Francisco Davis because he was the top salesman. I didn't care how late it was or what type of menial tasks I had to perform. It was worth staying late to have a ten-minute conversation with Francisco or even just be in the room when he made his follow-up calls. All I was looking for was how to feed my mind and see things I could do better.

Successful people are busy, so you have to *offer them value*. It can't hurt to offer to buy them coffee or lunch, but it's even better to do something that improves their business. Volunteer to edit their proposals or do research. Offer to stay late and write their thank-you notes while you listen to them make sales calls. You might be surprised what you may have to offer. Especially if you are under thirty, you probably know more about social media than just about everyone over forty does. Offer to help them set up their social media pages for their business. Ideally, the relationship will become a win-win. You get to learn from being in the other person's presence, and he or she benefits from your skills and willingness to work.

■ ■ ■ ■ ■

One last example is NBA coach Steve Kerr. Yes, him again, the same guy who made Andre Iguodala feel *needed* on Golden State's way to an NBA championship. In his first five seasons as a head coach, Kerr led the Warriors to the NBA finals every single year and won three championships. After five grueling seasons, including the last one in which he witnessed Klay Thompson, Kevin Durant, and DeMarcus Cousins sustain awful injuries (and the latter two leave the team via free agency), you might think that he would have spent the summer of 2019 getting some well-deserved rest.

In the summer of 2019, Team USA was preparing for the FIBA World Cup. I'm a huge basketball fan, and I couldn't even tell you what FIBA stands for. There's no glory, no Olympic medal, and little recognition to be had from coaching the team. In fact, so many NBA stars refused to play that there was only a handful of All-Stars on the roster. But since Gregg Popovich, arguably the NBA's best coach, was the head coach, Steve Kerr put his vacation aside in order to be an assistant to Popovich. He couldn't resist the opportunity to shadow greatness.

"This is an incredible opportunity and one I'm extremely grateful for," Kerr said. "I had the good fortune to participate in our USA Basketball program as an amateur, and to have the chance to return to the world stage three decades later and work under Pop, one of my former coaches and a mentor, is a tremendous honor."

If you want to gain power, you must create opportunities to shadow others. If you want to be exceptional, even after winning championships, you must jump on every opportunity you can to shadow powerful leaders.

Leadership Is Knowing What Drives People

In this, our final chapter, we keep coming back to ideas we've already looked at and are now taking to the next level. In chapter 2, we talked about knowing what drives you. Now we're going to examine what motivates others. We touched on some of these things when discussing the Nine Love Languages of Entrepreneurs, but this is next level.

When I was twenty-two years old, working at Morgan Stanley Dean Witter as an adviser, I spoke to two audiences in a span of a month. The first was a group of seniors who wanted to learn about better alternatives for retirement. I spent the majority of my time speaking to them about what it would feel like to be able to live in a 10,000-square-foot home with a Ferrari parked outside and an Amex black card in their wallet. They looked at me as if I had lost it—until they stopped paying attention altogether.

A couple of weeks later, I spoke to a group of salespeople who were in their late twenties to early thirties and decided to take a completely different approach. I asked them to think about what it would feel like to one day be able to send their kids and grandkids to the best universities without worrying about how much it would cost. Or having enough money in a retirement account to draw $10,000 a month for the rest of their lives, while living comfortably near a golf course. Again, I lost them all.

At the time, I had a manager who was trying to motivate me. All she talked about were the things that moved *her*. As you can imagine, she lost me. When I reflected, it made me realize why I had lost both audiences. Just as she didn't speak to what drove me, I hadn't spoken to what drove each audience.

The ultimate power move is getting the most out of people. It's also the move that will—now I'm speaking for myself—bring the most fulfillment. Seeing people finally get the light to turn on and succeed is what I live for most. It's also the reason this book is in your hands.

A great leader is someone who sets a great example and earns moral authority. A great leader is someone who is able to get others to do things they wouldn't do on their own. There are many people out there who set a great example yet still struggle with why their team doesn't follow their example. Setting an example alone is not enough. Great leaders eventually learn how to drive people to their own standard of excellence. This isn't an easy task, which makes it a high-paying skill. Anyone who learns how to move people has a skill set that's transferable to any industry.

Again, let's look at the four areas that drive people. Then we'll speak specifically about how to lead those who are driven by each category.

THE FOUR AREAS THAT DRIVE PEOPLE

ADVANCEMENT

- Next promotion
- Completing a task
- Meeting a deadline
- Reaching a goal as a team

INDIVIDUALITY

- Lifestyle
- Recognition
- Security

MADNESS

- Opposition
- Competition
- Control
- Power and fame
- Proving others wrong
- The need to avoid embarrassment
- Mastery
- Desire to be the best (break records)

PURPOSE

- History
- Helping others
- Change
- Impact
- Enlightenment/self-actualization

WHAT DRIVES YOU CHANGES AT EACH PHASE OF YOUR LIFE.

- **Advancement.** People driven by this see reaching new heights as the best form of motivation. Constantly have the next goal or position set up for them to keep moving up, or they'll get bored.
- **Individuality.** The language to speak to this group is what their future life can look like if they give everything they have: cars, prestige, going to the best restaurants, traveling, associating with celebrities, and so on. As long as they know that the lifestyle they're motivated by can eventually be reached by working with you, they'll do their part to help grow the company.
- **Madness.** People driven by this see unconventional factors as the best form of motivation. They are driven by having an enemy, by

facing an opponent. They will be bored out of their minds if you don't constantly find them a new enemy or target to reach.

- **Purpose.** People driven by this want to be part of something bigger than they are, but they also want the history books to write about them (in the company's history books or in industry papers). This group may be the smallest of the bunch, but if you're lucky enough to attract one to your organization, get ready to experience a massive explosion.

Understand, Position, and Lead— but Do Not Try to Fix

No matter whom you are managing, remember that the fastest way to lose them or frustrate them is to try to change them. I've made this mistake too many times in my career. Instead, find what drives them and position them in a way to win at the highest level. It may require you to change the lens through which you view them.

Stop trying to fix people. Thinking you can change or fix people is delusional behavior. When I started in business, I was guilty of this all the time. I pushed people hard when they were coming up short, because I assumed that that was what they wanted. I figured that if they were messing up, they'd appreciate my feedback, harsh as it might have been, and would change and become the performers I needed them to be.

This is delusional. I realized that I couldn't change people; they had to possess the inner drive to fix their own mistakes. Once I realized that, I began to manage people more effectively. I stopped trying to solve other people's problems. Instead, I realized that what they wanted is someone to listen to them, someone to ask them questions, someone to nudge them in the right direction. People want to be heard. Taking the time to understand them is critical for effective leadership. After that, if they possess an inner drive to excel, they'll self-correct. They'll do their part in achieving their best.

■ ■ ■ ■ ■

By digging deeper into power plays, we now have a different lens through which to view all human interactions. Whether it's leverage in a negotiation or your first meeting with an influencer, taking the time to see where the power lies—and acting accordingly—is what will make you a grand master. If you want to develop this ability, the most powerful move you can make is to shadow great leaders. Whatever the situation, do your best to be around people who have the skills and success that you are seeking.

Last, keep that chart of what drives people close by. Remember that everyone is motivated by different things and that your job as a leader is not to drive them (or, worse, fix them), it's to *understand* them and help align the chess pieces in front of them so they can maximize their potential.

MOVE 5

Master Power Plays

HOW TO BEAT GOLIATH
AND CONTROL THE NARRATIVE

1. Identify the next Goliath for you and your company to go after. Create a strategy to control the narrative. Minimize distractions and anything that stands in the way of your beating Goliath.

STUDY MOBSTERS:
HOW TO SELL, NEGOTIATE, AND INFLUENCE

2. Instead of thinking only about what's in it for you, think about how to find wins for your strategic partners. Before your next meeting, go through all seven steps of preparation. In every negotiation, be aware of who has leverage. Don't overnegotiate when you're lacking it, and don't bully when you have it, especially if you view the other person as a long-term strategic partner.

CULTIVATE YOUR POWER,
AND STAY BATTLE TESTED

3. Constantly study leverage. Watch every interaction between people, countries, and businesses to see if you can determine who has the leverage and if that person or entity is using it to gain power. Also, shift your approach to finding ways to help others rather than using a shotgun approach to getting business. Lastly, value people so deeply that you are constantly looking to see what drives them and how you can help steer them based on their motivations.

Conclusion

Checkmate

As someone who didn't finish school, I think it's so important
to become a lifelong learner and embrace an endless curiosity
about the world.

—Richard Branson

We've come a long way together. If you're not a sports fan, you may
have heard one too many sports analogies. I share what I know, and
I can't help but keep finding parallels between business and sports.
So please indulge me one last time, because there was a man named
Andrew Bynum who was once to basketball what Magnus Carlsen
is to chess. I know that may sound as though I'm giving Bynum too
much credit, but stay with me.

Bynum was blessed with unworldly talent. In 2005, when he was
only seventeen, he was the first-round pick of my beloved Los An-
geles Lakers. The late, great Kobe Bryant was still in his prime, and
I couldn't wait for that seven-foot behemoth to dominate the NBA.
On paper, Bynum had the raw talent to be as good as Shaquille
O'Neal. On the court, he showed flashes of one day being a Hall of
Famer.

Bynum started out as a damn good basketball player. He helped
the Lakers win NBA titles in 2009 and 2010. In 2012, before he

turned twenty-five, he was selected All-NBA. He seemed on course to win more championships and be a fixture on All-NBA teams.

Then it all went straight to hell.

He had some injuries, and he was traded to the 76ers. He bounced around the league, and then, in 2013, while playing for the Cavaliers, he was suspended. The reason was disturbing: during a practice, he shot the ball every time he touched it, no matter where he was on the court. I didn't just see that as a middle finger to his coaches and teammates; I saw it as complete disrespect for the game of basketball. Never mind the championships, the accolades, the tens of millions of dollars; at age twenty-six, Bynum had completely ruined his career and disgraced the game of basketball.

Why?

I've never met Bynum, so I can only speculate. The way I see it, the reason Bynum underachieved is that he did not love the game. How could he respect something that he never loved?

Sometimes it's tough to love something that comes too easily. You see this in business all the time. You often see it in children of wealthy families who have been given a big inheritance. When the struggle is removed from life—when we didn't have to *earn* it— people start to feel entitled and take things for granted. It's one of the laws of human nature.

Why am I talking so much about Andrew Bynum? Because the number one factor in reaching your potential is simple: *It must matter to you.* History books are filled with individuals who did impossible things simply because it mattered to them. I hope that something tugs at Bynum's heart to the point where he'd be willing to give his best.

You have to want success. You have to want it so badly that it hurts. Persistence, dedication, drive—these are traits that all elite people from athletes to chess masters to CEOs have. I know I keep reminding you how hard it is, because I know that you're going to need another gear to take your talent to the highest level imaginable.

Leveling Up Means
Starting Over at the Bottom

To reach your capacity, you're going to have to "compete up" and not be afraid. Seek to beat your prior best in all areas. The irony is that each time you step up, you have to start at the bottom.

The king of grade school becomes low man on the totem pole the day he goes to middle school. When he finally climbs back up to the top of the ladder, high school starts and he's back at the bottom again. Your career is going to feel similar: each time you advance, you'll officially be at the bottom of the next level. One of the biggest fears that holds people back from moving up is that they won't get respect. Let's look at this chart to see what I mean.

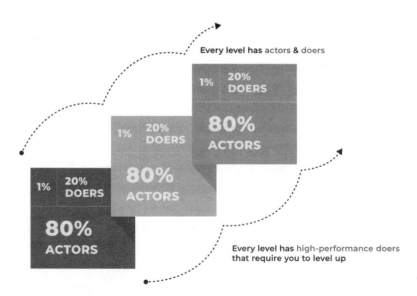

Every level has actors & doers

1% | 20% DOERS

80% ACTORS

Every level has high-performance doers that require you to level up

The key to getting in the 1 percent is continually investing in learning and growth. Large corporations invest in their talent. They groom promising junior employees for leadership, sending them for expensive training and assigning them experienced mentors. If you don't have the luxury of a large corporation investing in your talent, you must still find ways to invest in yourself.

For some reason, most of us think we're afraid of challenges. But when we're not being challenged, we get bored. Then we stagnate. If we aren't challenged, we also often don't realize what's inside of us and how much we are capable of accomplishing. Any entrepreneur who wants to stay sane needs to let go of the silly notion that challenges are scary. Challenges never stop coming, so you'd better learn to love them and thrive on them. Every struggle is an opportunity to grow and improve.

Every move up will make you feel as though you're in over your head. You will be tested. Again, what will determine your success is if it matters to you.

Use Entrepreneurship to Solve the World's Problems

I've said countless times that many of the world's problems are going to be solved by entrepreneurs. The simple reason is that entrepreneurs are problem solvers. They look at something complex, study it, simplify it, and ultimately find a way to solve it. Entrepreneurs can solve health, economic, environmental, and educational challenges.

Often, the first motivation for somebody who's never been an entrepreneur to become one is to make a lot of money so he or she can have a bigger house, a bigger car, and other toys. There's nothing wrong with that. But your mission has to be bigger. Know that the world today is counting on us to solve big problems that will never stop coming.

The game of business can be ugly at times. The start-up graveyard is filled with companies run by well-intentioned, talented people who just weren't prepared to handle the chaos of building a business. If you can take being pushed to your limits, beaten down by Goliath, and ostracized by friends and still stay true to your mission, it will be worth it. I don't mean that *eventually* it will be worth it; I mean that every day you fight for something, every day you live according to your future truth, every day you guide people to be their best, you will feel the rewards.

The world needs you. It needs your ideas, your passion, and your heart.

You have all the information needed to master the five key moves:

- how to know yourself
- how to reason
- how to build your team
- how to use strategy to scale
- how to make power plays

All the questions, all the tools, all the stories are there to help you. But ultimately, you're going to benefit only if you apply what you've learned in this book. It's now time to identify your next moves.

At a minimum, list five. If you aspire to think like a grand master, challenge yourself to list fifteen. As you're doing so, consider the concept of sequencing. You may be tempted to make move fifteen your third move. Instead, focus on the bigger picture. Remember, it's the moves in the right sequence that will make you a grand master. That's how you end up winning in the war room, boardroom, and bedroom.

PLANNING YOUR NEXT MOVES

AMATEUR LEVEL	1
	2
	3
PRO LEVEL	4
	5
MASTER	6
	7
	8
	9
	10
GRAND MASTER	11
	12
	13
	14
	15

Acknowledgments

Patrick Bet-David

Since I'm a by-product of six major things in my life, I'll use six categories to thank everything and everyone for whom I am thankful.

Genes. It all started with my parents, Gabreal Bet-David and Diana Boghosian. I wouldn't be who I am without them.

Culture. I have to thank five cultures that have made me who I am today. I'm half Armenian, half Assyrian, and I lived in Tehran, Iran, for ten years before seeking asylum in Erlangen, Germany, and eventually ending up in the United States. Each of those cultures has had a major influence on the way I view life.

Experiences. They say great actors are those who have lived a life with many different experiences filled with both pain and joy. I have to say that the same applies to the world of business. I'm grateful for every single event that's happened in my life, even though I didn't appreciate all of them while they were happening. I wouldn't be who I am today without having lived through a war in Iran, having lived in a refugee camp, or having served in the army. All of those experiences and more have made me who I am today.

Choices. I've made many bad choices and a few good ones. Some felt like great choices at first until I realized they weren't, and some felt like bad choices that turned out okay. All of them have taught me lessons that I cherish today. Some cost me money, some cost me relationships, some made me money, some helped me build relationships. All of them helped me become who I am today.

People. This also falls into a few categories. I have to start off by thanking my wife, Jennifer, who has had my back since day one. My life changed the day I met her. She gave birth to our three children, Patrick, Dylan, and Senna, each of whom has changed my life in his or her own unique way.

I have to thank my first best friend, my older sister, Polet Bet-David. Her husband, Siamak Sabetimani, became the brother I never had. Before I had my own three kids, I fell in love with theirs, Grace and Sean Sabetimani.

I'm immensely grateful for the leadership team of PHP Agency who bought into the vision I cast when all the odds were against us. There's no way in the world we could have built an agency of fifteen thousand insurance agents without the heart, focus, and talent of our leadership team: Sheena and Matt Sapaula, Jose and Marlene Gaytan, and many others.

Finding a Running Mate is tough, but Mario Aguilar has been exactly that on many projects, including helping to put together the content of this book.

This book would have never happened without my agent, Scott Hoffman.

I also have to thank my collaborator, Greg Dinkin, who helped bring structure and organization to my ideas and experiences. A special thanks to those who helped organize my thoughts when we were stuck on an idea or a chapter of the book: Maral Keshishian, Tigran Bekian, Tom Ellsworth, David Moldawer, and Kai Lode.

I'm grateful to the publisher, Jennifer Bergstrom, and our brilliant editors, Karyn Marcus and Rebecca Strobel. Much thanks to Lynn Anderson and Eric Raymer for their incredible attention to detail.

I wouldn't be writing this book or creating new content if it weren't for the millions of Valuetainers and entrepreneurs who follow the content on a monthly basis. I'm grateful for you. You energize me in ways that words can't describe.

Too often we recognize those who loved us and supported us and we forget those who were our competitors, haters, or critics. Those who have doubted me have a special place in my heart. I was tempted to list their names, but I would need several pages to list them all. Just know that I love you and I'm extremely thankful for you.

Inspiration. Last but not least, there've been a handful of moments when I was inspired to do something big with my life. I felt as though several experiences kept pulling me in, even though initially I didn't want to commit to them. Now that I look back, I'm glad I chose to commit and give my best. Such moments of inspiration are why I feel that my tank is always full and why I'm excited to get up every morning to fulfill the next vision that I'm creating.

Greg Dinkin (Collaborator)

You may be wondering, as I was when I first met Pat: Is this guy for real? As a poker champion and author of *The Poker MBA*, I have a finely tuned BS meter. I'm constantly looking to catch people in a bluff and test their authenticity.

In May 2019, a month after I started working with Pat, I attended the Vault conference in Dallas. At his opening strategy session, Pat fielded questions from dozens of the attendees. In doing so, he would remember specific details about their businesses. "Oh, yeah," he would say. "We talked two years ago about your comp plan. Have you been tracking it?" Or "I remember our email exchange about how you need to invest more in analytics. Have you pulled the trigger yet? No? Why not?"

I was astounded by his memory and even more impressed with his business acumen. Then it dawned on me that he had been mentoring dozens of entrepreneurs—for free, simply from his heartfelt desire to give back—while running his business, raising three kids, and expanding his knowledge base (I've never met anyone who reads more and works harder on himself).

Any doubt I had about Pat being in it—making videos for Valuetainment, giving workshops, and writing this book—for the right reasons was erased. As I witnessed that night and continued to see for the next year, Pat is as genuine, authentic, and caring as they come.

If I had to boil down his success to one characteristic, it's that he cares deeply about people accomplishing their dreams. As much as we did our best to include every ounce of Pat's knowledge on the page, it would be impossible to express his love and commitment to people—and why it's the secret sauce that makes him, at least in my view, one of the greatest living leaders on the planet.

Imagine a person who takes the time to truly get to know you, who asks questions to help you uncover exactly who you want to be—often leading you to remember and express your wildest ambition. Then imagine him supporting you with resources and coaching, while at the same time holding you accountable to being the best version of yourself at a level you may not even know you can attain. Then imagine seeing him demand even more of himself than he's demanding of you. How could you not reach great heights? It's no accident that Pat has taken dozens of people without college degrees and molded them into millionaires. Love matters, for sure. Combine it with accountability, leadership, and an example to follow, and incredible success follows.

I feel lucky to have had a front-row seat to observe such an impressive human being. Imagine being a basketball player and getting to shadow LeBron James for a year. If it seems as though I'm laying it on thick, it's because I'm overflowing with gratitude. This started out as just a writing project for me, and it ended up becoming a PhD program in unleashing human potential. As a result, I've become both a better coach/leader and a better version of myself. Seeing how many people are already benefiting from Pat's knowledge was a great motivator to help give you every bit of wisdom from Pat's toolbox.

In addition to my thanks to Pat, I want to thank Mario Aguilar for being the consummate professional. The ultimate consigliere, he was a huge asset at every stage of this process. I'm grateful for savant agent Scott Hoffman for following his instinct that Pat and I would be a good match. I also appreciate the support of my family and friends. Mom, Dad, Andy, Jayme, Leslie, Drew, Logan, Thea, Michelle, Cully, Josh, Bryan, Paul, Charlie, Mark, Monique, George, Chris, Stuckey, and Frank each contributed in his or her own unique way.

APPENDIX A

■　■　■　■　■

PERSONAL
IDENTITY
AUDIT

PERSONAL IDENTITY AUDIT

1. How do you think the world views you?

2. How do you view yourself?

3. How is the "public you" different from the "private you"?

4. What conditions produce the BEST VERSION OF YOU?
   (The version of you who competes and gets the highest results.)

   - ☐ Competition
   - ☐ Fear of loss
   - ☐ A setback
   - ☐ A victory
   - ☐ Having someone believe in you
   - ☐ A point to prove

5. Name a ninety-day period of your career during which you were the hungriest to succeed. What drove you?

6. How do you handle a public loss?

7. Do you have a tendency of blaming others for your lack of effort or discipline? If yes, why?

8. Do you feel you're entitled to things without earning them?

9. How difficult a personality do you have?

   - ☐ Very difficult
   - ☐ Difficult
   - ☐ Somewhat difficult
   - ☐ Easygoing
   - ☐ Very easygoing

10. Do you get along with people like yourself or can there be only one of you in the room?

11. Who do you speak to the most when you're losing?

☐ People ahead of you
☐ People at the same level as you
☐ People not yet at your level
☐ No one

12. Who are you secretly envious of that no one knows about? Don't worry about writing this one down. No one will know your answer but you. How is your relationship with the person you're most envious of? How much of that envy is due to your not willing to do the work that the other individual is willing to do?

13. What type of people annoy you the most and why?

14. What type of people do you like the most and why?

15. Who do you collaborate with the most?

16. What qualities and traits do you admire most in others?

17. How do you handle pressure?

18. How often do you challenge your own vision to help improve your perspective?

19. What brings out the worst side of you? Why?

20. What brings out the best side of you? Why?

21. What do you value the most in business and in life?

22. What do you fear the most in your line of business?

23. What accomplishment are you most proud of and why?

24. Who do you want to be?

25. What kind of life do you want to live?

APPENDIX B

■ ■ ■ ■ ■

SOLVE FOR *X* WORKSHEET

SOLVE FOR *X* WORKSHEET

Issue:

INVESTIGATE	SOLVE	IMPLEMENT
URGENCY 0–10	**WHO'S NEEDED?**	**WHOSE BUY-IN IS NEEDED?**
TOTAL IMPACT POTENTIAL GAIN: POTENTIAL LOSS:	**LIST OF SOLUTIONS**	**ASSIGNED RESPONSIBILITIES**
REAL CAUSE OF ISSUE(S)	**POTENTIAL NEGATIVE CONSEQUENCE(S)**	**NEW PROTOCOLS**
Why? Why? Why?		

Recommended Reading

PBD's Top 52 Business Books

1. *Blue Ocean Strategy: How to Create Uncontested Market Space and Make the Competition Irrelevant* by W. Chan Kim and Renée Mauborgne
2. *Principles: Life and Work* by Ray Dalio
3. *The Five Temptations of a CEO: A Leadership Fable* by Patrick Lencioni
4. *Built to Sell: Creating a Business That Can Thrive Without You* by John Warrillow
5. *Competitive Strategy: Techniques for Analyzing Industries and Competitors* by Michael E. Porter
6. *Multipliers: How the Best Leaders Make Everyone Smarter* by Liz Wiseman
7. *Only the Paranoid Survive: How to Exploit the Crisis Points That Challenge Every Company* by Andrew S. Grove
8. *Positioning: The Battle for Your Mind* by Al Ries and Jack Trout
9. *The Five Dysfunctions of a Team: A Leadership Fable* by Patrick Lencioni
10. *The Lean Startup: How Today's Entrepreneurs Use Continuous Innovation to Create Radically Successful Businesses* by Eric Ries
11. *The ONE Thing: The Surprisingly Simple Truth Behind Extraordinary Results* by Gary Keller

31. *Business Model Generation: A Handbook for Visionaries, Game Changers, and Challengers* by Alexander Osterwalder and Yves Pigneur

32. *Growing Pains: Transitioning from an Entrepreneurship to a Professionally Managed Firm* by Eric G. Flamholtz and Yvonne Randle

33. *High Output Management* by Andrew S. Grove

34. *Rich Dad, Poor Dad* by Robert T. Kiyosaki

35. *Trump: The Art of the Deal* by Donald J. Trump

36. *The Hard Thing About Hard Things: Building a Business When There Are No Easy Answers* by Ben Horowitz

37. *The Hypomanic Edge: The Link Between (a Little) Craziness and (a Lot of) Success in America* by John D. Gartner

38. *The Law of Success: The Master Wealth-Builder's Complete and Original Lesson Plan for Achieving Your Dreams* by Napoleon Hill

39. *The E-Myth Revisited: Why Most Small Businesses Don't Work and What to Do About It* by Michael E. Gerber

40. *Originals: How Non-Conformists Move the World* by Adam Grant

41. *Poor Charlie's Almanack: The Wit and Wisdom of Charles T. Munger, Expanded Third Edition* edited by Peter D. Kaufman

42. *Decisive: How to Make Better Choices in Life and Work* by Chip Heath and Dan Heath

43. *Ego Is the Enemy* by Ryan Holiday

44. *Elon Musk: Tesla, SpaceX, and the Quest for a Fantastic Future* by Ashlee Vance

45. *Lincoln on Leadership: Executive Strategies for Tough Times* by Donald T. Phillips

46. *Michael Jordan: The Life* by Roland Lazenby

47. *The CEO Next Door: The 4 Behaviors That Transform Ordinary People into World-Class Leaders* by Elena L. Botelho and Kim R. Powell

48. *Power vs. Force: The Hidden Determinants of Human Behavior* by David R. Hawkins

49. *The 48 Laws of Power* by Robert Greene
50. *I Love Capitalism!: An American Story* by Ken Langone
51. *Barbarians to Bureaucrats: Corporate Life Cycle Strategies* by Lawrence M. Miller
52. *How to Win Friends and Influence People* by Dale Carnegie

Other Books Referenced

- *The 5 Love Languages: The Secret to Love That Lasts* by Gary Chapman
- *The 7 Habits of Highly Effective People: Powerful Lessons in Personal Change* by Stephen R. Covey
- *101 Questions to Ask Before You Get Engaged* by H. Norman Wright
- *The Big Short: Inside the Doomsday Machine* by Michael Lewis
- *Difficult Conversations: How to Discuss What Matters Most* by Douglas Stone, Bruce Patton, and Sheila Heen
- *A First-Rate Madness: Uncovering the Links Between Leadership and Mental Illness* by Nassir Ghaemi
- *From Worst to First: Behind the Scenes of Continental's Remarkable Comeback* by Gordon Bethune
- *How to Stop Worrying and Start Living: Time-Tested Methods for Conquering Worry* by Dale Carnegie
- *The Intelligent Investor: The Definitive Book on Value Investing* by Benjamin Graham
- *Moneyball: The Art of Winning an Unfair Game* by Michael Lewis
- *The Power of Vulnerability: Teachings on Authenticity, Connection, and Courage* by Brené Brown
- *Powerful: Building a Culture of Freedom and Responsibility* by Patty McCord
- *Scaling Up: How a Few Companies Make It . . . and Why the Rest Don't* by Verne Harnish

- *The Secret* by Rhonda Byrne
- *Steve Jobs* by Walter Isaacson
- *Thank God It's Monday: How to Prevent Success from Ruining Your Marriage* by Pierre Mornell
- *The Toyota Way: 14 Management Principles from the World's Greatest Manufacturer* by Jeffrey Liker
- *Traction: Get a Grip on Your Business* by Gino Wickman
- *What Would the Rockefellers Do? How the Wealthy Get and Stay That Way, and How You Can Too* by Garrett B. Gunderson and Michael G. Isom
- *What Would the Founders Do? Our Questions, Their Answers* by Richard Brookhiser
- *Winners Never Cheat: Everyday Values That We Learned as Children (but May Have Forgotten)* by Jon M. Huntsman

For more content, visit the Valuetainment YouTube channel: https://www.youtube.com/c/valuetainment

About the Author

Patrick Bet-David went from escaping war-torn Iran to founding his own financial firm, raising tens of millions of dollars, and creating Valuetainment, the leading YouTube channel for entrepreneurs. His unorthodox approach to business and life has created compelling interviews with Ray Dalio, Kevin Hart, the late Kobe Bryant, President George W. Bush, and a host of other luminaries. His content on social media has been viewed over a billion times.

Patrick never obtained a college degree and went from the army to selling health club memberships before selling financial services. At age thirty, Bet-David founded PHP, a financial services agency. He lives in Dallas with his wife and three children.